SPINK'S STANDARD CATALOGUE OF BRITISH AND ASSOCIATED
ORDERS, DECORATIONS AND MEDALS WITH VALUATIONS

The Royal Order of
Victoria and Albert
3rd Class

Empress of India
Medal, 1877
(reverse)

The George Cross

SPINKS

# Standard Catalogue of British *and associated* Orders · Decorations & Medals *with valuations*

A. R. Litherland
B. T. Simpkin

SPINK     London 1990

Published by Spink & Son Ltd.
5, 6 & 7 King Street, St. James's
London, SW1Y 6QS

British Library Cataloguing in Publication Data
Litherland, A. R. (Andrew R.)
Spink's catalogue of British orders, decorations and
medals.-6th. ed.
1. Honours. British decorations, medals and orders
I. Title II. Simpkin, B. T. (Brian T.) III. Joslin, E.
C. (Edward Charles) 1924-. Spink's catalogue of
British and associated orders, decorations and
medals 737.2

ISBN 0 907605 32 X

Designed by Paul Sharp

Printed in Great Britain by Grillford Ltd
Granby, Milton Keynes, MK1 1QZ

# Contents

## Acknowledgements

The editors would like to acknowledge the following for their valued assistance and advice given during the preparation of this catalogue.

T J Davies       D Mahoney
N Dix       J D O'Malley
Mrs J E Doel       D H Saville
W H Fevyer       E G Ursual
R Kirch       C Vivian

We would also like to thank the others not named who contributed to this updated catalogue.

The editors would like to give special acknowledgement to E C Joslin Esq L.V.O. upon whose previous four editions this work is based and for the assistance he has given throughout.

Photographs supplied by the Hayward-Scarlett Picture Library, London Stamp Exchange and Spink & Son Medal Department.

# Collecting

Many collectors are familiar with the earlier Standard Catalogues which were first pioneered by Spink & Son Ltd in 1969. However, it has been apparent for some time that the collector now requires a more detailed and sophisticated price catalogue, considerably wider in scope and superior than all previous publications.

Nevertheless, in preparing this work, the authors have taken into account the need to introduce this fascinating collecting series to the general public and satisfy those who have family orders or medals in their possession which need identifying and valuing. It is hoped that this publication will, therefore, satisfy the needs not only of the general public, but also both new and experienced collectors.

The collecting of medals as a hobby has been practised for over a hundred years, but it is only in the last fifty years that we have seen an increased activity in this field. The series of orders, decorations and medals, particularly the British series (the issue of which has always been restricted to the actual recipients), represents our Island's proud heritage of naval, military and air achievements during the last two hundred years. The possession of these awards helps to recall a particular war, campaign or action and helps to keep alive the services of a particular officer, man or regiment or perhaps some outstanding act of gallantry. With our diminishing armed forces, these medals serve as a constant reminder of the outstanding and yet often forgotten deeds of our ancestors, such as:

1   Nelson's defeat of the French at the Battle of the Nile, thus saving Egypt and, indirectly, India from French conquest.
2   Nelson's overwhelming defeat of the combined French and Spanish fleets at Trafalgar which finally ruled out Napoleon's invasion plans for these islands.
3   The masterly retreat and evacuation at Corunna in 1809 under the leadership of General Sir John Moore.
4   Wellington's brilliant campaigns against the previously all-victorious French Army in Spain and Portugal from 1809-14.
5   The charge of the Light Brigade at Balaklava.
6   The heroic defence of Rorke's Drift, 1879, by 139 men, when surrounded by an overwhelming force of about 3000 Zulu warriors.
7   The retreat from Mons by the 'Contemptible Little Army' in the face of overwhelming German superiority.
8   The Falkland Islands conflict—and countless others.

Such is the wealth of material available covering outstanding events in our history that the collector, whether well-established or one who has recently taken up the hobby, is in need of a price catalogue such as those that can be found for stamps, coins and other collecting fields.

The first collectors were few in number, being mostly wealthy people. Many built large collections which would be impossible to form today, partly due to current price structure, but mainly because the amount of material at that time seldom becomes available today. The collectors of that era often dealt with their own favourite dealer and these again were few and far between. Today there are far more collectors and dealers representing a remarkable cross-section of the community, both in this country and abroad.

# *What to Collect*

The range of British orders, decorations and medals is considerable. Therefore, right at the very outset, one should give thought as to what to collect so as to obtain maximum enjoyment and satisfaction from the hobby. There is a very wide basis for the formation of a collection and one probably cannot go far wrong by choosing one or a combination of the following as a guide:

A collection based on a particular family name; it follows that if the name is unusual the potential for collecting is rather limited.

A collection of a particular series is also a popular theme, possibly based on the following:

a) **Orders**   There is a very wide range covering the various classes, civil and military divisions from different periods. A collection of Orders often makes a most eye-catching display.

b) **Gallantry Awards**   This is another wide ranging theme but often made managable by a collector restricting himself to a particular service and/or period. The research potential for these awards is often considerable and most rewarding.

c) **Campaign Medals**   Although it is often tempting to collect one of each type, especially in the early years, it soon becomes a somewhat daunting task. A more realistic way would be to collect to a particular regiment, a specific war or campaign, a certain period or geographical area. These too provide vast research potential.

d) **Coronation & Jubilee Medals**   This is an interesting and generally manageable theme covering the various Royal commemorative medals issued for wearing.

e) **Long & Meritorious Service Medals**   The range of Long & Meritorious Service Medals is considerable covering the Services in the UK and the Empire/Commonwealth.

f) **Life-Saving Medals**   A fine and interesting series of humanitarian awards with the opportunity for original research not only into individual acts of gallantry but also research into the lesser known Societies that issued the awards.

The collectors purchasing power will obviously govern to a certain extent what is collected.

# Factors Governing Price Structure

When studying price structure of various awards the following should be considered:

1 **Authenticity**

It is recommended that collectors, particularly those starting a collection, should always make purchases through a reputable and established dealer or auction house who have the knowledge and integrity to provide a guarantee of authenticity.

2 **Renaming**

A collector should ensure that the naming on any medal is not defective as this will have an adverse effect on value. The term 'Renamed' implies that the original naming has been removed and the medal re-impressed or re-engraved with new details. This renaming was often performed by the issuing body to correct errors. Alternatively this may have been carried out by the recipient who had lost or had his medal stolen, then replaced it and had it renamed with his service details.

3 **Conditions**

Although the condition of medals is not as important as with coins it is recommended that collectors, where possible, buy medals and especially orders in the best condition. This will pay dividends when a collector wishes to sell or part-exchange.

The undermentioned abbreviations are those normally used to describe conditions:

FDC—Fleur de Coin (faultless or mint condition)

EF—Extremely Fine

VF—Very Fine

F—Fine

Worn.

Collectors should bear in mind that rarity or historical importance may override condition criteria.

4 **Numbers issued**

The numbers issued of any particular medal will have a bearing on its value. It should be noted however that the number of medals to have survived could be considerably less.

5 **Rank and Unit**

It is fair to say that a medal awarded to an officer commands a higher price than one awarded to an 'other rank'. The more senior the rank the higher the price. Officers medals have in general more research potential.

Medals awarded to British units generally command a higher price than those to some colonial units, this is due to a lack of research potential for medals awarded to natives.

6 **Groups**

There is a indefinable group premium often placed upon a group of medals above the sum total of their individual values. This reflects complete, long and unusual service.

7  **Multiple Bars**

Although multiple bar medals are generally more valuable collectors should not make the mistake of adding together the value of each single bar to obtain a total value.

8  **Documentation**

Original documentation always enhances the value of a medal or group. It is particularly important in the case of unnamed gallantry awards and medals where it helps substantiate the name of the recipient.

9  **Research**

The researching of a medal recipient often provides much of the enjoyment for a medal collector. In addition research often pays dividends, uncovering such information as casualties, further service and personal details.

10 **Desirability**

Although a medal may be numerically rare this may not be reflected in its value if it is from a less sought after series. Anniversaries, new publications, films and collectors' whims may be responsible for new trends.

---

## *Points to bear in mind when using the Spink Catalogue*

First and foremost the prices in this catalogue should be used as a *guide only*. These prices have been obtained by studying the catalogues of specialist dealers and auction houses, and also our own experience. The price quoted is the current market value of a piece in average (VF) condition, awarded to a recipient of the lowest rank, from a common unit unless stated otherwise.

**Orders:** prices against all Orders are based on the standard government issues. Prices will vary depending upon the period and quality of manufacture.

**Gallantry awards:** prices here will vary considerably depending on the specific citation details and theatre of war. Prices quoted are for an 'average' award and this should always be taken into account.

# *The order of wearing Orders, Decorations and Medals*

Victoria Cross (V.C.)
George Cross (G.C.)
Order of the Garter (K.G.)
Order of the Thistle (K.T.)
Order of St. Patrick (K.P.)
Order of the Bath (G.C.B., K.C.B. and D.C.B., and C.B.)
Order of Merit (O.M.; ranks next after G.C.B.)
Order of the Star of India (G.C.S.I., K.C.S.I. and C.S.I.)
Order of St. Michael and St. George (G.C.M.G., K.C.M.G. and D.C.M.G., and C.M.G.)
Order of the Indian Empire (G.C.I.E., K.C.I.E. and C.I.E.)
Order of the Crown of India (C.I.)
Royal Victorian Order (G.C.V.O., K.C.V.O. and D.C.V.O., and C.V.O.)
Order of the British Empire (G.B.E., K.B.E. and D.B.E., and C.B.E.)
Order of the Companion of Honour (C.H.; ranks next after G.B.E.)
Distinguished Service Order (D.S.O.)
Royal Victorian Order (L.V.O., M.V.O. Class IV)
Order of the British Empire (O.B.E.)
Queen's Service Order (Q.S.O.)
Imperial Service Order (I.S.O.)
Royal Victorian Order (M.V.O. Class V)
Order of the British Empire (M.B.E.)
Baronet's Badge
Knight Bachelor's Badge
Indian Order of Merit (Military) (I.O.M.), Order of Burma (for gallantry) (O.B.)
Royal Red Cross (Class I; R.R.C.)
Distinguished (formerly Conspicuous) Service Cross (D.S.C.)
Military Cross (M.C.)
Distinguished Flying Cross (D.F.C.)
Air Force Cross (A.F.C.)
Royal Red Cross (Class II; A.R.R.C.)
Order of British India (O.B.I.)
Kaisar-i-Hind Medal
Order of Burma (for good service) (O.B.)
Order of St. John
Albert Medal (A.M.)
Union of South Africa King's (Queen's) Medal for Bravery, in gold
Distinguished Conduct Medal (D.C.M.)
Conspicuous Gallantry Medal (C.G.M.)
George Medal (G.M.)
King's (Queen's) Police Medal, for Gallantry (K.P.M., K.P.F.S.M., Q.P.M.)
Queen's Fire Service Medal, for Gallantry (Q.F.S.M.)
Edward Medal (E.M.)
Royal West African Frontier Force Distinguished Conduct Medal (D.C.M.)
King's African Rifles Distinguished Conduct Medal (D.C.M.)
Indian Distinguished Service Medal (I.D.S.M.)
Burma Gallantry Medal (B.G.M.)

Union of South Africa King's (Queen's) Medal for Bravery, in silver
Distinguished Service Medal (D.S.M.)
Military Medal (M.M.)
Distinguished Flying Medal (D.F.M.)
Air Force Medal (A.F.M.)
Constabulary Medal (Ireland)
Board of Trade Medal for Saving Life at Sea (S.G.M.)
Indian Order of Merit (Civil) (I.O.M.)
Empire Gallantry Medal (E.G.M.)
Indian Police Medal for Gallantry
Burma Police Medal for Gallantry
Ceylon Police Medal for Gallantry
Sierra Leone Police Medal for Gallantry
Sierra Leone Fire Brigade Medal for Gallantry
Colonial Police Medal for Gallantry
Queen's Gallantry Medal (Q.G.M.)
Royal Victorian Medal (in gold, silver or bronze)
Queen's Service Medal (Q.S.M.)
Uganda Services Medal (if awarded for gallantry)
British Empire Medal (B.E.M.)
Canada Medal (C.M. or M. du C.)
Life Saving Medal of the Order of St. John
King's (Queen's) Police Medal for Distinguished Service (K.P.M., K.P.F.S.M., Q.P.M.)
Queen's Fire Service Medal for Distinguished Service (Q.F.S.M.)
King's (Queen's) Medal for Chiefs
War Medals (in order of date of campaign)
Polar Medals (in order of date)
Imperial Service Medal
Police Medals for Meritorious Service
Uganda Services Medal (if awarded for meritorious service)
Badge of Honour
Jubilee, Coronation and Durbar Medals
King George V Long and Faithful Service Medal
King George VI Long and Faithful Service Medal
Queen Elizabeth II Long and Faithful Service Medal
Meritorious Service Medals
Efficiency and Long Service Decorations and Medals, Medals for Champion Shots, Independence Medals, etc.
Other Commonwealth Orders, Decorations and Medals (instituted since 1949, otherwise than by the Sovereign) and awards by the States of Malaysia and the State of Brunei
Foreign Orders (in order of date of award)
Foreign Decorations (in order of date of award)
Foreign Medals (in order of date of award)

# Ribands

Widths of Ribands used with Insignia and on Riband Bars

| | with Insignia | on Uniform |
|---|---|---|
| K.G. | 4″ | not worn |
| K.T. | 4″ | not worn |
| K.P. | 4″ | not worn |
| G.C.B. | 4″ | 1½″ |
| G.C.B. (Dame Grand Cross) | 2¼″ | 1½″ |
| K.C.B. | 2″ | 1½″ |
| D.C.B. | 1¾″ | 1½″ |
| C.B. | 1½″ | 1½″ |
| O.M. | 2″ | 2″ |
| G.C.S.I. | 4″ | 1½″ |
| K.C.S.I. | 2″ | 1½″ |
| C.S.I. | 1½″ | 1½″ |
| G.C.M.G. | 4″ | 1½″ |
| G.C.M.G. (Dame Grand Cross) | 2¼″ | 1½″ |
| K.C.M.G. | 2″ | 1½″ |
| D.C.M.G. | 1¾″ | 1½″ |
| C.M.G. | 1½″ | 1½″ |
| G.C.I.E. | 4″ | 1½″ |
| K.C.I.E. | 2″ | 1½″ |
| C.I.E. | 1½″ | 1½″ |
| G.C.V.O. | 3¾″ | 1¼″ |
| G.C.V.O. (Dame Grand Cross) | 2¼″ | 1¼″ |
| K.C.V.O. | 1¾″ | 1¼″ |
| D.C.V.O. | 1¾″ | 1¼″ |
| C.V.O. | 1¾″ | 1¼″ |
| L.V.O. (M.V.O. 4th cl.) | 1¼″ | 1¼″ |
| M.V.O. (5th cl) | 1¼″ | 1¼″ |
| Royal Victorian Medal | 1¼″ | 1¼″ |
| G.B.E. | 4″ | 1½″ |
| G.B.E. (Dame Grand Cross) | 2¼″ | 1½″ |
| K.B.E. | 1¾″ | 1½″ |
| D.B.E. | 1¾″ | 1½″ |
| C.B.E. | 1¾″ | 1½″ |
| O.B.E. | 1½″ | 1½″ |
| M.B.E. | 1½″ | 1½″ |
| B.E.M. | 1¼″ | 1¼″ |
| C.H. | 1½″ | 1½″ |
| D.S.O. | 1⅛″ | 1⅛″ |
| C.I. | 1½″ | 1½″ |

**Order of St John**

| | | |
|---|---|---|
| Bailiff Grand Cross | 4″ | 1½″ |
| Dame Grand Cross | 2¼″ | 1½″ |
| Knight of Justice | 2″ | 1½″ |

| | | |
|---|---|---|
| Dame of Justice | 1¼" | 1¼" |
| Knight of Grace | 2" | 1½" |
| Dame of Grace | 1¼" | 1¼" |
| Chaplain | 2" | 1½" |
| Commander (Brother) | 1½" | 1½" |
| Commander (Sister) | 1¼" | 1¼" |
| Officer (Brother) | 1½" | 1½" |
| Officer (Sister) | 1¼" | 1¼" |
| Serving Brother | 1½" | 1½" |
| Serving Sister | 1¼" | 1¼" |

**ORDER OF THE GARTER**
Lesser George sash badge

**ORDER OF THE GARTER**
Breast star

**ORDER OF THE GARTER**
Garter

ORDER OF THE
THISTLE
Knight's collar
chain with collar
badge, breast star
and sash badge

ORDER OF THE THISTLE
Sash badge

ORDER OF THE THISTLE
Breast star

ORDER OF ST PATRICK
Knight's collar chain, collar bad
and sash badge

ORDER OF ST PATRICK
Knight's breast star and sash badge

ORDER OF ST PATRICK
The Usher at Arms Badge

ORDER OF THE BATH
K.B. (pre 1815) badge and star

ORDER OF THE BATH
G.C.B. military collar,
collar badge, sash badge and
breast star

ORDER OF THE BATH
G.C.B. civil collar, collar badge,
sash badge and breast star

THE ROYAL GUELPHIC ORDER G.C.H. collar, G.C.H. military sash badge and breast star

ORDER OF ST MICHAEL
AND ST GEORGE
G.C.M.G. collar, sash badge
and breast star

ORDER OF ST MICHAEL
AND ST GEORGE
K.C.M.G. breast star

ORDER OF ST MICHAEL
AND ST GEORGE
G.C.M.G. sash badge

22

**ORDER OF THE STAR OF INDIA**
G.C.S.I. collar, collar badge,
sash badge and breast star

**ORDER OF THE STAR OF INDIA**
C.S.I. breast badge

**ORDER OF THE
CROWN OF INDIA**

ORDER OF THE INDIAN EMPIRE
G.C.I.E. collar, sash badge
and breast star

ORDER OF THE INDIAN EMPIRE
C.I.E. 1st issue breast badge

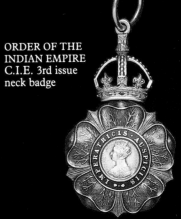

ORDER OF THE
INDIAN EMPIRE
C.I.E. 3rd issue
neck badge

ROYAL FAMILY ORDER
Elizabeth II

ROYAL FAMILY ORDER
George VI

ROYAL FAMILY ORDER
George V

ROYAL ORDER OF
VICTORIA AND ALBERT

ROYAL VICTORIAN ORDER G.C.V.O. collar, sash badge and breast star

ROYAL VICTORIAN
ORDER
M.V.O. 4th Class
(since 1988 L.V.O.)

ROYAL VICTORIAN
ORDER
M.V.O. 5th Class

ROYAL VICTORIAN
MEDAL

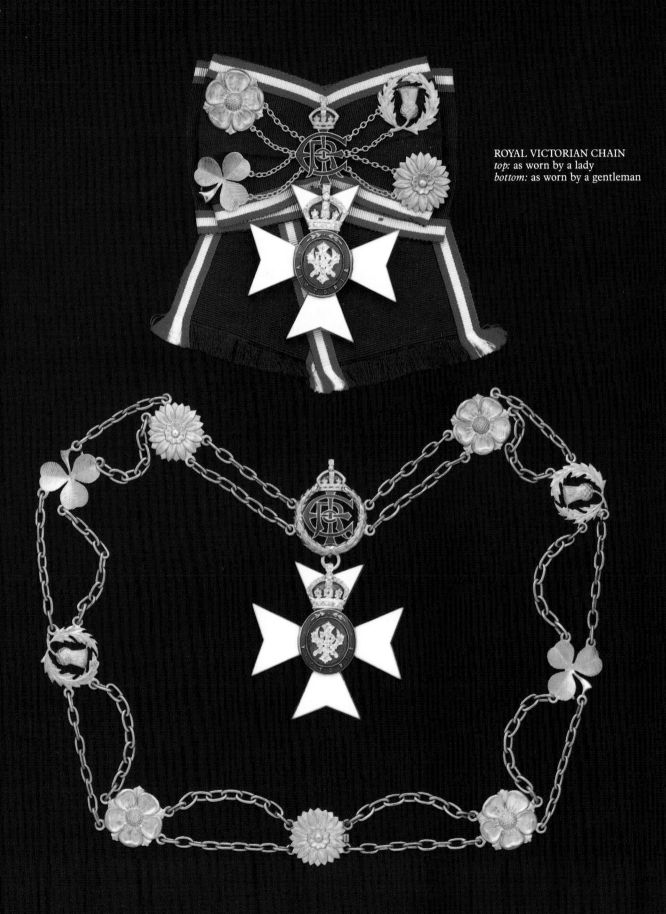

ROYAL VICTORIAN CHAIN
*top:* as worn by a lady
*bottom:* as worn by a gentleman

ORDER OF THE BRITISH EMPIRE
G.B.E. collar, sash badge and breast
star 2nd type civil

ORDER OF THE BRITISH EMPIRE 1st
type
K.B.E. civil neck badge and breast star
C.B.E. military neck badge
O.B.E. military and M.B.E. military
breast badges.

ORDER OF MERIT
civil

ORDER OF THE COMPANION OF
HONOUR Ladies badge

BARONETS BADGE
United Kingdom type

BARONETS BADGE OF
NOVA SCOTIA

AFGHANISTAN, ORDER OF THE
DOORANIE EMPIRE
Commanders badge (left)

ORDER OF ST JOHN
Knight of Grace neck badge and
breast star (right)

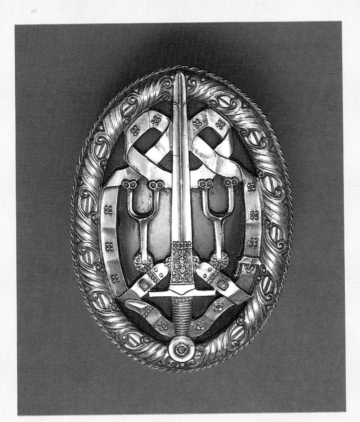

KNIGHT BACHELOR'S BADGE

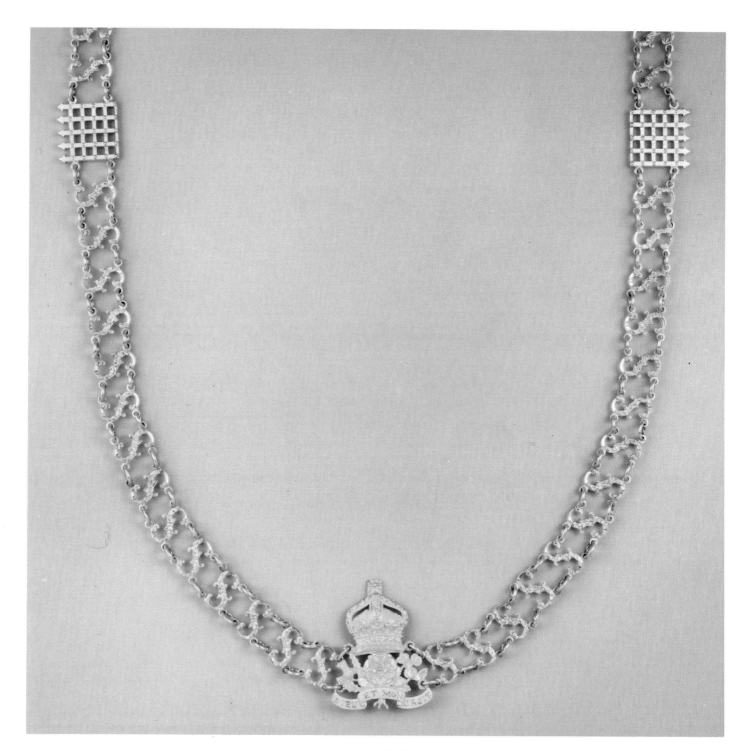

COLLAR OF S'S

# Orders Decorations & Medals

## with valuations

# Orders of Knighthood

Prices of gold insignia are based on the period 1860-87. Earlier insignia will be more expensive.

Complete sets of first and second class insignia in their original cases command a premium above the price of individual stars and badges.

The dates given are those of the foundation and abolition of the orders.

In the case of the lesser orders, insignia are returnable on promotion to a higher class. All collar chains are returnable, though the St Michael and St George could be retained up to 1948.

---

## 1 The Most Noble Order of the Garter (K.G.) 1348

This is one of the 'great' Orders, the others being the Thistle and the Patrick.

The Garter was founded by King Edward III and as it is the premier Order of Great Britain, it commands the very highest respect.

The Order consists of twenty-five Knights only and is the personal gift of the Sovereign and, due to the small number of Knights, it is one of the rarest orders in existence today. Unlike many other orders, the Garter has never been suspended, having been awarded continuously since the middle of the fourteenth century.

In addition to the twenty-five Knights, there are a small number of 'extra' Knights who invariably are non-Christians such as the late Emperor of Japan Hirohito and two past sovereigns of Turkey. Sir Winston Churchill, probably one of the most outstanding commoners to be awarded the Order in recent years, was awarded the insignia originally presented to one of his forebears, namely the 1st Duke of Marlborough, who was admitted to the Order in 1702.

The Garter sash is worn over the left shoulder which is opposite to the lesser orders. The motto of the Garter is *'Honi soit qui mal y pense'* or 'Evil be who evil thinks'.

The officially issued insignia of this Order have always been returnable to the Crown by the heirs of the recipients. Before the latter part of the nineteenth century, however, when insignia was more frequently worn than is now the custom, Knights often purchased additional stars and badges at their own expense. This practice can also be explained by the fact that there were no metal stars furnished by the Crown until 1858, and also by the desire of the Knights to have more splendid badges than the rather plain officially issued specimens. Privately commissioned insignia of these orders occasionally appear on the market, the price of these pieces largely depending on their age and quality.

*The early and more outstanding of the privately made pieces may be expected to cost more. The prices below are for standard insignia similar to those officially awarded.*

*Prices are for insignia without pedigree; insignia proved to have been worn by outstanding personalities can be expected to be of greater value.*

| | |
|---|---:|
| Collar chain | £50,000 |
| Collar badge (The George) | £25,000 |
| Star (in metal, early 20th-century) | £3000 |
| Star (embroidered, in very fine condition) | £1000 |
| Sash badge (The Lesser George, early 20th-century) | £9000 |
| Garter (with embroidered lettering in very fine condition) | £800 |
| Garter (with *gold* lettering, buckle and tab) | £2000 |
| Officers badges | £9000 |

## 2   *The Most Ancient and the Most Noble Order of the Thistle (K.T.)* 1687

The usually accepted date of the institution of this Order is 1687, the Order having been revived by Queen Anne in 1703. However, it has been suggested by some authorities that the Order was founded as far back as 787. The motto of the Order is *'nemo me impune lacessit'* or 'No-one provokes me with impunity'.

The Order is restricted to sixteen distinguished Scotsmen, thus making it more exclusive than the Garter and probably the rarest order in Europe, if not the world. Occasionally, extra Knignts who are selected members of royal families are awarded the Order. The only foreigner to have been made a Knight for over two hundred years is King Olaf of Norway, who was admitted as an extra Knight in 1962. Unlike the Garter, which is occasionally awarded to non-Christians, the Thistle is restricted in this respect.

As with the Garter, all the Thistle insignia are returnable and the only pieces that come on to the market are invariably the unofficially produced pieces. As with the Garter, the sash riband is worn over the left shoulder, resting on the right hip.

| | |
|---|---:|
| Collar chain | £50,000 |
| Collar badge | £20,000 |
| Star (in metal, early 20th-century) | £3000 |
| Star (embroidered, in very fine condition) | £800 |
| Sash badge (gold) | £6000 |
| Officers badge | £5000 |

# 3 *The Most Illustrious Order of St Patrick (K.P.)*

1783-1974

The Order of St Patrick was instituted on February 5th 1793, by King George III to provide Irish peers with a suitable award for distinguished services. The Order was intended to be for the peers of Ireland what the Garter and the Thistle were for those of England and Scotland. From 1833 the maximum number of knights at any one time was set at twenty-two.

For the first time since its institution in 1783, the Order of St Patrick now has no Knights as no new non-royal knights have been created since 1922 when the Union of Ireland with Great Britain was dissolved. Three royal Knights, sons of King George V, were created after 1922—the Prince of Wales, later the Duke of Windsor (1927), the Duke of York, later George VI (1936) and the Duke of Gloucester (1934).

During the Second World War, a number of distinguished service leaders whose families were associated with Northern Ireland would probably have qualified as knights. It was suggested that the Order be kept alive by such appointments but the separation of the North and South of Ireland made the revival impracticable. It is ironic that the legend of the Order is *'quis separabit'*— 'Who shall separate'! The 9th Earl of Shaftesbury was the longest surviving recipient of the Order; he was awarded the honour in 1911 and died fifty years later in 1961.

Unlike the other two great Orders, the Garter and the Thistle, the sash for this Order is worn as with other lesser orders, over the right shoulder.

| | |
|---|---|
| Collar chain | £40,000 |
| Collar Badge | £18,000 |
| Star (in metal) | £3000 |
| Star (embroidered, in very fine condition) | £300 |
| Sash badge | £8500 |
| Officers badge | £5000 |

# 4 *The Most Honourable Order of the Bath* 1725

The Order was founded during the time of the Prime Minister Sir Robert Walpole as an order with one class and one division only, recipients being known as K.Bs, or simply Knights of the Bath.

The title of the Order always seems remarkably strange, but this was derived from the ancient ritual of bathing or cleansing which was symbolic of washing away any impurities before admission to the Order.

In 1815, after the conclusion of the Napoleonic Wars, the Prince Regent (later George IV) found it necessary to reward many distinguished officers of both the Navy and the Army, consequently the Order was enlarged by creating two divisions, military as well as civil, with the military embracing three classes. These were the G.C.B. (Knight Grand Cross), K.C.B. (Knight Commander) and the C.B. (Companion). In 1847 it was found necessary to enlarge the civil division to three classes which then corresponded with the military division. All badges were produced in gold prior to 1887, since when they have always been in silver gilt. In 1917 the third class badge (C.B.) of this Order was altered from a breast badge, worn the same way as a medal, into a badge worn around the neck.

Admission to the Order is currently granted rather sparingly, and since 1971 women have also been admitted. The Bath is probably the most highly regarded of the lesser orders. The motto of the Order is *'Tria juncta in uno'* 'Three joined in one', namely England, Scotland and Ireland.

Until 1857 the insignia of all grades of both divisions were returnable by the heirs of the recipients and then reissued. However, after that year they were allowed to be retained by the families. These days, the insignia are returnable only upon promotion in the Order although, as with all other orders the collar chain has to be returned.

**Knight of the Bath (K.B.)**

| | |
|---|---|
| Collar chain | £35,000 |
| Collar badge | £5000 |
| Star (metal) | £3500 |
| Star (embroidered, in very fine condition) | £500 |
| Oval gold sash badge without enamel (similar to the later civil division) | £5000 |

*Insignia after 1815*

MILITARY DIVISION

*Prices for gold badges are based on those issued just prior to 1887, earlier insignia can be expected to be more valuable; complete cased sets would command a further premium*

**Knight Grand Cross (G.C.B.)**

| | |
|---|---|
| Collar chain (gold) (no distinction between military and civil) | £25,000 |
| Collar chain (silver gilt) | £14,000 |
| Collar badge (gold) | £4250 |
| Collar badge (silver gilt) | £2000 |
| Star | £850 |
| Star (embroidered, in very fine condition) | £400 |
| Sash badge (gold and enamel) | £3000 |
| Sash badge (silver gilt and enamel) | £1200 |

**Knight Commander (K.C.B.)**

| | |
|---|---|
| Star | £450 |
| Star (embroidered, in very fine condition) | £300 |
| Neck badge (gold and enamel) | £1200 |
| Neck badge (silver gilt and enamel) | £500 |

**Companion (C.B.)**

| | |
|---|---|
| Breast badge (gold and enamel) | £750 |
| Breast badge (silver gilt and enamel) | £350 |
| Neck badge (silver gilt and enamel) | £280 |

CIVIL DIVISION

**Knight Grand Cross (G.C.B.)**

| | |
|---|---|
| Collar chain (gold) | £25,000 |
| Collar chain (silver gilt) (no distinction between military and civil) | £14,000 |
| Star (metal) | £500 |
| Sash/collar badge (gold) | £1500 |
| Sash/collar badge (silver gilt) | £525 |

**Knight Commander (K.C.B.)**

| | |
|---|---|
| Star (metal) | £250 |
| Neck badge (gold) | £600 |
| Neck badge (silver gilt) | £200 |

**Companion (C.B.)**

| | |
|---|---|
| Breast badge (gold) | £425 |
| Breast badge (silver gilt) | £150 |
| Neck badge (silver gilt) | £130 |
| Officers badge | £3000 |

# 5 *The Royal Guelphic Order* 1815-37

Instituted by the Prince Regent (later George IV) and awarded by the Crown of Hanover to both British and Hanoverian servicemen and civilians for distinguished services to Hanover.

By the Hanoverian law of succession, a woman could not ascend the throne, consequently, upon the death of William IV, Queen Victoria could not adopt the title of Sovereign and the Duke of Cumberland, fifth son of George III, became King of Hanover. From then on, the Guelphic Order became a totally Hanoverian award.

As with the Order of the Bath, which the insignia rather resembles from a design point of view, the Order comprised three classes, having both military and civil divisions. The motto of the Order is *'Nec aspera terrent*—'Difficulties do not terrify'.

The majority of the recipients during the early years were distinguished British and Hanoverian officers who had fought Napoleon, many Hanoverian regiments having fought with distinction under Wellington in both the Spanish Peninsula and at Waterloo.

The prices of insignia listed below have been based on the period 1815-37, all insignia being London made.

The lower classes of the award, namely the Knight and the Knight Commander, do from time to time come on to the market, particularly the civil ones. However, many military division awards are often accompanied by other decorations.

| **Knight Grand Cross (G.C.H.)** | *1 Military* | *2 Civil* | **Knight Commander (K.C.H.)** | | |
|---|---|---|---|---|---|
| Gold collar. (No distinction between military and civil) | | | Star | £950 | £700 |
| | £8500 | £8500 | Neck badge (gold and enamel) | £2500 | £1300 |
| Silver gilt/copper gilt collar. (No distinction between military and civil) | £4250 | £4250 | | | |
| Collar badge (gold and enamel 2.6in. dia.) | £3750 | £3000 | **Knight (K.H.)** | | |
| Star | £1200 | £900 | Breast badge (gold and enamel) | £1800 | £1000 |
| Sash badge (gold and enamel) | £4000 | £3000 | Breast badge (silver and enamel) | £1000 | £750 |

## 6 *The Most Distinguished Order of St Michael and St George* 1818

Founded in 1818 by the Prince Regent, and awarded as a token of appreciation for services rendered by the population of Malta and the Ionian Islands in the Mediterranean, which in 1815 had been formed as an independent kingdom under the protection of the United Kingdom. The islands, which were acquired as a result of the Napoleonic Wars, were then very strategically placed, thus making them important to Great Britain.

Towards the end of the nineteenth century, due to the growing extent of the British Empire, the Order was then extended to those who had rendered distinguished services in the colonies and in foreign affairs generally. The motto, *'Puspicium melioris aevi*—'Token of a better age', was adopted at the time of the institution of the Order.

The Order of St Michael and St George comprises three classes, namely G.C.M.G. (Knight Grand Cross), K.C.M.G. (Knight Commander) and C.M.G. (Companion). Up to 1891 the insignia was returnable upon promotion or death of the recipient, however, after this date they were returnable only upon promotion within the Order. Since 1948 the collar chains have been returnable upon the death of the recipient.

As with all British insignia, these were awarded in gold and enamel prior to 1887, since then all awards have been in silver gilt and enamel. In more recent years, the insignia have been awarded to ladies but to date only four Grand Crosses have been issued. Insignia awarded to ladies are slightly smaller in size. In 1917 the third class badge (C.M.G.) of this Order was altered from a breast badge, worn the same way as a medal, into a badge worn around the neck.

**Knight Grand Cross (G.C.M.G.)**

| | | | |
|---|---|---|---|
| Collar chain | £1500 | Neck badge (gold and enamel) | £1200 |
| Star | £600 | Neck badge (silver gilt and enamel) | £300 |
| Sash badge (gold and enamel) | £5000 | | |
| Sash badge (silver gilt and enamel) | £750 | **Companion (C.M.G.)** | |
| | | Breast badge (gold and enamel) | £650 |
| **Knight Commander (K.C.M.G.)** | | Breast badge (silver gilt and enamel) | £350 |
| Star (introduced 1859) | £350 | Neck badge (silver gilt and enamel) | £220 |

*All prices are based on insignia awarded to gentlemen.*

## 7 *The Most Exalted Order of the Star of India* 1861-1947

Founded in 1861 as a reward for services in connection with India. After the Indian Mutiny of 1857-58, the British Crown accepted responsibility for the administration of the Indian subcontinent, taking over the duties from the private trading company, known as the Honourable East India Company. It was quickly realized that it was necessary to have an order connected solely with India, as a mark of the Government's esteem for the loyal princes and others. The insignia are the most magnificent of all British Orders, especially the Knight Grand Commander (G.C.S.I.), which, as it was awarded to the Viceroy and Indian princes, was of gold and enamel, lavishly set with diamonds. The motto of the Order 'Heavens Light Our Guide' is set onto a pale blue enamelled ribbon, the letters being in gold set with diamonds.

Prior to the independence of India in 1947, all insignia of this Order was returnable by the heirs of the recipients. However, after 1947, the Order was no longer awarded and the recipients or their families were allowed in certain cases to purchase the star and badges of any of the applicable three classes, but not the Grand Commander gold and enamel collar chain, consequently, these collar chains seldom, if ever, appear on the market.

The first class of this and the Order of the Indian Empire was designated Knight Grand Commander, thus removing the Christian designation of Knight Grand Cross, the Order being given mainly to Hindus and Muslims.

| | |
|---|---|
| Knight Grand Commander (G.C.S.I.) gold and enamel collar chain | £35,000 |
| Knight Grand Commander (G.C.S.I.) star and sash badge | £34,000 |
| Knight Commander (K.C.S.I.) star and neck badge | £4,500 |
| Companion (C.S.I.) breast badge | £3,000 |
| Companion (C.S.I.) neck badge | £1,800 |

## 8 *The Most Eminent Order of the Indian Empire*

1878-1947

Originally this Order consisted of Companions only, but was then enlarged in 1887 to the three traditional classes. This was the second of the Indian orders founded by Queen Victoria when she adopted the title 'Empress of India'. Hence the motto *'Imperatricis auspicus'*—'Under the auspices of the Empress'.

The Order was discontinued in 1947 due to independence being granted to India and Pakistan; the Order is the fourth and final senior British Order which has been discontinued owing to political or dynastic reasons, the others being the Orders of St Patrick, Guelphic and Star of India.

The design of the Order, like the Star of India, came about as it was necessary to omit a cross, which is the traditional basis for the designs of British orders. A cross would not have been accepted by the non-Christian recipients and consequently, unlike other orders, it did not have a patron saint. The Order was intended to serve as a junior award to the Order of the Star of India, a certain proportion of the Indian Empire Order was awarded to officers of the two services. The third-class badge of this Order, like all other orders, was worn on the breast, the same way as a medal, but in 1917 it was altered for wear around the neck. Prior to the independence of India in 1947, the first and second classes were returnable by the recipients' executors upon their death. However, as with the Star of India, the recipients or their families were allowed to purchase the stars and badges, but not the Knight Grand Commander's silver gilt collar chain.

| | |
|---|---|
| Knight Grand Commander (G.C.I.E.) silver gilt collar chain | £15,000 |
| Knight Grand Commander (G.C.I.E.) star and sash badge | £6000 |
| Knight Commander (K.C.I.E.) star and neck badge | £1800 |
| Companion (C.I.E.) 1st issue breast badge with 'INDIA' on the petals of the lotus flower | £1000 |
| Companion (C.I.E.) 2nd issue (smaller size) breast badge | £380 |
| Companion (C.I.E.) 3rd issue (smaller size) neck badge | £300 |

## 9 *The Royal Family Order*

There are three Orders (nos. 9, 10 & 11) associated with the Court which are only awarded to ladies. The first is the Royal Family Order, which is worn only by the Queen and the female relatives of the Sovereign: special badges of distinction are awarded to their ladies-in-waiting. The modern Royal Family Order consists of badges set with diamonds which in turn invariably surround the portrait of the Sovereign. These insignia very seldom come on to the market and it would be pointless to attempt to price them.

This Order is worn by the Queen and the female relatives of the Sovereign. Special badges are also given to ladies-in-waiting. These insignia seldom appear on the market.

## 10 *The Royal Order of Victoria and Albert* 1862

This Royal Family Order for Ladies was instituted by Queen Victoria on February 10th 1862 and consists of four classes. It was awarded to Ladies as a mark of personal regard and favour. The first and second classes were restricted to Royalty both British and foreign. The third and fourth classes were granted to Ladies of high distinction and probably members of Her Majesty's Household.

The Insignia of the first, second and third classes consists of an onyx cameo with the busts of Queen Victoria and Prince Albert in profile, facing to the left, surmounted by a Crown; the first and second classes being set in diamonds, and the third class in pearls and diamonds. The fourth class Badge is in the form of a monogram, 'V. & A.', in pearls and rubies, also surmounted by a Crown.

| | |
|---|---|
| 1st class | £25,000 |
| 2nd class | £18,000 |
| 3rd class | £12,000 |
| 4th class | £4,500 |

## 11 *The Imperial Order of the Crown of India* 1878-1947

This Ladies Order was instituted on 1st January 1878 by Queen Victoria to commemorate the occasion of Her Majesty's assumption of the title 'Empress of India'. The Order was awarded to British and Indian Ladies who merited distinction for devoted service for the advancement and benefit of India.

The badge consists of the Royal Cypher in diamonds, pearls and turquoises encircled by a border set with pearls, surmounted by the Imperial Crown, jewelled and enamelled. The badge is worn from a bow of light blue watered ribbon, edged with white.

| | |
|---|---|
| Breast Badge | £8,000 |

## 12 *The Royal Victorian Order* 1896

This was the last of the Orders instituted during the nineteenth century, having been introduced in 1896 towards the very end of the reign of Queen Victoria.

At the time of the introduction of this Order, prime ministers and governments were increasing their influence over the distributions of awards and distinctions. The Victorian Orders and Medals were introduced, therefore, so as to be totally outside the jurisdiction of members of government—the award being the sole prerogative of the Sovereign. From the very beginning, the Order consisted of five classes plus three different classes of medals, which are available to both ladies and gentlemen.

Ladies' insignia are similar in size to the gentlemen's but the collar is smaller, the G.V.C.O. star is also slightly smaller and the sash is only 2.25in. wide. The badges of the lower grades are suspended from a bow except when worn in uniform.

All insignia are in silver, gilt and enamel. The majority are numbered and are returnable on promotion.

| | Gentleman | Ladies |
|---|---|---|
| Knight Grand Cross (G.C.V.O.) collar chain | £7500 | £9000 |
| Knight Grand Cross (G.C.V.O.) sash badge and breast star | £950 | £1300 |
| Knight Commander (K.C.V.O.) neck badge and breast star | £550 | £800 |
| Commander (C.V.O.) neck badge | £240 | £300 |
| Member (4th class) (M.V.O.) breast badge (L.V.O. since 1988) | £150 | £200 |
| Member (5th Class) (M.V.O.) breast badge | £150 | £200 |

## 13 *The Royal Victorian Medal*

The Royal Victorian Medal is a private medal issued by the Sovereign to both men and women who have rendered personal services. To distinguish between British and foreign recipients of the medal King George VI in 1951 decreed that foreign recipients should wear the medal from a ribbon with an additional central white stripe. These foreign recipients are referred to as 'associates'. In 1983 the order for wearing the Royal Victorian Medal was changed, and the medal was no longer worn after campaign medals but before them.

| *Victoria* | | | *Edward VIII* | |
|---|---|---|---|---|
| Silver | £85 | | Silver (2 issued) | £1800 |
| Bronze | £60 | | | |
| | | | *George VI* | |
| *Edward VII* | | | Silver gilt | £80 |
| Silver | £85 | | Silver | £55 |
| Bronze | £55 | | Bronze (4 issued) | £700 |
| *George V* | | | *Elizabeth II* | |
| Silver gilt | £80 | | Silver gilt | £95 |
| Silver | £60 | | Silver | £70 |
| Bronze | £45 | | Bronze | £50 |

## 14 *The Royal Victorian Chain* 1902

The Royal Victorian Chain was introduced by Edward VII in 1902 and is only awarded to selected foreign Princes and very high ranking members of the Royal Household. The chain is not strictly speaking part of the Royal Victorian Order.

| | |
|---|---|
| Gentlemen's collar with standard C.V.O. badge | £9000 |
| Gentlemen's collar (1921 issue with diamonds to crown and cypher) | £12,000 |
| Ladies' bow arrangement (1902-21 with a standard C.V.O. badge without diamonds) | £9000 |
| Ladies' bow arrangement (1921 issue with diamonds to crown and cypher) | £12,000 |

## 15 *The Order of Merit* 1902

In spite of the fact that this is a relatively modern order, it is one of the most coveted of British distinctions. It was introduced by King Edward VII in 1902 being a very special distinction awarded to those supreme in the fields of art, music and literature, and is also, from time to time, awarded to military leaders in time of war. The military division is distinguished by crossed swords that pass through the centre of the neck badge. This is another order which again is limited, this time to twenty-four members as well as an additional limited number of foreign recipients. As with the Royal Victorian Order, the Order of Merit is the sole gift of the Sovereign but carries no rank apart from the initials O.M. after the name. This award is also presented to ladies, recipients being Florence Nightingale in 1905, Professor Dorothy Hodgkin in 1965 and Dame Veronica Wedgwood in 1969. Other well-known public figures that were awarded this distinction were Sir Winston Churchill, General Eisenhower (later President of the USA), Field Marshal Alexander and Admiral of the Fleet Earl Mountbatten. The ribbon is interesting in that the blue represents the Order of the Garter, and the red, the Order of the Bath.

It is particularly difficult to assess the value of the military division of this Order, as invariably when then do appear on the market they are accompanied by other decorations and medals forming part of a group.

The numbers awarded during the different reigns are shown in brackets, but in addition ten honorary awards have been presented, as follows:
Edward VII (3), George V (2), George VI (2) and Elizabeth II (3).

| *Military* | | *Civil* | |
|---|---|---|---|
| Edward VII (7) | £6000 | Edward VII (17) | £4000 |
| George V (7) | £6000 | George V (28) | £3800 |
| George VI (8) | £6000 | George VI (22) | £4000 |
| Elizabeth II (2) | £8000 | Elizabeth II (41) | £3000 |

## 16 *The Most Excellent Order of the British Empire* 1917

This is the junior of all the British Orders, having been founded as recently as 1917. The Order was introduced owing to the very large demand for honours and awards created by the First World War—the Order of the Bath (military division) having been created in 1815 for the very same reasons following the Napoleonic Wars. The Order, as well as the Medals of the Order, is awarded for service to the State and Commonwealth generally, and is given to a very wide range of people (both civilians and service personnel) in all walks of life for valuable work in the social services, entertainment and local government.

When the Order was instituted in 1917, Britannia appeared in the centres of both stars and badges. The ribbon was purple, with a central scarlet stripe added for the military division. In 1937, joint effigies of King George V and Queen Mary replaced Britannia, the rays of the stars were altered from a fluted effect to faceted or chipped and the ribbon was changed to rose pink with pearl-grey edges. While the insignia for both the civil and military divisions is the same, the ribbon for the latter includes an additional central pearl-grey stripe.

Ladies' insignia are similar to the gentlemen's but the collar and G.B.E. star are smaller, the sash is 2.25in. in width, and the badges of the lower grades are suspended from a bow, except when worn in uniform.

In 1957 a silver crossed oak leaf emblem was instituted for wear on the ribbon of the Order and riband bar, civil or military, in recognition of gallantry. The award of the emblem for gallantry ceased in 1974 with the introduction of the Q.G.M.

A recipient of the B.E.M. appointed to the Order may retain and wear both awards. A member of the Order awarded both civil and military divisions may also retain and wear both awards. A person awarded the Order with emblem for gallantry may on promotion for 'meritorious service' wear the emblem on the higher award.

| Gentlemen | 1st type | 2nd type | Ladies | | |
|---|---|---|---|---|---|
| Knight Grand Cross (G.B.E.) collar | £6000 | £6000 | Dame Grand Cross (G.B.E.) collar | £7500 | £7500 |
| Knight Grand Cross (G.B.E.) sash badge and star | £950 | £1100 | Dame Grand Cross (G.B.E.) sash badge and star | £1500 | £1500 |
| Knight Commander (K.B.E.) neck badge and star | £325 | £350 | Dame Commander (D.B.E.) neck/breast badge and star | £450 | £500 |
| Commander (C.B.E.) neck badge | £120 | £140 | Commander (C.B.E.) neck/breast badge | £125 | £135 |
| Officer (O.B.E.) breast badge | £40 | £45 | Officer (O.B.E.) breast badge | £50 | £50 |
| Member (M.B.E.) breast badge | £40 | £45 | Member (M.B.E.) breast badge | £50 | £50 |

## 17 *Medal of the Order of the British Empire* 1917-1922

The Medal of the Order of the British Empire was instituted in June 1917 as a lower award connected with the Order. The medal was produced in silver and issued unnamed and was worn from a plain purple ribbon. In December 1918 a military division was created and whilst civil awards retained the plain purple ribbon, military awards were distinguished by the addition of a central red stripe. Nearly 2000 medals were issued between 1917 and 1922 when the medal was replaced by the Empire Gallantry Medal and British Empire Medal.

| Medal | £60 |
|---|---|

## 18 *Medal of the Order of the British Empire for Gallantry* 1922-1940 *Empire Gallantry Medal*

The Medal of the Order of the British Empire for Gallantry commonly referred to as the Empire Gallantry Medal, was instituted together with the British Empire Medal by a Royal Warrant dated 29th December 1922. These two medals replaced the original Medal of the Order which had been introduced in 1917. The Empire Gallantry Medal had both civil and military divisions and was awarded for specific acts of gallantry.

The medal was struck in silver and was issued named in serif capitals engraved around the edge. The ribbon was originally plain purple for civil and purple with a central red stripe for military awards. In common with the Order, in July 1937 the ribbon was changed, becoming pink with grey edges for civil awards and having an additional central grey stripe for military awards. The Empire Gallantry Medal was similar to the British Empire Medal, it differed only in having the word 'GALLANTRY' in the obverse exergue below Britannia and by having a suspension ornamented by laurel leaves. In 1933 to further emphasize the difference, a silver laurel branch emblem was introduced for wear on the ribbon. A smaller version was worn on the riband bar.

In 1940 the Empire Gallantry Medal was superseded by the George Cross. Recipients of the E.G.M. were to exchange their Medals for the George Cross, but not all E.G.M.s were exchanged or returned.

A total of 130 medals were issued, 64 being civil, 62 military and 4 honorary.

| | |
|---|---|
| George V | £3000 |
| George VI | £3000 |

## 19 *Medal of the Order of the British Empire for Meritorious Service* 1922 *British Empire Medal*

The Medal of the Order of the British Empire for Meritorious Service is usually referred to as the British Empire Medal. Together with the Empire Gallantry Medal it was instituted in December 1922 replacing the earlier Medal of the Order of the British Empire. The medal is awarded for meritorious service to both civil and military personnel. The medal may be worn if the recipient is promoted to a higher grade of the Order.

The medal is struck in silver and is issued named in engraved capitals around the edge. For ribbon details see—Empire Gallantry Medal. The British Empire Medal is very similar to the Empire Gallantry Medal, it differs by having in the obverse exergue the words 'MERITORIOUS SERVICE' and by having a suspension ornamented by oak leaves. A silver bar bearing oak leaves was established in March 1941 as an award for further acts of meritorious service.

In December 1957 an emblem of crossed silver oak leaves was introduced for wear on the ribbon to denote gallantry. A smaller version was worn on the riband bar. Such awards for gallantry ceased in 1974 with the introduction of the Queen's Gallantry Medal.

| | Military | Civil |
|---|---|---|
| George V | £180 | £120 |
| George VI GRI cypher | £100 | £60 |
| George VI GVIR cypher | £160 | £90 |
| Elizabeth II | £100 | £50 |
| Elizabeth II with gallantry emblem | £450 | £300 |

## 20 *The Order of the Companion of Honour* 1917

This is sometimes regarded as a junior Order of Merit which had been introduced in 1902. The C.H. badge was founded by King George V in 1917 at the same time as the Order of the British Empire. It was restricted to fifty companions but increased to sixty-five members in 1943, and is awarded to men and women who perform special services of national importance. The award is made on the recommendation of prime ministers of the countries of the British Commonwealth, in accordance with the following statutory quotas:
UK—45, Australia—7, New Zealand—2, Other Commonwealth countries—11.

In over half a century, very few recipients have received both the Order of Merit and the Companion of Honour, but among those who have are Lord Atlee, Field Marshal Smuts, Walter de la Mare, Henry Moore, Benjamin Britten, Sir Winston Churchill, G. P. Gooch, Lord Blackett, E. M. Forster, Graham Greene and Sir Michael Tippett.

| | |
|---|---|
| Gentlemen | £1500 |
| Ladies | £2000 |

## 21 *The Baronet's Badge* 1629

The first badge of this Order was instituted in 1629 by the Baronets of Scotland who were known as 'Baronets of Nova Scotia', owing to a grant of lands in Nova Scotia made to them by James I in 1624. It was almost three hundred years before King George V granted permission for the Baronets of England, Ireland, Great Britain and of the United Kingdom to wear distinctive badges to indicate their rank.

The Scottish Baronets wore a badge with a distinctive design, which was a crowned shield carrying the cross of St Andrew. The remaining badges, authorised in 1929, contain on a central shield the crowned arms of Ulster, surrounded by a border of roses (England), of shamrocks (Ireland), of roses and thistles combined (Great Britain), or roses, thistles and shamrocks combined (United Kingdom). These badges are engraved on the reverse with the recipient's title and date of institution.

| Baronets of: | Gold | Silver-gilt |
|---|---|---|
| Scotland (Nova Scotia) late 18th and early 19th century examples | £3000 | — |
| Scotland (Nova Scotia) late 19th and 20th century example | £2000 | £1000 |
| England (rose surround) | £950 | £500 |
| Ireland (shamrock surround) | £950 | £500 |
| Great Britian (rose and thistle surround) | £950 | £500 |
| United Kingdom (rose, thistle and shamrock surround) | £950 | £500 |

## 22 *The Knight Bachelor's Badge* 1929

Authorised by King George V in 1929 at the same time as the later issue of Baronet's Badges. The Imperial Society of Knights Bachelors obtained the permission of the King to wear a distinctive badge so as to distinguish their rank, thus bringing them into line with the Baronets. The first model was of a larger type worn on the breast by means of a reverse pin, this measuring 3in. × 2in. In 1933 it was reduced in size and then in 1974 it was reduced even further and adapted for wear around the neck from a ribbon. Although the Queen in 1974, gave permission for badges to be worn around the neck, as knights felt at a disadvantage to the wearers of other neck badges, it is now becoming fashionable for knights to wear the breast badge. The title 'Knight Bachelor' was introduced by King Henry III to signify that the title dies with the holder.

| | |
|---|---|
| 1st type breast badge (1929) | £150 |
| 2nd type breast badge (smaller) (1933) | £130 |
| 3rd type (smaller) neck badge (1974) | £150 |

## 23 *The Order of St John of Jerusalem* 1888

This Order was incorporated by Royal Charter during the reign of Victoria in 1888. The insignia is unique in that it is not awarded by the Crown but by the Order itself on the authority of the Sovereign. As a result, the Order can be regarded as a semi-private order.

The Order is given for voluntary work in connection with activities in hospitals, and ambulance and relief work. Recipients who are not British subjects, or who are non-Christians, are made associates of the Order, and their insignia used to be distinguished by the fact that the normal plain black watered ribbon had a central white stripe. Now all ribbons of the Order are the same.

| | Gold | Silver gilt/ Silver | Base metal |
|---|---|---|---|
| Bailiff Grand Cross, sash badge and star (G.C.St.J.) | £1500 | £900 | — |
| Dame Grand Cross, sash badge and star (G.C.St.J.) | £1500 | £600 | — |
| Knight of Justice, neck badge and star (K.St.J.) | £750 | £300 | £175 |
| Dame of Justice, breast badge and star (D.St.J.) | £750 | £300 | £200 |
| Knight of Grace, neck badge and star (K.St.J.) | — | £300 | £150 |
| Dame of Grace, breast badge and star (D.St.J.) | — | £300 | £175 |
| Commander (Brother), neck badge (C.St.J.) | — | £150 | £60 |
| Commander (Sister), breast badge (C.St.J.) | — | £85 | £60 |
| Officer (Brother/Sister), breast badge, plain silver cross, 1926-36 | — | £30 | — |
| Officer (Brother), breast badge, enamelled cross (O.St.J.) | — | £45 | £30 |
| Officer (Sister), breast badge, enamelled cross (O.St.J.) | — | £45 | £30 |
| Serving Brother/Sister 1st type (S.B.St.J.; S.S.St.J.) | — | £45 | £30 |
| Serving Brother/Sister skeletal type, 1939-47 | — | £30 | — |
| Serving Brother/Sister 2nd type, plain cross (similar to officers badge 1926) | — | — | £30 |

## 24 *The Order of the Dooranie Empire (Afghanistan)*

1839

This Order has been included here as, when it was originally instituted in 1839 by the Shah of Afghanistan, it was to be conferred as a reward to British officers only for services to Afghanistan. British officers were awarded 5 first class, 19 second and 36 third class, the insignia being an imitation of the Guelphic Order of Hanover. Insignia of the Order, more particularly the third class, do from time to time come onto the market, and are often associated with groups. (The campaign medal awarded at the time is No. 95.)

| | |
|---|---|
| Grand Cross, star and badge | £7500 |
| Knight Commander, star and badge | £5000 |
| Commander | £2500 |

*Prices are based on 1839 issues proved to have been awarded to British officers.*

# *Decorations*

Prices for gallantry awards are based on general citations (where applicable), ie, without detail in the London Gazette of a specific act of gallantry. Prices can be considerably enhanced by the particular act of gallantry, the rarity of the award for a particular campaign, combinations of decorations in a group being another important factor. Readers *must* bear in mind that the undermentioned prices are base prices.

## 25 *The Victoria Cross* 1856

This, the foremost British and Commonwealth gallantry decoration, is awarded for very exceptional gallantry and as such, is the most prized gallantry award that any subject of the realm can earn.

Introduced in 1856 towards the end of the Crimean War, and made retrospective to 1854, it was deemed by Queen Victoria that the cross should be simple in design and must be made out of the bronze cannon captured from the Russians during the Crimean War. Queen Victoria took a great deal of interest in the award and personally invested 67 of the 111 Crimea recipients at a parade held in Hyde Park in June 1857.

Originally, Naval recipients wore the cross from a blue ribbon and those of the Army from a crimson ribbon, it was not until 1918 that the crimson ribbon became standard for all services. Since 1918, when the ribbon is worn alone a miniature of the Cross is fixed to it to make it more distinctive.

The V.C. is always issued named with the recipients details engraved on the reverse of the suspension bar and the date(s) of the act of gallantry engraved in the centre reverse of the Cross.

A total of 1354 awards have been given, which includes three bars and from the time of institution until 1908, eight had been forfeited for misconduct. The Army have been awarded 832, Royal Navy 107, RAF 31, RM 10, Civilians 4, the remainder being awarded to Commonwealth units. The youngest recipient was only just over fifteen years of age and the oldest sixty-nine. Three have been awarded to father and son, while four have been awarded to brothers.

This is probably the most difficult item of all to value, as so much depends on various factors, such as the branch to which awarded (Navy, Army, RAF, Imperial, Commonwealth or Indian troops); the regiment in which the recipient was serving and the total number awarded to the regiment; the theatre of war and the number awarded for the particular action; the citation details; whether officer or other rank; the condition; the composition and number of other medals that might accompany the award and the biographical details of the recipient.

| Pre-1914 | £10,000 |
| 1914-18 | £10,000 |
| 1939-45 | £25,000 |

## 26  *The New Zealand Cross* 1869

This decoration for gallantry is unique to the Commonwealth of New Zealand and was awarded on twenty-three occasions only for bravery during the period of the second Maori war which lasted from 1860-72, although, in actual fact, the last award was not approved until as late as 1910.

The decoration came about through an Order in Council made at Government House, Wellington on the 10th March 1869, it being the intention of New Zealand that this would be a purely local and unofficial award, in the same manner as those awarded by societies such as the Royal Geographical and Royal Humane, and therefore not to be confused or compared with those awards issued by the Crown. The award came about as local volunteer forces did not qualify for the Victoria Cross.

Awards were made immediately and before the approval of London could be obtained, whereupon the Secretary of State in London, Earl Granville, reacted rather promptly and sent a despatch to the Governor which read, 'I am unwillingly constrained to observe that in complying with this natural desire to reward local forces, you have overstepped the limits of the authority confided to you by Her Majesty. The authority inherent in the Queen as the fountain head of honour throughout her Empire has never been delegated to you and you are, therefore, not competent as Her Majesty's representative to create any of those titular or decorative distinctions which, in the British Empire, have their source, and are valuable because they have their source, in the grace of the Sovereign.' After this rather severe dressing down, the Queen eventually gave her blessing to the New Zealand Cross, but, due to the fact that the New Zealand local forces were disbanded later on, the Cross by 1911 had fallen into disuse.

The riband was the same as the V.C. but without the later bronze emblem. Crosses were issued named with the recipients' rank, name, unit and the date of the act of gallantry engraved on the reverse.

| | |
|---|---|
| Original | £20,000 |
| New Zealand Mint replica | £500 |

## 27  *The George Cross* 1940

Instituted in September 1940 as a reward to civilians and to members of the armed forces for acts of the greatest heroism or of the most conspicuous courage. A highly prestigious award, it ranks second only to the Victoria Cross.

By the terms of a Royal Warrant of January 1941, the George Cross replaced the Empire Gallantry Medal. Holders of the EGM received the George Cross in exchange. By a Royal Warrant of December 1971 living recipients of the Albert and Edward Medals were permitted to exchange these medals for the George Cross.

Excluding these exchange awards and the unique award to the Island of Malta, over 150 George Crosses have been awarded since 1940, of these 106 were awarded between 1940 and 1947. 4 awards have been made to women.

The Cross is struck in silver and the reverse is always engraved, giving the recipient's name, rank and date of announcement in the 'London Gazette'.

Exchange awards have the date of the act engraved in place of the 'London Gazette' entry.

| Service awards, from 1940 | £4500 |
|---|---|
| Civilian awards, from 1940 | £3250 |
| Service exchange awards, pre-1940 | £2500 |
| Civilian exchange awards, pre-1940 | £1500 |

## 28 *The Distinguished Service Order* 1886

Following the campaigns of the mid-nineteenth century such as the Crimea and the Indian Mutiny, it was realized that there was no adequate reward for distinguished service for presentation to junior officers, apart from the Victoria Cross—in the case of senior officers, membership to the Order of the Bath was available. As a result, the D.S.O. was introduced in 1886.

The design of the Order has remained basically constant. Originally produced in gold and enamel it was changed in 1889 to silver-gilt and enamel, in common with other British awards. There have been six reverse types, with the royal cypher changing: VRI, EviiR, GvR, GRI (1938-1948), GviR (1949-1952), EiiR. There have also been minor changes to the obverse crown: crown with flattened arches (Victoria issues); crown with rounded arches (later Victoria and Edward VII issues); larger crown (later issues). Throughout its history the Order has always been issued unnamed. From about 1938 onwards, the year of award was engraved on the reverse of the suspension bar. A top brooch bar forms an integral part of the Order. For further awards a silver-gilt bar bearing a crown was issued; from 1938 onwards the bars were dated on the reverse with the year of award.

Of the more scarcer types, approximately 153 gold Victorian, a minimum of 78 Edward VII and approximately 63 2nd type George VI D.S.Os were awarded.

Approximately 1170 silver-gilt Victorian D.S.Os were awarded for the 2nd Boer War.

Approximately 9900 George V D.S.Os, 770 first bars, 76 second bars and 7 third bars were awarded for the 1st World War.

Approximately 4880 George VI 1st type D.S.Os, 500 first bars, 59 second bars and 8 third bars were awarded for the 2nd World War.

| | Unnamed single | Attributable group |
|---|---|---|
| Victoria (gold) | £1500 | £1800 |
| Victoria (silver-gilt) | £450 | £600 |
| Edward VII | £950 | £1500 |
| George V | £320 | £450 |
| George VI (1st type) | £450 | £550 |
| George VI (2nd type) | £1200 | £2000 |
| Elizabeth II | £950 | £1500 |

## 29 *The Imperial Service Order and Medals* 1902

Prior to the creation of the Order of the British Empire in 1917, there was no way of rewarding the efforts of the very many lesser members of the civil service in both administrative and clerical posts throughout the country, and indeed the Empire. The Imperial Service Order was established by King Edward VII in August 1902 so as to fill this gap in the awards system. In August 1908, the Order was extended to include women.

Twenty-five years service was the usual requirement, though in India the period was twenty years and sixteen years in countries with unhealthy climates. The prescribed period could however be waived for those performing eminently meritorious service.

The Order came in one class. That awarded to gentlemen had a central gold plaque bearing the Royal Cypher and the legend 'For Faithful Service', set upon a silver eight pointed star, the uppermost point being replaced by a crown suspension. That awarded to women is similar except that it has a silver wreath in place of the star.

For lower grades of the civil service the Imperial Service Medal was available being awarded under similar conditions as the I.S.O. Originally the I.S.M. was of the same design as the Order except that the plaque was silver and the star or wreath bronze. In 1920 the I.S.M. was changed to a silver circular medal; the obverse bearing the monarch's head or bust, the reverse depicting a man at rest with 'For Faithful Service' in the exergue. The medal was named around the edge.

| *Order* | |
|---|---|
| Edward VII (Gentlemen) | £110 |
| Edward VII (Women) | £300 |
| George V (Gentlemen) | £75 |
| George V (Women) | £200 |
| George VI (Gentlemen) | £95 |
| George VI (Women) | £150 |
| Elizabeth II (Gentlemen) | £95 |
| Elizabeth II (Women) | £120 |

| *Medal* | |
|---|---|
| Edward VII (Gentlemen) | £35 |
| Edward VII (Women) | £100 |
| George V (1st issue, star shaped, Gentlemen) | £20 |
| George V (1st issue, with wreath, Women) | £90 |
| George V (2nd issue circular) | £12 |
| George VI | £12 |
| Elizabeth II | £12 |

## 30 *The Indian Order of Merit* 1837

This is the oldest gallantry award, having been introduced as far back as 1837 by the Honourable East India Company, which at that time was responsible for the administration of the Indian subcontinent. However, it did not become an official award until after the H.E.I. Company's forces were taken over by the Crown following the conclusion of the Indian Mutiny. The award was originally known as the 'Order of Merit' but with the introduction of the British Order of Merit (No. 15) in 1902, the title of this Order was altered to the 'Indian Order of Merit'.

Three classes were originally introduced, the first in gold, and the second and third basically in silver, all with obverse centres enamelled. Promotion in the Order was dependant upon successive acts of gallantry. Recipients were entitled to higher pay and pensions. In 1902, a civil division of the Order was introduced to correspond with the military division. In 1911, Indian troops became eligible for the Victoria Cross and the first class in gold was abolished, so the remaining two classes were re-designated as the new first and second class. The civil division which had been introduced in 1902 was reduced to one class only in 1939, as was the military division in 1944.

Apart from the Royal Mint and the Calcutta Mint, the insignia was made by a number of manufacturers especially immediately after the Indian Mutiny. Some pieces are hallmarked and command a premium. The insignia made by the firm of J. W. Benson Ltd, Ludgate Hill, London, has the firm's name and address engraved at the lower end of the backplate. These too command a premium.

The numbers awarded (given below) are approximate.

---

*Military*

Centres read 'Reward of Valor', star body 38mm. in diameter and fitted with a three pronged ribbon brooch bar unless stated otherwise.

| | | |
|---|---|---:|
| 1837-1912: | 1st Class in gold, 42 awarded | £1800 |
| | 2nd Class in silver with a gold centre and wreath, 130 awarded | £500 |
| | 3rd Class in silver, 2740 awarded | £140 |
| 1912-1939: | 1st Class in silver with a gold centre and wreath, reverse engraved '1st Class', 26 awarded | £850 |
| | 2nd Class in silver, reverse engraved '2nd Class', 1215 awarded | £130 |
| 1939-1945: | 1st Class in silver with a gold centre and wreath, reading 'Reward of Gallantry', Reverse engraved '1st Class', 2 awarded | £2500 |
| 1939-1944: | 2nd Class in silver, centre reading 'Reward for Gallantry', Reverse engraved '2nd Class', 332 awarded | £250 |

| | | |
|---|---|---:|
| 1945-1947: | Single Class only, in silver with a gold centre and wreath and a crown above the laurel wreath, centre reading 'Reward for Gallantry', diameter of the whole increased to 44mm. Without three pronged ribbon brooch bar | £750 |

*Civil*

Centres read 'For Bravery'. The 1902-1939 issues are 35mm. in diameter

| | | |
|---|---|---:|
| 1902-1939: | 1st Class in gold with ERI or GRI cyphers, none awarded | — |
| | 2nd Class in silver with a gold centre, none awarded | — |
| | 3rd Class in silver, 29 awarded | £550 |
| 1939-1947: | Single Class, reduced to 26mm. diameter in silver with a gold centre and wreath, 10 awarded | £900 |

## 31 *The Royal Red Cross* 1883

Prior to the South African Campaign 1877-9 nurses had not been considered eligible for war medals; however, it was decided that they would qualify for campaign medals, which then raised the question of a special distinction. As a result, Queen Victoria in 1883 approved the institution of the Royal Red Cross for award to British and foreign ladies for exceptional service in the field of naval and military nursing. Since 1977 the decoration has also been available to male nurses. When first issued the award was in gold and enamel but, after 1887, in common with other British decorations, the awards were issued in silver-gilt and enamel. In 1920 it was stated that awards could also be made for exceptional acts of bravery.

Some 240 were awarded prior to 1914, 940 for the First World War, 40 between the wars and 380 for 1939-46.

Due to the vastly expanded nursing services called for by the First World War, a second class or Associate Royal Red Cross was introduced in 1915 and just over 5000 A.R.R.Cs were awarded. This compares with less than 1000 awarded for the Second World War.

Issues of the R.R.C. and A.R.R.C. dating from 1938 onwards have the year of award engraved on the reverse lower arm.

Bars for the 1st class were instituted in 1917; to 1920 79 had been awarded, for the period 1940-46 17 were issued. Holders of the 2nd class entitled to a further award received promotion to the 1st class.

| *1st class* (R.R.C.) | | Bars to the 1st class (including the original cross, Geo. V) | £250 |
|---|---|---|---|
| Victoria, gold and enamel | £950 | | |
| Victoria, silver gilt and enamel with gold centre | £400 | *2nd class* (A.R.R.C.) | |
| Edward VII, silver gilt and enamel | £400 | George V, silver and enamel | £40 |
| George V, silver gilt and enamel | £150 | George VI 1st type, silver and enamel | £65 |
| George VI 1st type 'GRI', silver gilt and enamel | £220 | George VI 2nd type, silver and enamel | £150 |
| George VI 2nd type 'GVIR' silver gilt and enamel | £400 | Elizabeth II, silver and enamel | £65 |
| Elizabeth II, silver gilt and enamel | £300 | | |

## 32 *The Conspicuous Service Cross* 1901
## *The Distinguished Service Cross* 1914

When first introduced in 1901 the decoration was known as the Conspicuous Service Cross. The award was available to warrant and subordinate officers of the Royal Navy for distinguished service; these ranks not being eligible for the D.S.O.

In 1914 the decoration was renamed the Distinguished Service Cross and eligibility was extended to all commissioned officers below the rank of Lieutenant-Commander. Second award bars were introduced in 1916 and in 1931 the award was extended to the Merchant Navy and the Fishing Fleets. During the Second World War, the coverage of the Cross was even further extended so as to include RAF officers serving with the fleet as well as army officers serving aboard merchant ships, who were manning the defensive anti-aircraft and anti-submarine guns.

The C.S.C. and D.S.C. were struck in silver, hallmarked on the reverse and issued unnamed. Crosses issued since 1940 have been dated on the reverse lower arm, similarly, bars have been dated on the reverse since this date.

Only eight of the original C.S.Cs were awarded up to 1914. For the First World War approximately 2000 D.S.Cs, 90 first bars and 10 second bars were awarded. During the period 1921-38 7 awards were made. For the Second World War approximately 4,500 D.S.C.s, 430 first bars, 44 second bars and a single third bar were awarded.

|  | Unnamed single | Attributable group |
|---|---|---|
| Edward VII | £1500 | £4500 |
| George V | £250 | £400 |
| George VI 1st type | £250 | £400 |
| George VI 2nd type 'GVIR' (1949-52) | £750 | £1500 |
| Elizabeth II | £500 | £1200 |

## 33 *The Military Cross* 1914

The Army, unlike the Royal Navy who possessed the Distinguished Service Cross, did not have a gallantry award for issue to the junior commissioned officers or warrant officers at the commencement of the 1914-18 war. The demands for such an award caused by the First World War made it necessary to institute such an award, and the Military Cross was introduced on 28th December 1914.

In common with the other awards normally reserved for one branch of the services, the M.C. has been awarded to the Royal Navy and members of the R.A.F. The award is also available to Commonwealth and colonial forces.

The M.C. is struck in silver and issued unnamed. Since about 1938 the year of award has been engraved on the lower arm of the reverse, bars have also been engraved on the reverse since that time.

During the period 1914-1920, over 37,000 M.Cs were awarded with approximately 2,900 first, 167 second and 4 third bars. Between the wars approximately 350 crosses and 31 first bars were awarded. For the Second World War approximately 11,000 M.Cs were awarded with 480 first and 24 second bars.

|  | Unnamed single | Attributable group |
|---|---|---|
| George V | £140 | £200 |
| George VI 1st type | £185 | £350 |
| George VI 2nd type 'GVIR' | £400 | £1000 |
| Elizabeth II | £400 | £1200 |

## 34 *The Distinguished Flying Cross* 1918

The Distinguished Flying Cross was introduced in 1918 as an award to officers and warrant officers of the R.A.F. for courage or devotion to duty performed whilst actually flying, on active operations against the enemy. During the Second World War eligibility was extended to equivalent ranks in the Army and Fleet Air Arm.

The silver Cross was originally worn from a ribbon of violet and white horizontal stripes, but in common with the other three Air Force awards this was altered in July 1919 to diagonal stripes running at an angle of 45 degrees down from left to right. Four issues are recognised by the cypher on the reverse, otherwise the design has remained constant. Since about 1939 the year of award has been engraved on the lower arm of the reverse and the reverse of any additional bars. The D.F.C. is issued unnamed.

From the time it was instituted until the Second World War just over 1200 Crosses, 88 first bars and 7 second bars were awarded. For the Second World War over 20,000 Crosses, 1550 first bars and 42 second bars were awarded.

|  | Unnamed single | Attributable group |
|---|---|---|
| George V | £400 | £800 |
| George VI | £300 | £450 |
| George VI, 2nd type 'GVIR' | £600 | £1500 |
| Elizabeth II | £500 | £1600 |

## 35 *The Air Force Cross* 1918

The Air Force Cross was introduced in 1918 as an award to officers and warrant officers of the R.A.F. for courage or devotion to duty performed whilst flying, when not on active operations against the enemy. During the Second World War eligibility was extended to equivalent ranks in the Army and Fleet Air Arm.

The silver Cross was originally worn from a ribbon of red and white horizontal stripes, but in common with other Air Force awards it was altered in July 1919 to diagonal stripes running at an angle of 45 degrees down from left to right. Four issues were made, recognised by different cyphers on the obverse arms and reverse centre. Since about 1939 the year of award has been engraved on the reverse lower arm and the reverse of any additional bars. The A.F.C. is issued unnamed.

From the time it was instituted until the Second World War over 830 crosses, 12 first bars and 3 second bars were awarded. For the Second World War 2000 crosses, 26 first bars and 1 second bar were awarded.

|  | Unnamed single | Attributable group |
|---|---|---|
| George V | £450 | £650 |
| George VI | £350 | £500 |
| George VI 2nd type | £600 | £900 |
| Elizabeth II | £500 | £750 |

## 36 *The Order of British India* 1837

This award was introduced by the Honourable East India Company in 1837 to reward its Indian officers for outstanding, long and meritorious service. The Order consists of two classes, both in gold with enamelled centres which were

worn around the neck. The ribbon was originally sky-blue but this was changed in 1838 to crimson. From 1939, when represented by ribbons only, the 1st class of the Order was distinguished by having two thin central blue stripes and the 2nd class by having a single stripe. From 1945 these ribbons replaced the plain crimson ribbon used when wearing the insignia.

An interesting aspect of this award is that, after the partition of India and Pakistan in 1946, the Pakistan Government ordered nine 1st class and fifty-one 2nd class from the London medallists Spink & Son Ltd for award to *British* officers who had rendered outstanding services to Pakistan. These contained a pale blue enamel centre (from 1939) and border. The donors and recipients of the award were thus completely reversed.

| | |
|---|---|
| 1st class 1st type, gold, light blue centres with dark blue garter surrounding | £450 |
| 1st class 2nd type (introduced 1939) gold, light blue centres and garter | £450 |
| 2nd class gold (without crown), dark blue centre | £320 |

## 37 *The Order of Burma* 1940

For administration purposes Burma became independent of British India in 1937 and as a result separate awards had to be introduced. The Order of Burma was established by George VI in 1940 at the same time as the Burma Gallantry Medal. The Order of Burma was awarded to a limited number of Governor's Commissioned Officers for long, faithful and honourable service in the Burma Army, Frontier Force and Military Police. By an amendment in 1945 the Order could also be awarded to the above in respect of gallantry or meritorious service. The Order became obsolete in 1947. Twenty-four are known to have been awarded.

| | |
|---|---|
| | £3,000 |

## 38 *The Kaiser-i-Hind Medal* 1890

Introduced by Queen Victoria in 1890 for award to those irrespective of nationality, colour, creed or sex who had performed useful public service in India; it was frequently given for social work and similar services.

The medal was originally issued in two classes—gold and silver. A third class in bronze was introduced in the reign of George V. A brooch bar forms an integral part of the Medal. Dated bars were awarded for additional service. Medals were issued unnamed. When awarded to service personnel or gentlemen the decoration was worn in the same way as a service medal, when worn by a lady on evening dress the badge was then suspended from a ribbon fashioned into a bow.

No further awards were made after 1947 following the independence and partition of the Indian subcontinent.

*George V 2nd issue*

| Victoria | | George V | |
|---|---|---|---|
| 1st class in gold | £650 | 2nd issue, smaller | |
| 2nd class in silver | £200 | and solid struck | |
| | | 1st class in gold | £575 |
| Edward VII | | 2nd class in silver | £130 |
| 1st class in gold | £600 | 3rd class in bronze | £110 |
| 2nd class in silver | £200 | | |
| | | George VI | |
| George V | | 1st class in gold | £575 |
| 1st issue, large | | 2nd class in silver | £130 |
| hollow type | | 3rd class in bronze | £110 |
| 1st class in gold | £500 | | |
| 2nd class in silver | £140 | | |

*George VI*

## 39 *The Albert Medal* 1866

The Albert Medal was instituted by a Royal Warrant of 7th March 1866 as a one-class award to recognise gallantry in saving life at sea. A year later the Royal Warrant was amended so as to include two classes: 'Albert Medal of the First Class' and 'Albert Medal of the Second Class'. By a Royal Warrant of 30th April 1877 the award was extended to recognise gallantry in saving life on land. In 1917 came a change in title, the Albert Medal 1st class becoming 'The Albert Medal in Gold', the 2nd class becoming 'The Albert Medal'. In 1949 the Albert Medal in Gold was abolished in favour of the George Cross and the Albert Medal (2nd class) was to be only awarded posthumously. In 1971 the award of the Albert Medal was terminated and all living recipient's were permitted to exchange their Medals for the George Cross.

The Albert Medal was named after Prince Albert, the Prince Consort, who died in 1861; the general esteem that this award quickly gained earned it the unofficial name of 'the civilian V.C.'.

The medal for saving life at sea is distinguished by the wording around the perimeter, 'FOR GALLANTRY IN SAVING LIFE AT SEA', has a central monogram of a 'V' and 'A' interwoven with an anchor set upon a blue enamel background and is worn from a blue and white ribbon. The medal for saving life on land has the legend, 'FOR GALLANTRY IN SAVING LIFE ON LAND', a central monogram of 'V' & 'A' upon a crimson enamel background, worn from a crimson and white ribbon.

The Albert Medal in gold is worked in gold and bronze, the Albert Medal (2nd class) is worked entirely in bronze. Medals of both classes are engraved on the reverse giving the recipient's name, details of the act and date.

Ribbon for the gold 1st class medal for sea was originally 16mm. wide blue with two white stripes, changing with the introduction of the 2nd class to 35mm. wide blue with four white stripes. The 2nd class remained 16mm. wide blue with two white stripes until 1904 when it was changed to 35mm. wide blue with two white stripes. The ribbon for the gold 1st class medal for land was 35mm. wide crimson with four white stripes, that for the 2nd class was originally 16mm. wide crimson with two white stripes changing in 1904 to 35mm. wide ribbon.

Numbers awarded given in brackets below:

|  | Civilian | Armed Forces |
|---|---|---|
| Albert Medal in Gold (1st class) for Gallantry in Saving Life at Sea [25] | £2400 | £2700 |
| Albert Medal (2nd class) for Gallantry in Saving Life at Sea [216] | £1500 | £1800 |
| Albert Medal in Gold (1st class) for Gallantry in Saving Life on Land [45] | £2000 | £2500 |
| Albert Medal (2nd Class) for Gallantry in Saving Life on Land [282] | £1000 | £1200 |

## 40 *The King's (later Queen's) Medal for Bravery* 1939

The medal, also known as the Woltemade Medal, was instituted in 1939 as an award to subjects of the Union of South Africa and dependent territories who endanger their own lives in saving or endeavouring to save the lives of others. It was awarded in gold and silver, in total 1 gold and 34 silver George VI medals were issued, only 1 silver medal was issued bearing the head of Elizabeth II— this for an act of heroism in March 1953. The ribbon is 44.5mm wide Royal blue with a thin orange stripe at the edge

|  | Gold | Silver |
|---|---|---|
| George VI | £5000 | £1000 |
| Elizabeth II | — | £3000 |

## 41 *The Distinguished Conduct Medal* 1854

Prior to the Crimean War, there were no official gallantry medals for other ranks of the British Army, although some regiments did issue unofficial gallantry medals at their own expense, which were invariably individually engraved.

It was the Crimean War which caused the D.C.M. to be instituted for other ranks only. Before 1894 the award was available to dominion and colonial forces, but after this date, each of the different countries had its own award, which invariably contained a distinctive title on the reverse.

Very few awards were given for some of the campaigns, which is illustrated by the price structure for the medals awarded for the various wars or campaigns as given below. Additional awards are represented by a bar attached to the ribbon—11 medals were awarded with *two* bars representing three awards. The first type of bar introduced in 1881 contained the date of the action in relief lettering, the present-day second action laurel bar was introduced in 1916. As with other service awards, the D.C.M. has been given to the Navy, principally to the R.N.V.R. battalions, who served on the Western Front throughout a considerable part of the First World War.

All D.C.M.s were issued named, generally impressed but in a range of styles throughout its history.

| Victoria | | |
|---|---|---|
| Crimea (800) | | £600 |
| Crimea - Heavy Brigade | | £3000 |
| Crimea - Light Brigade | | £5000 |
| Indian Mutiny (17) | | £3000 |
| I.G.S. 1854-95 | | £1000 |
| Abyssinia 1867-68 (7) | | £2000 |
| Ashantee 1873-74 (33) | | £1500 |
| S. Africa 1877-79 (16) | | £2200 |
| Afghanistan 1878-80 (61) | | £1000 |
| S. Africa 1880-81 (20) | | £1200 |
| Egypt 1882-89 (134) | | £1000 |
| I.G.S. 1895-1901 | | £750 |

| | |
|---|---|
| Sudan 1896-97 | £750 |
| S. Africa 1899-1902 (2,090) | £350 |
| China 1900 | £2000 |
| Edward VII | £300 |
| George V, uncrowned head (1914-18 War etc) (25,000) | £140 |
| George V, uncrowned head (1914-18 War etc) to R.N.V.R. Battalions | £400 |
| George V, crowned head (1930-37) (14) | £2500 |
| George VI, INDIAE IMP Imp legend (1937-47) | £900 |
| George VI, INDIAE IMP deleted (1948-52) (25) | £2000 |
| Elizabeth II, D.G.BR:OMN:REGINA F:D legend (26) | £2000 |
| Elizabeth II, DEI. GRATIA REGINA F:D, legend | £2000 |

## 42 *The Distinguished Conduct Medal (Dominion & Colonial)* 1895

By a Royal Warrant of 31st May 1895 medals for Distinguished Conduct, Meritorious Service and Long Service were introduced to Warrant Officers, N.C.O.s and men of the colonial forces. The qualifications being as far as possible similar to those governing the award of comparable medals to U.K. forces. Prior to this time the Imperial issue of the D.C.M. had been used for all awards whether U.K. or Colonial. The ribbon and design of the Colonial D.C.M. was as for the Imperial issues except for the the name of the country on the medal reverse. In the event only Canada and Natal issued medals of this type, though specimens were struck for Cape of Good Hope, New Zealand, New South Wales, Queensland and Tasmania.

| Canada | Victoria | Rare |
|---|---|---|
| Natal | Victoria | Rare |
| | Edward VII | £2500 |
| Specimens | | £500 |

## 43 *The Distinguished Conduct Medal (W.A.F.F. & K.A.R.)*

Instituted in the early 1900s, both medals were awarded until 1942 when they were replaced by the standard imperial issue D.C.M. Essentially similar to the Imperial issue, the medals differed by having a distinctive ribbon and a reverse with the words 'West African Frontier Force' or 'King's African Rifles'.

Approximate numbers awarded K.A.R. Edward VII 2; George V 190 plus 8 x 1st bars, W.A.F.F. Edward VII 55 plus 1 x 1st bar; George V 165 plus 7 x 1st bars 1 x 2nd bar.

| | K.A.R. | W.A.F.F. |
|---|---|---|
| Edward VII | £1500 | £800 |
| George V | £600 | £700 |

## 44 *The Conspicuous Gallantry Medal (Royal Navy 1855 and Royal Air Force 1943)*

The Naval Medal was introduced in 1855 to reward gallantry by Petty Officers, N.C.O.s and other ranks of the R.N & R.M. The medal utilized was the Naval M.S.M., having on the obverse the head of Queen Victoria with '1848' beneath the truncation and the M.S.M. die struck reverse, 'Meritorious Service' being erased and 'Conspicuous Gallantry' engraved in its place, the die struck word 'For' remaining.

The award of the medal lapsed at the end of the Crimean War and it was then instituted on a more permanent basis in 1874 following the successful conclusion of the Ashantee War 1873-74. At that time a special die was introduced so that the medal was awarded with normal relief wording on the reverse reading, 'For Conspicuous Gallantry' and the obverse was without the year '1848'.

Only twelve of the original Crimean period awards were issued to eleven recipients (one recipient twice). Since 1874 the decoration has been given very sparingly, only 236 being given in all, including 108 for the First World War, 72 for the Second World War, and 1 for the recent Falkland Islands conflict.

During the Second World War, it was realized that the Distinguished Flying Medal was not sufficient to cover the deeds performed by NCOs and men of the R.A.F. Consequently, the C.G.M. was extended to the R.A.F, this being senior to the existing D.F.M. The R.A.F. award is the same as the Naval medal in all respects except that it is worn with a light blue ribbon with dark blue edges as opposed to the Naval white with dark blue edges. From 1943-45 only 111 awards were given which is very few when one considers the vastly enlarged Royal Air Force at that time. Between 1946 and 1979 only one medal was awarded, this was in 1968 to the Royal Australian Air Force for Vietnam.

R.N. C.G.M.s were issued named, either impressed or engraved according to the period. R.A.F. medals were issued engraved.

| *C.G.M. (R.N. & R.M. 1855)* | |
|---|---|
| Victoria 1st issue '1848' type (11) | £1800 |
| Victoria 2nd issue (51) | £1500 |
| Edward VII (2) | £3500 |
| George V (110) | £1500 |
| George VI (72) | £2000 |
| Elizabeth II (1) | Rare |
| | |
| *C.G.M. (R.A.F. 1943)* | |
| George VI (111) | £3000 |
| Elizabeth II (1) | Rare |

### 45 *The George Medal* 1940

Instituted at the same time as the George Cross, the medal was awarded for acts of great bravery. It was intented primarily as a civilian award but could well be awarded to members of the military services for actions when purely military awards would not normally be granted. Bars were awarded for further acts of bravery.

The medals are struck in silver and are always issued named. There are four obverse types and a single reverse common to all.

Approximately 2000 George Medals and 25 first bars have been awarded.

|  | Service | Civilian |
|---|---|---|
| George VI | £650 | £450 |
| Elizabeth II | £950 | £800 |

### 46 *The King's Police Medal* 1909
### *The King's Police and Fire Brigade's Medal* 1940
### *The Queen's Police Medal* 1954
### *The Queen's Fire Service Medal* 1954

Instituted by Royal Warrant of 7th July 1909 as a reward for Police and Fire Services of G.B. and the dominions for gallantry or distinguished service. Prior to 1933 there was no wording on the reverse to distinguish those medals awarded for gallantry and those for distinguished service. The ribbon was originally blue with silver edges, in 1916 an additional central silver stripe was added. By a Royal Warrant of 12th December 1933 two reverse types were introduced with the words 'FOR GALLANTRY' & 'FOR DISTINGUISHED SERVICE' Medals for gallantry were worn from ribbon having an additional thin red stripe bisecting the silver. The title of the medal was changed in 1940 to that of 'King's Police and Fire Brigade's Medal'. Since 1950 medals for gallantry could only be awarded posthumously.

By a Royal Warrant of 19th May 1954 the above medal was replaced by two distinct medals for police and fire services. The Queen's Police Medal had two reverses: 'FOR GALLANTRY' & 'FOR POLICE DISTINGUISHED SERVICE', the ribbons remained unchanged. The Queen's Fire Service Medal had two reverses: 'FOR GALLANTRY' & 'FOR DISTINGUISHED FIRE SERVICE'. The ribbon for distinguished service was red with three yellow stripes, for gallantry the yellow was bisected by a thin dark blue stripe.

By the 1909 Warrant bars were awarded for further acts of gallantry; originally the bars were dated, from 1934 onwards they had the usual laurel leaf design. These silver medals were always issued named in serif capitals giving details of name, rank and service or force.

| King's Police Medal | | Queen's Police Medal | |
|---|---|---|---|
| Pre-1933 General issues | | For Gallantry | |
| Edward VII | £400 | Elizabeth II | £600 |
| George V 1st type Coinage Head | £125 | | |
| George V 2nd type Crowned Bust | £250 | For Distinguished Police Service | |
| | | Elizabeth II | £150 |
| Post-1933 For Gallantry | | | |
| George V 2nd type | £400 | Queen's Fire Service Medal | |
| George VI 1st type | £500 | For Gallantry | |
| George VI 2nd type | £700 | Elizabeth II | — |
| Post-1933 For Distinguished Service | | For Distinguished Fire Service | |
| George V 2nd type | £200 | Elizabeth II | £200 |
| George VI 1st type | £125 | | |
| George VI 2nd type | £200 | | |

## 47 *The King's Police Medal (South African issue)* 1937

Instituted by a Royal Warrant of 24th Sept. 1937 to reward members of the South African Police for courage and devotion to duty. In 1938 the award was extended to include the Police Force of S. W. Africa. Two bilingual reverse types were issued: 'FOR BRAVERY VIR DAPPERHEID' and 'FOR DISTINGUISHED SERVICE VIR VOORTREFLIKE DIENS'. Medals were awarded under similar conditions as for the unilingual issue which they replaced. Three obverse types were issued: George VI 1st type 'GEORGIUS VI REX ET IMPERATOR' 1937-49 (10 Gall. 13 Dist. Serv.) George VI 2nd type 'GEORGIUS VI REX' 1950-52 (1 Dist. Serv.), Elizabeth II 1953-60 (20 Gall. 3 Dist. Serv.). The medals became obsolete in 1960.

| For Gallantry | |
|---|---|
| George VI | £750 |
| Elizabeth II | £600 |
| For Distinguished Service | |
| George VI | £400 |
| Elizabeth II | £1000 |

## 48 *The Edward Medal* 1907

The medal was introduced in 1907 as, prior to this date, the only available decoration for civilians for saving life was the Albert Medal which was only sparingly granted. When the medal was first suggested, its object was to reward acts of gallantry in endeavouring to save life in mines and quarries. However in 1909 a second issue for industry was introduced, the two being distinguished by different reverses. In addition there were two different reverse types for the Medal for Industry, the first type issued between 1910 and 1912. Both the Medal for Mines and Industry came in two classes—being in silver and bronze. Originally designated 'The Edward Medal of the First and Second Class' their title was changed in 1917 to 'The Edward Medal in Silver' and 'The Edward Medal'. Two bars were awarded, both to silver medals for mines. Medals were issued engraved around the edge giving the recipients name and by the mid-1930s the date and possibly the place.

When the George Cross and George Medal were introduced in 1940, awards for civilian acts of courage and devotion became confusing. Consequently, in 1949, King George VI decreed that the silver Edward Medal should cease and that all future bronze medals should be awarded posthumously. In 1971 the award of the Edward Medal was terminated and all living recipients were permitted to exchange their Medal for the George Cross.

Approximate numbers issued: 77 silver and 318 bronze medals for mines; 25 silver and 163 medals for industry.

| Mines Issue | silver | bronze | Industry issue | silver | bronze |
|---|---|---|---|---|---|
| Edward VII 1907-10 | £550 | £300 | Edward VII 1910 | £1000 | £700 |
| George V 1st type (Coinage Head) 1911-30 | £550 | £300 | George V 1st type obv. 1st type rev. 1911 | £1000 | £700 |
| George V 2nd type (Crowned bust) 1931-36 | £800 | £450 | George V 1st type obv. 2nd type rev. 1912-30 | £700 | £300 |
| George VI 1st type 1937-48 | £700 | £450 | George V 2nd type obv. 2nd type rev. 1931-36 | £1000 | £700 |
| George VI 2nd type 1949-52 | £1000 | £600 | George VI 1st type 1937-48 | £1000 | £700 |
| Elizabeth II 1st and 2nd type 1953-71 | none awarded | £700 | George VI 2nd type 1949-52 | none awarded | £1000 |
| | | | Elizabeth II 1st & 2nd type | none awarded | £1000 |

*Mines*

*Industry 1st type*

*Industry 2nd type*

## 49  *The Indian Distinguished Service Medal* 1907

Instituted by a Royal Warrant of 25th June 1907, it was introduced as an award to recognize the distinguished services of Indian comissioned and non-commissioned officers and men of the regular land forces in India. Later, in 1929, the award was extended to the Indian Marines and in 1940 to the Indian Air Force. In 1944 it was extended yet again to include the Hong Kong and Singapore Royal Artillery. The medal became obsolete in 1947.

The medal was struck in silver and issued named either engraved or impressed. There were four obverse types and a single reverse type. A bar for further distinguished service was introduced in 1917 of the same type as for the D.C.M. and M.M. Some I.D.S.Ms. were supplied with a laurelled brooch bar.

Approximate numbers awarded: Edward VII 140, George V 1st type 3800, George V 2nd type 140, George VI 1190. A total of 49 bars were awarded.

| | |
|---|---|
| Edward VII | £450 |
| George V 1st type 'KAISAR-I-HIND' | £95 |
| George V 2nd type | £320 |
| George VI | £120 |

## 50  *The Burma Gallantry Medal* 1940

Burma ceased to be part of British India on 1st April 1937. By Royal Warrant of 10th May 1940 the Burma Gallantry Medal was instituted. It was awarded for conspicuous gallantry and could be conferred by the Governor of Burma upon the Governor's Commissioned and Non-Commissioned Officers and other ranks of the Burma Army, the Frontier Force, Military Police, the Burma Royal Naval Volunteer Reserve and Burma Auxiliary Air Force. By an amendment in 1945 the B.G.M. was made available only to Non-Commissioned Officers and other ranks in the above units. The award of the Medal ceased in 1947 when Burma was granted independence. During its lifetime just over 200 awards were made with a further 3 second award bars.

| | |
|---|---|
| | £1500 |

## 51  *The Distinguished Service Medal* 1914

Instituted in October 1914, it was intended to supplement the Conspicuous Gallantry Medal being awarded for bravery in action with the enemy but of a lesser degree than that for the C.G.M. A bar was approved in 1916 for further acts of bravery. Originally awarded to R.N. & R.M. Petty Officers, N.C.O.s and men, eligibility was extended during the Second World War to cover not only Army and R.A.F. personnel serving aboard ships, but was extended to include also the Merchant and Dominion Navies.

The medal was issued named, First World War examples being impressed in capitals, often giving the name of the ship, sometimes the location of the action or the type of operation undertaken and date. Second World War examples are named in impressed or engraved capitals. First World War bars are dated on the reverse with the date of the action, whilst Second World War bars are undated.

During the First World War approximately 4,100 medals, 67 first bars and 2 second bars were awarded. For the Second World War approximately 7,100 medals, 153 first bars, 4 second bars and 1 third bar were awarded.

| | |
|---|---|
| George V, 1st type, uncrowned head (1914-37) | £180 |
| George V, 2nd type, crowned head (1930-37)    probably never issued | |
| George VI, 1st type, with 'Ind.Imp' in legend (1938-49) | £200 |
| George VI, 2nd type, without 'Ind.Imp' in legend (1949-53) | £1000 |
| Elizabeth II, 1st type, with 'Br.Omn' in legend (1953-57) | £1500 |
| Elizabeth II, 2nd type, without 'Br.Omn' in legend (1957- ) | £1500 |

## 52 *The Military Medal* 1916

This medal was introduced by Royal Warrant of 25th March 1916 as an award to Army N.C.O.s and men for individual or even associated acts of bravery in the field. In June of that year it was extended to women. Bars were awarded for further acts of bravery.

There are six obverse heads and legends and four reverse types with differing cyphers. Medals were issued named in impressed capital letters although some Second World War issues to the Indian Army are found with the capitals engraved. Medals awarded to foreign troops during the First World War were issued unnamed.

During the First World War approximately 115,600 medals were issued in addition to 5,796 first bars, 180 second bars and 1 third bar. Some 300 medals and 4 first bars were issued between the Wars. Over 15,000 medals were issued during the Second World War with 177 first bars and 1 second bar.

| | |
|---|---|
| George V, 1st type, uncrowned head (1916-30) | £60 |
| George V, 1st type, uncrowned head (1916-30) | |
|    Commonwealth unit | £80 |
| George V, 1st type, uncrowned head (1916-30) with bar | £150 |
| George V, 1st type, uncrowned head (1916-30) | |
|    to the RNVR Battalions | £150 |
| George V, 2nd type, crowned head (1930-38) | £1000 |
| George VI, 1st type with 'Ind.Imp' in legend (1938-48) | £200 |
| George VI, 2nd type, without 'Ind.Imp' in legend (1948-53) | £750 |
| Elizabeth II, 1st type, with 'Br.Omn' in legend (1953-58) | £800 |
| Elizabeth II, 2nd type, without 'Br.Omn' in legend (1958- ) | £800 |

## 53  *The Distinguished Flying Medal* 1918

The Distinguished Flying Medal was introduced in 1918 at the same time as the D.F.C., A.F.C. & A.F.M. It was awarded to non-commissioned officers and men of the R.A.F. for courage or devotion to duty performed whilst flying, on active operations against the enemy. During the Second World War eligibility was extended to equivalent ranks in the Army and Fleet Air Arm.

The silver oval medal was originally worn from a ribbon of violet and white horizontal stripes similar to but thinner than that of the D.F.C. In common with the other Air Force awards this was altered in July 1919 to diagonal stripes running at an angle of 45 degrees down from left to right. There have been five obverse and two reverse types. Obverse—George V 1st type Coinage head (1918-30), George V 2nd type, Crowned bust (1930-38), George VI 1st type 'Ind.Imp.' (1938-49), George VI 2nd type without Ind.Imp' (1949-53), Elizabeth II. Reverse—George V undated reverse, George VI and Elizabeth II reverse dated '1918'. All D.F.Ms were issued named, those for the First World War were impressed in large serif capitals, those for the Second World War were engraved. Since 1939 second award bars have been dated on the reverse.

For the First World War approximately 100 medals and 2 first bars were awarded, between the World Wars a further 80 medals and 2 first bars were awarded. For the Second World War over 6,500 medals, 60 first and 1 second bar were awarded.

| | |
|---|---|
| George V 1st type | £650 |
| George V 2nd type | £1500 |
| George VI 1st type | £450 |
| George VI 2nd type | £1200 |
| Elizabeth II | £1250 |

## 54  *The Air Force Medal* 1918

The Medal was introduced in 1918 and was awarded to non-commissioned officers and men of the R.A.F. for courage or devotion to duty performed whilst flying when not on active operations against the enemy. During the Second World War eligibility was extended to include equivalent ranks of the Army and Fleet Air Arm.

The medal was originally worn from a ribbon of red and white horizontal stripes similar, but thinner than, that of the A.F.C. In common with other Air Force awards this was altered in July 1918 to diagonal stripes running at an angle of 45 degrees down from left to right. There have been five obverse types, as for the D.F.M. and two reverse types—George V issues having an undated reverse, George VI and Elizabeth II issues with the reverse dated '1918'. All A.F.Ms were issued named, as for the D.F.M.

For the First World War just over 100 Medals and 2 first bars were awarded. Between the World Wars a further 106 Medals and 3 bars, and for the Second World War 259 Medals were awarded.

| | |
|---|---|
| George V 1st type | £600 |
| George V 2nd type | £1000 |
| George VI 1st type | £450 |
| George VI 2nd type | £600 |
| Elizabeth II | £650 |

## 55 *The Constabulary Medal (Ireland)* 1842

Instituted in 1842 as a reward for gallantry and meritorious service to members of the Irish Constabulary. With a change in regulations in 1872 it was then awarded solely for gallantry. It was first awarded in 1848 and the last award was in 1922, the year the Royal Irish Constabulary was disbanded.

A silver medal, the obverse design varied. Early awards had a harp incorporating a female figure with a crown and wreath and the inscription 'REWARD OF MERIT IRISH CONSTABULARY'. Later versions had a plain harp with a different crown and wreath and the legend, 'REWARD OF MERIT ROYAL IRISH CONSTABULARY'. The force became 'Royal' in 1867 but some medals issued after this date and one as late as 1921 had the pre-1867 title. Within a wreath of laurel and shamrock the reverse was engraved with details of the recipient, rank, name number, date and sometimes place of action. The suspension was originally a fixed straight bar but by 1876 a swivelling silver wire suspension had been introduced. The ribbon was originally light blue but was changed to green in 1872. Bars for second awards were introduced in 1920.

Approximately 315 medals were awarded, mostly for the Easter Rising 1916 (23) and the Civil War 1920 (180) 1921 (55). 7 second award bars or second medals were awarded.

£1000

## 56 *The Indian Police Medal* 1932

The Indian Police Medal was instituted by Royal Warrant of 23rd February 1932 as a reward for Indian Police Forces and Fire Brigades for gallantry or valuable services. The Indian Police and Fire Services were also entitled to receive the K.P.M. but this was restricted to fifty awards per year. Two hundred Indian Police Medals could be awarded each year. The bronze medal was issued named around the edge in italic script giving details of name, rank and force. Two obverse types were issued: George V crowned and robed bust and George VI 1st type legend. Until Dec. 1944 there was one reverse type reading: 'FOR DISTINGUISHED CONDUCT', thereafter there were two types: 'FOR

GALLANTRY' and 'FOR MERITORIOUS SERVICE' as appropriate. The medal had a fixed straight bar suspension. Prior to Dec. 1944 the ribbon for all medals had a crimson centre flanked by bands of dark blue and silver grey, thereafter, whilst medals for meritorious service retained the same ribbon, those for gallantry had an additional silver stripe bisecting the blue. Bronze bars for further acts of gallantry or merit could be awarded. The medals continued to be awarded after the creation of the Dominion of India in 1947 but ceased when India became a Republic in 1950.

| | | | |
|---|---|---|---|
| George V rev. FOR DISTINGUISHED CONDUCT | £300 | George VI rev. FOR GALLANTRY | £450 |
| George VI rev. FOR DISTINGUISHED CONDUCT | £300 | George VI rev. FOR MERITORIOUS SERVICE | £300 |

## 57 *The Burma Police Medal* 1937

The medal was instituted by a Royal Warrant of 14th December 1937 following the separation of Burma from India and was abolished in 1948. The medal was open to all ranks, European and Burmese, of the civil and military police, frontier force and fire brigades. Awards were made for gallantry or meritorious service, with a maximum of 25 awards per year. The medal was in bronze and had one reverse type with legend 'FOR DISTINGUISHED CONDUCT' with 'BURMA' above and 'POLICE' below.

Approximately 53 awards were made for gallantry, 80 for meritorious service with a further 8 unclassified.

| | |
|---|---|
| If awarded for Gallantry | £750 |
| If awarded for Meritorious Service | £600 |

## 58 *The Colonial Police Medal* 1938

The Colonial Police Medal was instituted by Royal Warrant on 10th May 1938. It was awarded to colonial police forces and fire-brigades for gallantry and meritorious service. The medals in silver were named around the edge with the

recipients rank, name and force. The reverse consisted of either (a) a police truncheon and wreath with circumscription 'COLONIAL POLICE FORCES FOR GALLANTRY' (or 'FOR MERITORIOUS SERVICE) or (b) a fireman's helmet, axe and wreath with circumscription 'COLONIAL FIRE BRIGADES FOR GALLANTRY' (or 'FOR MERITORIOUS SERVICE'). Bars were awarded for further acts of gallantry. The ribbon for the Colonial Police Medal for Meritorious Service is blue with green edges with a thin silver stripe separating the colours. For gallantry a thin red line bisects the green.

| George VI | Police | Fire |
|---|---|---|
| For Gallantry | £250 | £900 |
| For Meritorious Service | £100 | £180 |
| | | |
| Elizabeth II | | |
| For Gallantry | £300 | £800 |
| For Meritorious Service | £100 | £180 |

## 59 *The Ceylon Police Medal* 1950

The medal was instituted by a Royal Warrant of 19th June 1950 and replaced the Colonial Police Medals for Gallantry and Meritorious Service. The Ceylon Police Medal was abolished in 1972. The medal was struck in silver with a straight bar swivelling suspender and with the recipients name and rank impressed around the edge. Two different reverse types were issued, one with the inscription 'FOR GALLANTRY', the other 'FOR MERIT'. The ribbon for the meritorious service medal was khaki with stripes of silver, light blue and dark blue towards the edge, for the gallantry medal thin red stripes bisect the silver.

A maximum of 10 awards for merit were allowed per year, with no restriction on the number of awards for gallantry.

| | |
|---|---|
| George VI FOR GALLANTRY | £750 |
| George VI FOR MERIT | £500 |
| Elizabeth II FOR GALLANTRY | £750 |
| Elizabeth II FOR MERIT | £500 |

## 60 *The Queensland Police Merit Medal* 1904

A silver medal instituted by the Queensland Government in 1904 awarded to members of the Queensland Police Force for meritorious service. It became obsolete with the introduction of the Colonial Police Medal in 1938

| | |
|---|---|
| Edward VII | £850 |
| George V | £850 |

## 61 *The Queen's Gallantry Medal* 1974

Introduced on 20th June 1974 as an award for exemplary acts of bravery. It was intended primarily as an award for civilians but military personnel are also eligible, for actions for which purely military awards are not normally granted. Both U.K. and Commonwealth citizens may receive the medal. With the introduction of the Q.G.M., awards of the Order of the British Empire and the British Empire Medal in respect of gallantry were terminated.

The medal is made of silver and is issued impressed around the edge with the recipient's name and when appropriate the military details. A bar is awarded for further acts of bravery. Since its introduction, less than 400 awards have been issued.

| | |
|---|---|
| Services | £700 |
| Civilians | £600 |

## 62 *The Allied Subject's Medal*

This medal was awarded to allied and neutral subjects in recognition of services to British prisoners of war and evadees during the First World War. Both humanitarian service and courage were rewarded.

The medal was struck in both silver and bronze and was issued unnamed. 134 silver and 574 bronze medals were issued, the majority going to Belgian and French nationals.

| | |
|---|---|
| Silver | £550 |
| Bronze | £350 |

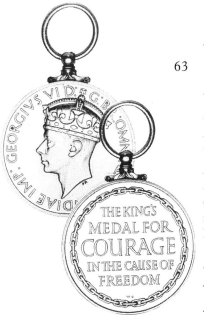

## 63 *The King's Medal for Courage in the Cause of Freedom* 1945

The medal was instituted by Royal Warrant dated 23rd August 1945. Together with the King's Medal for Service in the Cause of Freedom, this was the Second World War counterpart to the First World War Allied Subjects Medal. The Medal for courage was awarded to foreign civilians and members of foreign armed forces. Awards to the latter were in respect of special or clandestine operations outside the scope of normal military duties. The medal was awarded specifically for acts of courage where life was risked or dangerous work under hazardous wartime circumstances undertaken in furtherance of the Allied cause.

Approximately 3,200 medals were awarded, the first issue taking place in 1947. Struck in silver, the medal was issued unnamed.

| | |
|---|---|
| | £300 |

## 64 *The British North Borneo Company Bravery Cross*

The cross for bravery was awarded in both silver and bronze and worn from a watered golden yellow ribbon. They were manufactured by Joseph Moore Ltd., of Birmingham and the silver crosses have on their reverse a Birmingham hallmark for 1890.

| | |
|---|---|
| Silver | £375 |
| Bronze | £250 |

## 65 *The Sea Gallantry Medal* 1854

The medal originated through the Merchant Shipping Act of 1854 and is the only gallantry medal to have been instituted by an Act of Parliament. The medal instituted was large—2.25 inches in diameter and was not intended for wear. It was issued in both silver and bronze and with two different obverse legends—one the 'Gallantry' medal read 'AWARDED BY THE BOARD OF TRADE FOR GALLANTRY IN SAVING LIFE', the 'Humanity' Medal had the legend 'AWARDED BY THE BOARD OF TRADE FOR SAVING LIFE AT SEA'. The 'Gallantry' medal was awarded to those who actually risked their life in saving others, the 'Humanity' medal was awarded to those who provided the services such as a captain of a ship. The 'Humanity' medal was awarded infrequently; the last award being 1893.

In 1904 smaller medals of 1.27 inches dia., which could be worn, were introduced replacing the earlier large type. There were two types of the small Edward VII medal, distinguished by the legend. Type 1 (1904-05) 'AWARDED BY THE BOARD OF TRADE FOR GALLANTRY IN SAVING LIFE', Type 2 (1906-1910) 'FOR GALLANTRY IN SAVING LIFE AT SEA'. The two types of the George VI medal are distinguished by the cypher below the bust: Type 1 (1937-47) 'G.R.I.', Type 2 1948-51 'GVIR'.

Medals, large and small were issued with engraved naming around the edge; the details usually given being the recipients name, name of the vessel and date.

Approximate numbers issued (silver/bronze): Victoria (both types) 500/750; Edward VII large type 11/23; Edward VII small type both obv. 70/78; George V 385/375; George VI 1st type 7/13; George VI 2nd type 0/6; Elizabeth II 19/9. Only one second action bar has been awarded, this being to Chief Officer James Whitely who was awarded the medal in 1917 and the bar in 1921.

| | silver | bronze |
|---|---|---|
| Victoria large 'Gallantry' medal | £300 | £180 |
| Victoria large 'Humanity' medal | £650 | £450 |
| Edward VII large 'Gallantry' medal | £700 | £500 |
| Edward VII small 1st type | £500 | £400 |
| Edward VII small 2nd type | £350 | £250 |
| George V | £250 | £250 |
| George VI 1st type | £600 | £550 |
| George VI 2nd type | — | £700 |
| Elizabeth II | £700 | £700 |

## 66 *The Sea Gallantry Medal (Foreign Services)* 1841

This medal was approved by Queen Victoria in 1841 to recognize the services rendered by foreigners to British subjects in distress. Some early awards were for services rendered on land. Medals were awarded in gold, silver and bronze. Originally a special reverse was struck for each occasion but this was found to be an unnecessary expense and in 1849 standard reverses were introduced. Medals issued prior to 1854 were 1.78in. in diameter and were not fitted with suspensions, though some were fitted privately. Post 1854 issued were 1.27in. in diameter and fitted with a suspension. Prior to 1922 the medal was worn from a plain crimson ribbon, thereafter the ribbon was light red having a white stripe near each edge, i.e. S.G.M. ribbon. Medals were issued named around the edge, with details of the recipients name, date and place or ship engraved on the large medal and the name and usually the date engraved or impressed on the small medal.

The large medal has one obverse and five reverse types:

1. Within the wreath, 'PRESENTED BY THE BRITISH GOVERNMENT', around the wreath an individually struck inscription. (1841-49 and occasionally beyond).

2. Within the wreath, 'VICTORIA REGINA CUDI JUSSIT MDCCCXLI'. Specimens only.

3. Within the wreath, as 1 above, around the wreath, 'FOR SAVING THE LIFE OF A BRITISH SUBJECT' (1849-54).

4. As above but with the inscription around the wreath being 'FOR ASSISTING A BRITISH VESSEL IN DISTRESS' (1849-54).

5. As above but with the inscription around the wreath being 'FOR SAVING THE LIVES OF BRITISH SUBJECTS' (1850-54).

The small medal has five obverse types plus variations to the Victoria issue head and legend, with four reverse types:

6. As 3 above (1854-c.1906).

7. As 4 above (1854-c.1896).

8. As 3 above (1854-c.1926).

9. Within the wreath 'FROM THE BRITISH GOVERNMENT', around the wreath, 'FOR GALLANTRY AND HUMANITY (1858-present).

Approximate numbers awarded. Large medals 100 gold, 120 silver 14 bronze. Large specimen medals 10 gold, 24 bronze.

|  | gold | silver | bronze |
|---|---|---|---|
| Victoria large medal | £2000 | £500 | £500 |
| Victoria small medal | £800 | £200 | — |
| Edward VII | £1200 | £300 | — |
| George V | £800 | £250 | — |
| George VI | — | £600 | — |
| Elizabeth II | Rare | £600 | — |

# Campaign Medals

Readers are recommended to study the 6th edition of *British Battles & Medals* by E. C. Joslin, A. R. Litherland and B. T. Simpkin, published by Spink & Son Ltd., for a comprehensive study of campaign medals. The number in brackets found after the name of the medal is that which is used in *British Battles and Medals*.

It must be understood that a number of the earlier campaign medals (Nos. 67 to 88 inclusive) were privately struck and in some cases later strikings have been made; *the prices given are based on original strikings.*

## The Honourable East India Company's Medals 1778-1837 *and early privately issued Campaign Medals (nos. 67-88)*

The Honourable East India Company was an association of merchant venturers formed in London in 1599. They formed the Company for the purpose of trading with the Far East and later assumed considerable power. The enormous power that the Company wielded until just after the Indian Mutiny (1856-57) made it necessary for them to maintain a considerable army and navy to guard not only its immediate local possessions and factories, but also to ensure continued safety by enlarging its territories until it reached a stage where the Company was controlling most of the Indian subcontinent. This in turn brought the Company frequently into conflict with neighbouring states and in addition it also had to contest territories claimed by the French and other nations.

We are indebted to the H.E.I.C., as it is normally known, for setting the example of issuing campaign or service medals long before the British Government's general issue to officers and men alike, namely for Waterloo in 1815.

The early medals, except for Burma 1824-26 were often of two sizes, sometimes in gold and silver with very simple ring suspenders and without standard ribbons as we know them today. Furthermore, they were issued unnamed; consequently, these earlier medals are listed separately.

In addition to the H.E.I.C., a number of private individuals and associations issued medals at their own expense; after the introduction of the official Government medal for Waterloo, private medals lapsed.

### 67 *Capture of Louisbourg Medal* 1758 (BBM 25)

This was in the nature of a gallantry or distinguished service medal being conferred on selected recipients only, who took part in the capture of Louisbourg in Canada from the French on 27th July 1758. Generals Amherst and Wolfe commanded the land forces and Admiral Boscawen the fleet.

| Gold | £10,000 | Silver | £1500 | Bronze | £600 |
|------|---------|--------|-------|--------|------|

### 68 *Carib War Medal* 1773 (BBM 26)

Silver and copper medals were awarded by the Legislative Assembly of the island of St Vincent to the Militia or Volunteers who had taken part in the campaign against the Caribs or natives of the Island who had been encouraged to rebel against the English by the French settlers.

| | Silver/Copper | £950 |
|---|---|---|

### 69 *Deccan Medal* 1778-84 (BBM 31)

These medals were struck in Calcutta and were either 40.5mm. or 32mm. in diameter; the larger size, a few of which were in gold, were issued to officers only. This was the first of the Company's general issue of medals, awarded for services in Western India and Gujerat, under the overall leadership of Warren Hastings.

The reverse contains a Persian inscription which, translated, reads: 'As coins are current in the world, so shall be the bravery and exploits of those heroes by whom the name of the victorious English nation was carried from Bengal to the Deccan. Presented in AD 1784 [Hegira 1199] by the East India Company's Calcutta Government.'

| | Gold | Silver |
|---|---|---|
| 40.5mm. | £5000 | £750 |
| 32mm. | (Not issued) | £300 |

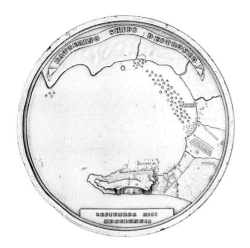

## 70 *Defence of Gibraltar Medals* 1779-83 (BBM 28,29)

The two most common medals awarded for the defence of Gibraltar are the silver ones presented to officers by Generals Picton and Eliott at their own expense. There were, however, other medals given for the same event. The Defence of Gibraltar was carried out by some 7000 British and Hanoverian troops against the combined forces of Spain and France, the French having some 40,000 troops in the initial assault.

| | |
|---|---|
| General Picton's Medal, silver | £550 |
| General Eliott's Medal, silver | £300 |

## 71 *Mysore Medal* 1790-92 (BBM 32)

Produced in two sizes, 43mm. and 38mm. in diameter, the large was awarded in gold and silver, the smaller in silver only. The medals were awarded to the officers and men employed by the H.E.I. Company under the leadership of Lord Cornwallis and Generals Meadows and Abercromby, for the defeat of the powerful Tippoo Sahib, ruler of Mysore.

| | Gold | Silver |
|---|---|---|
| 43mm. dia. | £5000 | £500 |
| 38mm. dia. | *(Not issued)* | £300 |

## 72 *Isle of St Vincent Medal* 1795 (BBM 33)

The issue of this bronze medal came about due to circumstances which were similar to those in 1773, which were commemorated by the Carib War Medal. Awarded to the officers and N.C.Os of the Corps of Natives which numbered 500 men, which was raised by Major Seton from among the slaves, the medal is often referred to as 'St Vincent's Black Corps Medal'.

The campaign was against the Caribs or natives and French troops.

| | |
|---|---|
| | £700 |

### 73 *Capture of Ceylon Medal* 1795 (BBM 34)

This was awarded for services during the capture of the island of Ceylon from the Dutch, the campaign resulting from the Napoleonic Wars.

Two medals were awarded in gold to Captains Barton and Clarke and approximately 121 in silver to native gunners of the Bengal Artillery.

| Gold (2) £10,000 | Silver (121) £950 |
|---|---|

### 74 *Mr Davison's Nile Medal* 1798 (BBM 37)

This medal was a personal award by Nelson's prize agent—a Mr Davison—to all the officers and men present. The admirals and captains were awarded the medal in gold which is, of course, very scarce. Other officers received silver medals, while petty officers were given gold-plated bronze medals and the remainder were issued with bronze medals. The reverse shows an interesting pictorial scene of the fleet in Aboukir Bay with an inscription. The official Government medals for the Nile were not issued for another fifty years and then they were issued only to the survivors living at that time.

| Gold | £8000 | Bronze gilt | £150 |
|---|---|---|---|
| Silver | £450 | Bronze | £90 |

### 75 *Seringapatam Medal* 1799 (BBM 38)

Tippoo Sahib, ruler of Mysore, who had been defeated during the campaign 1790-92, was attacked by the Company's forces due to his hostile movements and his negotiations with the French. The medals were awarded to both British and Indian regiments for the capture of the fortress of Seringapatam on the 4th May. The left wing of the forces was under the command of Lt-Col the Honourable Arthur Wellesley, later the Duke of Wellington, this being one of the actions which later gained him the nickname of 'The Sepoy General'. The Company took over the administration of the territory following this campaign, thus enlarging the Company's 'Empire'. As a result of the capture of the fortress, prize money was distributed with some £100,000 being given to the Commander-in-Chief and the princely sum of £7 to private soldiers!

The medals, struck in England, were 48mm. in diameter and those in Calcutta 45mm. in diameter. They were struck in gold, silver gilt, silver, bronze and pewter, although the smaller 45mm. was produced in gold and silver only.

| | Gold | Silver Gilt | Silver | Bronze | Pewter |
|---|---|---|---|---|---|
| | (113) | (185) | (3636) | (5000) | (45,000) |
| 48mm. | £3000 | £375 | £300 | £150 | £120 |
| 45mm. | £3000 | *(Not issued)* | £220 | *(Not issued)* | *(Not issued)* |

### 76 *Earl St Vincent's Medal* 1800 (BBM 39)

Awarded by Admiral Earl St Vincent to the crew of his ship HMS *Ville de Paris* who remained loyal during the mutiny of the fleet in the Mediterranean, which followed the infamous mutiny of the home fleet anchored off The Nore in 1797. Awarded in silver, although it is thought that a few gold specimens were presented to selected people holding high office.

| | |
|---|---|
| Gold   £5000 | Silver   £450 |

### *Honourable East India Company's Egypt Medal*

1801 (BBM 40)

Medals were issued by the Hon. East India Company to both the British and Indian regiments that had set out from India to assist the troops from the UK during their capture of Egypt, which had been occupied by Napoleon's troops. An expedition to conquer the country was despatched from England under General Abercrombie, and additional forces were sent from India and also the Cape of Good Hope, under the command of General Baird. Sixteen medals were issued in gold and 2200 in silver, the medals being 48mm. in diameter. In addition, the Sultan of Egypt awarded a medal in various sizes to the majority of officers present (No. 78), and the Highland Society presented medals at their own expense (No. 79).

| | |
|---|---|
| Gold (16)   £5000 | Silver (2200)   £375 |

### 78 *Sultan's Medal for Egypt* 1801 (BBM 41)

This is often referred to as an Order, as it was issued in four different sizes or classes but it is in actual fact a service or campaign medal, awarded by Sultan Selim III to officers and N.C.Os who took part in the Egyptian campaign of 1801, when the French forces were expelled. The medal, which was suspended from a gold chain and hook, came in four sizes, namely 2.1in. 54mm.; 1.9in. 48mm.; 1.7in. 43mm.; and 1.4in. 36mm. diameter. All were given in gold to officers according to rank, but the smaller size was also awarded in silver to N.C.Os.

| | |
|---|---|
| Gold, 2.1in., 54mm.£1500 | Gold, 1.4in., 26mm. £500 |
| Gold, 1.9in., 48mm. £750 | Silver, 1.4in., 36mm.£500 |
| Gold, 1.7in., 43mm. £600 | |

## 79 *The Highland Society Medal* 1801 (BBM 42)

This medal, which was awarded in gold, silver and bronze, was struck by the Highland Society of London for possible award to The Prince Regent and General Sir Ralph Abercromby's sons. It is believed that some of the medals were presented by the Highland Society of London at a much later date as gifts to individuals who had served the Society, and these appear on the market from time to time.

| Gold | £4000 | Silver | £250 | Bronze | £150 |
|------|-------|--------|------|--------|------|

## 80 *Mr Boulton's Trafalgar Medal* 1805 (BBM 43)

Mr Boulton, a manufacturer in Birmingham, at his own expense issued medals in various metals to the survivors of the Battle of Trafalgar. The medal is unusual in that around the edge there is an inscription, 'From M. Boulton to the Heroes of Trafalgar'. It was given in silver, and white metal, according to the rank of the recipient. Specimens in bronze gilt and bronze are also found.

| Gold | £9000 | Pewter | £150 |
|------|-------|--------|------|
| Silver | £750 | Bronze gilt/bronze specimens | £200 |

## 81 *Mr Davison's Trafalgar Medal* 1805 (BBM 44)

This was the second of two medals issued privately by Mr Davison, who was Nelson's prize agent, the first being for the Nile in 1798. This Trafalgar Medal was only issued in pewter and was awarded unnamed but is found engraved on the reverse

| | £600 |
|--|------|

## 82 *Medal for the Capture of Rodrigues, Isle of Bourbon and Isle of France* 1809-10 (BBM 47)

Awarded by the Hon. East India Company to its forces from the Bombay and Bengal presidencies for the capture of the three islands of Rodrigues, Bourbon and France, which took place between July 1809 and the end of 1810. Forty-five medals were awarded in gold and just over 2000 in silver; the medal is 1.9in., 49mm. in diameter and bears on the obverse a native holding a Union flag while standing before a gun. The reverse contains a wreath and a Persian inscription as well as one in English similar to the title above. Assistance was given by British troops and ships from the Royal Navy, who were not awarded any medals.

| Gold (45)  £5000 | Silver (2156)  £400 |
|---|---|

## 83 *Spanish Medal for Bagur and Palamos* 1810 (BBM 50)

Awarded by the Spanish Government to the crews of the *Ajax, Cambrian* and *Kent*. Eight medals were issued in gold to senior officers, while the remainder were awarded silver medals.

Some 600 seamen and marines landed to capture merchant ships which were tied up to the quays, although it transpired that the landing parties were driven through the town and eventually managed to return to their ships after suffering heavy casualties.

| Gold (8)  £4000 | Silver (600)  £400 |
|---|---|

## 84 *Java Medal* 1811 (BBM 51)

This medal was awarded by the H.E.I.C. for the capture of Java from Holland which had at that time become part of Napoleon's empire. The capture of Java was part of the British Government's policy of dominating the Far East at a time when European forces were largely contained in Europe by the Royal Navy's blockade.

One hundred and thirty-three gold medals were issued and approximately 6519 silver (750 of these to Europeans), and these were awarded to officers and men of the Company's forces. The British forces were awarded medals much later on, in 1847—the Naval and Military General Service Medal with bar Java; the General and Field officers, as well as Naval captains, had previously been awarded gold medals. The obverse of the Company's medal depicts an attack on Fort Cornelis during the campaign and the reverse contains English and Persian inscriptions.

| Gold (133)  £5000 | Silver (6519)  £350 |
|---|---|

## 85 *Nepaul War Medal* 1814-16 (BBM 73)

This medal, 2in., 51mm. diameter, was awarded in silver, being issued to native troops only; approximately 300 were awarded. The medal was awarded for the campaign in Nepaul under Generals Marley, Gillespie (who was killed), and Ochterlony. The campaign was necessary so as to pacify the Rajah of Nepaul who had refused to ratify a treaty which had previously been signed by his ambassadors. The campaign was also undertaken so as to combat the frequent border raids made on the Company's territories by the Nepalese. Since the date of the Treaty, Gurkha troops from Nepaul have been recruited into both the Indian and British Armies and their outstanding bravery and loyalty have become legendary.

The obverse of the medal contains a scene of hills and stockades and the reverse a Persian inscription. The British troops and also the native troops who did not receive this medal were, in 1851, awarded the Army of India Medal with bar Nepaul. The Nepaul Medal was struck by the Calcutta Mint and was normally worn suspended by a cord which passed through a loop attached to the award.

| | |
|---|---|
| Silver (300) | £500 |

## 86 *Ceylon Medal* 1818 (BBM 74)

This particular medal was issued by the Ceylon Government for gallant conduct during the Kandian rebellion. Forty-seven are supposed to have been issued (gold 2, silver 45), the regiments present being the 19th, 73rd Foot (2nd Battalion, the Black Watch) 83rd Foot, the 1st and 2nd Ceylon Regiments, 7th, 15th and 18th Madras N.I.

| | |
|---|---|
| Silver (45) | £1000 |

## 87 *Burma Medal* 1824-26 (BBM 75)

This medal was authorized by the Honourable East India Company in 1826, being awarded to native officers and men in the Company's service, and was the first of the Company's 'modern' smaller size standard medals as we know them today. The war resulted from repeated acts of aggression by the Burmese on the borders adjacent to the East India Company's territory.

The obverse depicts the elephant of Ava kneeling before the British lion with palm trees and the Union flag, and an inscription is contained in the exergue. The reverse contains a scene of the storming of the pagoda at Rangoon. The medal was awarded to the Bengal and Madras Armies; native officers were presented with a gold medal, and the native troops a silver one. Approximately 750 gold medals were issued and 24,000 silver. The British troops involved were later, in 1851, issued with the Army of India Medal with bar Ava.

| | | | | | |
|---|---|---|---|---|---|
| Gold (750) | £2500 | Silver gilt | £300 | Silver (24,000) | £250 |

### 88 *Coorg Medal* 1837 (BBM 78)

Awarded in gold and silver, only 44 of the gold and 300 of the silver being issued. The obverse depicts a Coorg warrior holding a knife in his raised right hand and musket in the left, with an inscription in Canarese which, translated, reads: 'A mark of favour given for loyalty to the Company's government in suppressing the rebellion in the months of April and May 1837'. The reverse contained war trophies and 'For Distinguished Conduct and Loyalty to the British Government of Coorg, April 1837'. The medal was issued solely to the Coorgs who remained loyal during the rebellion and was not awarded to the Company's regular or irregular forces.

Like many of the East India Company's medals, restrikes are found, many of which have die flaws.

| | | | |
|---|---|---|---|
| Gold (44) | £5000 | Silver (300) | £350 | Bronze specimen £120 |

---

# Official Medals and Later Private Issues (nos. 89-182)

### 89 *Naval Gold Medal* 1795-1815 (BBM 52, 53)

This medal was introduced in 1795, two years after the commencement of the Napoleonic Wars and eighteen years before the equivalent Army Gold Crosses and Medals. The Naval Gold Medals were first introduced for award to admirals and captains of ships following Lord Howe's fleet victory over the French off Ushant on 1st June 1794, this generally being known as 'The Glorious 1st June'. The larger medals, which are 2in., 51mm. in diameter were awarded to admirals, and the smaller medals, 1.3in., 38mm. to captains. Both medals were glazed on the obverse and reverse and were individually engraved on the reverse with details of the action and the recipient's name.

The whole series of medals is rare and consequently valuable, with only 23 of the larger and 116 of the smaller having been awarded. Following the victory in 1815, the medals were discontinued and successful officers after that date were awarded the Order of the Bath.

Officers who received the Naval Gold Medal also received, if they were living in 1847, the silver Naval General Service Medal for the action. Army officers who qualified for the military Gold Medals and Crosses did not receive the equivalent bars to their Military General Service Medal authorized in 1847.

---

| Small gold medal | Large gold medal | | |
|---|---|---|---|
| 1.3in. dia. (116) £10,000 | 2in. dia. (23) £30,000 | *Hermione* 1799 (1:-) | Banda Neira 1811 (1:-) |
| Only awarded for a few of the actions which were commemorated by | | Trafalgar 1805 (27:3) | Capture of *Rivoli* 1812 (1:-) |
| the silver N.G.S. Medal issued in 1848, namely: | | 4 Novr 1805 (4:-) | Capture of *Chesapeake* 1813 (1:-) |
| 1 June 1794 (17:8) | Capture of *Thetis* 1808 (1:-) | St Domingo 1806 (8:2) | Capture of *L'Etoile* 1814 (1:-) |
| *St Vincent* 1797 (15:6) | Capture of Badere Zaffer 1808 (1:-) | Curacao 1807 (4:-) | *Endymion* with *President* 1815 (1:-) |
| *Camperdown* 1797 (15:2) | Capture of *Furieuse* 1809 (-:1) | *Numbers in brackets indicate small and large medals awarded thus:* | |
| Nile 1798 (14:1) | *Lissa* 1811 (4:-) | *Trafalgar 27 small and 3 large medals* | |

## 90 *Naval General Service Medal* 1793-1840 (BBM 54)

The medal was not authorized until as late as 1847 and then it was only issued to those *still* surviving. Due to illiteracy, lack of communication and of publicity, many entitled to receive the award would not have claimed their medals and, as a result, the numbers issued for some of the approved actions were extremely small indeed. The medal was originally intended to cover the period of the Napoleonic Wars, namely 1793-1815, but the medal was then extended to cover the period up until 1840 so as to reward those that took part in the Battles of Algiers (1816), Navarino (1827) and Syria (1840). Some 20,933 medals were issued, but the majority had a single bar only; the maximum number of bars issued with one medal was seven, and only 2 were awarded; 4 medals had six bars and 14 medals were awarded with five bars.

The N.G.S. Medal is particularly interesting in that it was issued for actions against a number of nations, namely France, Holland, Spain, Denmark, Sweden, Turkey, Egypt, Algiers, USA and Russia, consequently, the medal is of intense interest to the collector. These actions, against all the major nations of the world at that time, were commemorated by the issue of 231 different bars. As with the majority of later medals, the medal was officially impressed, and the details can easily be checked against medal rolls.

A selection of bars should give a general idea of price structure and for this purpose we have chosen bars covering general fleet actions, frigate actions and boat service engagements. Only single bar medals have been priced. The collector should bear in mind that *one cannot assess the value of a multiple bar medal by a simple addition of the values of the single bars.* In cases such as this, one's assessment should be based on the rarest bar and then add a proportion only of the value of any further bars.

Collectors must bear in mind that with this series in particular, one cannot assess a value simply based on the number of bars issued, otherwise Trafalgar would be of less value than, say, Algiers or Navarino and the Boat Service bar for 14th December 1814 would be less than that for all the other Boat Service bars listed. Various factors are taken into account such as the action itself, ie, whether it is a popular bar such as Trafalgar and which nation we engaged; those for services against the USA in the 1812—14 War are more in demand due to the interest of collectors in both countries. Another factor is the number of bars awarded to the ship aboard which the recipient served, and the part the ship played in the action.

*Numbers in brackets indicate bars issued.*

| Fleet Actions | | Frigate Actions | |
|---|---|---|---|
| 1 June 1794 (540) | £600 | Mars 21 April 1798 (26) | £900 |
| 14 March 1795 (95) | £750 | Lion 15 July 1798 (23) | £900 |
| 23 June 1795 (177) | £600 | Acre 30 May 1799 (41) | £750 |
| St Vincent (348) | £500 | London 13 March 1806 | |
| Camperdown (298) | £700 | (27) | £825 |
| Nile (326) | £550 | Curacao 1 Jany 1807 | |
| Egypt (618) | £350 | (65) | £700 |
| Copenhagen 1801 (555) | £500 | Stately 22 March 1808 | |
| Gut of Gibraltar (142) | £500 | (31) | £825 |
| Trafalgar (1710) | £750 | Lissa (124) | £500 |
| 4 Novr 1805 (296) | £400 | | |
| Martinique (486) | £300 | *Boat Service Actions* | |
| Basque Roads (529) | £350 | 16 July 1806 (51) | £650 |
| Guadaloupe (483) | £300 | 1 Novr 1809 (110) | £600 |
| Java (665) | £300 | 28 June 1810 (25) | £900 |
| St Domingo (396) | £420 | 29 Sepr 1812 (25) | £850 |
| St Sebastian (293) | £300 | 2 May 1813 (48) | £650 |
| Algiers (1328) | £280 | 8 April 1814 (24) | £1900 |
| Navarino (1142) | £300 | 14 Decr 1814 (205) | £700 |
| Syria (6978) | £120 | | |

List of all bars and numbers awarded:

Nymphe
  18 June 1793 (4)
Crescent
  20 Octr 1793 (12)
Zebra
  17 March 1794 (2)
Carysfort
  29 May 1794 (583)
1 June 1794 (540)
Romney
  17 June 1794 (2)
Blanche
  4 Jany 1795 (5)
Lively
  13 March 1795 (3)
14 March 1795 (95)
Astraea
  10 April 1795 (2)
Hussar
  17 May 1795 (1)
Thetis
  17 May 1795 (2)
17 June 1795 (41)
23 June 1795 (177)
Dido
  24 June 1795 (1)
Lowestoffe
  24 June 1795 (6)
Spider
  25 Aug 1795 (1)
Port Spergui
  17 March 1796 (4)
Indefatigable
  20 April 1796 (6)
Santa Margarita
  8 June (1796) (3)
Unicorn
  8 June 1796 (4)
Southampton
  9 June 1796 (4)
Dryad
  13 June 1796 (5)
Terpsichore
  13 Octr 1796 (3)
Lapwing
  3rd Decr 1796 (2)
Blanche
  19th Decr 1796 (2)
Minerve
  19 Decr 1796 (4)
Amazon
  13 Jany 1797 (6)
Indefatigable
  13 Jany 1797 (6)
St Vincent (348)
  (14 Feb 1797)
Nymphe
  8 March 1797 (4)
San Fiorenzo
  8 Mar 1797 (8)

Camperdown (298)
  (11 Octr 1797)
Phoebe
  21 Decr 1797 (5)
Mars
  21 April 1798 (26)
Isle St Marcou
  6 May 1798 (3)
Lion
  15 July 1798 (23)
Nile (326)
  (1 Augt 1798)
Espoir
  7 Augt 1798 (1)
12 Octr 1798 (74)
Fisgard
  20 Octr 1798 (9)
Sybille
  28 Feby 1799 (12)
Acre
  30 May 1799 (41)
Schiermonnikoog
  12 Aug 1799 (9)
Arrow
  13th Sepr 1799 (2)
Surprise with Hermione (7)
  (25th Octr 1799)
Speedy
  6 Novr 1799 (3)
Courier
  22 Novr 1799 (3)
Viper
  26 Decr 1799 (1)
Fairy
  5 Feby 1800 (3)
Harpy
  5 Feby 1800 (3)
Loire
  5 Feby 1800 (1)
Peterel
  21 March 1800 (2)
Penelope
  30 March 1800 (11)
Vinciego
  30 March 1800 (2)
Capture of the Désirée (21)
  (8 July 1800)
Seine
  20 Augt 1800 (7)
Phoebe
  19 Feby 1801 (6)
Egypt (618)
  (8 March-22 Sept 1801)
Copenhagen 1801 (555)
  (2 April 1801)
Speedy
  6 May 1801 (7)
Gut of Gibraltar
  12 July 1801 (142)

Sylph
  28 Sepr 1801 (2)
Pasley
  28 Octr 1801 (4)
Scorpion
  31 March 1804 (4)
Centurion
  18 Sept 1804 (9)
Acheron
  3 Feby 1805 (2)
Arrow
  3 Feby 1805 (8)
San Fiorenzo
  14 Feby 1805 (12)
Phoenix
  10 Augt 1805 (26)
Trafalgar (1710)
  (21 Octr 1805)
4 Novr 1805 (296)
St Domingo (396)
  (6 Feby 1806)
Amazon
  13 March 1806 (29)
London
  13 March 1806 (27)
Pique
  26 March 1806 (8)
Sirius
  17 April 1806 (10)
Blanche
  19 July 1806 (22)
Anson
  23 Augt 1806 (6)
Arethusa
  23 Augt 1806 (6)
Curacao
  1 Jany 1807 (65)
Pickle
  3 Jany 1807 (2)
Hydra
  6 Augt 1807 (11)
Comus
  15 Augt 1807 (10)
Louisa
  28 Octr 1807 (1)
Carrier
  4 Novr 1807 (1)
Sappho
  2 March 1808 (4)
San Fiorenzo
  8 March 1808 (16)
Emerald
  13 March 1808 (16)
Childers
  14 March 1808 (4)
Nassau
  22 March 1808 (31)
Stately
  22 March 1808 (31)

Off Rota
  4 April 1808 (19)
Grasshopper
  24 April 1808 (7)
Rapid
  24 April 1808 (1)
Redwing
  7 May 1808 (7)
Virginie
  19 May 1808 (21)
Redwing
  31 May 1808 (5)
Seahorse wh.
  Badere Zaffere (32)
  (6 July 1808)
Comet
  11 Augt 1808 (3)
Centaur
  26 Augt 1808 (41)
Implacable
  26 Augt 1808 (41)
Cruizer
  1 Novr 1808 (4)
Amethyst wh. Thetis (31)
  (10 Novr 1808)
Off the Pearl Rock
  13 Decr 1808 (14)
Onyx
  1 Jany 1809 (5)
Confiance
  14 Jany 1809 (8)
Martinique (486)
  (24 Feby 1809)
Horatio
  10 Feby 1809 (13)
Superieure
  10 Feby 1809 (1)
Amethyst
  5th April 1809 (26)
Basque Roads 1809 (529)
  (12 April 1809)
Castor
  17 June 1809 (5)
Pompee
  17 June 1809 (21)
Recruit
  17 June (1809) (5)
Cyane
  25 and 27 June 1809 (5)
L'Espoir
  25 and 27 June 1809 (5)
Bonne Citoyenne
  wh. Furieuse (12)
  (6th July, 1809)
Diana
  11 Septr 1809 (5)
Anse la Barque
  18 Decr 1809 (40)
Cherokee
  10 Jany 1810 (4)

Scorpion
12 Jany 1810 (5)
Guadaloupe (483)
(5 Feby 1810)
Firm
24 April 1810 (1)
Surly
24 April 1810 (1)
Sylvia
26 April 1810 (1)
Spartan
3 May 1810 (30)
Royalist
May and June 1810 (3)
Amanthea
25 July 1810 (23)
Banda Neira (68)
(9 Augt 1810)
Otter
18 Sepr 1810 (8)
Staunch
18 Sepr 1810 (2)
Boadicea
18 Sepr 1810 (15)
Briseis
14 Octr 1810 (2)

Lissa (124)
(13 March 1811)
Anholt
27 March 1811 (40)
Off Tamatave
20 May 1811 (79)
Hawke
18 Augt 1811 (6)
Java (665)
(July-18 September 1811)
Locust
11 Novr 1811 (2)
Skylark
11 Novr 1811 (4)
Pelagosa
29 Novr 1811 (64)
Victorious with
Rivoli (67)
(22 Feby 1812)
Weazel
22 Feby 1812 (6)
Griffon
27 March 1812 (7)
Rosario
27 March 1812 (7)

Malaga
29 April 1812 (17)
Growler
22 May 1812 (1)
Northumberland
22 May 1812 (63)
Off Mardoe
6 July 1812 (47)
Sealark
21 July 1812 (4)
Royalist
29 Decr 1812 (3)
Weazel
22 April 1813 (5)
Shannon wh. Chesapeake
(42) (1 June 1813)
Pelican
14 Augt 1813 (4)
St Sebastian (293)
(8 Sepr 1813)
Thunder
9 Octr 1813 (7)
Gluckstadt
5 Jany 1814 (42)
Cyane
16 Jany 1814 (7)

Venerable
16 Jany 1814 (42)
Eurotas
25 Feby 1814 (32)
Hebrus with L'Etoile (40)
(27 March 1814)
Cherub
28 March 1814 (7)
Phoebe
28 March 1814 (31)
The Potomac
17 Aug 1814 (108)
Endymion wh. President (58)
(15 Jany 1815)
Gaieta
24 July 1815 (88)
Algiers (1328)
(27 Augt 1816)
Navarino (1142)
(20 Octr 1827)
Syria (6978)
(4 Novr 1840)

---

BOAT SERVICE:

*Numbers in brackets indicate numbers issued*

15 Mar 1793 (1)
17 Mar 1794 (29)
29 May 1797 (3)
9 June 1799 (4)
20 Dec 1799 (3)
29 July 1800 (4)
29 Aug 1800 (25)
27 Oct 1800 (5)
21 July 1801 (7)
27 June 1803 (5)
4 Nov 1803 (1)
4 Feb 1804 (10)
4 June 1805 (10)
16 July 1806 (51)
2 Jan 1807 (3)
21 Jan 1807 (8)
13 Feb 1808 (2)
10 July 1808 (8)
11 Aug 1808 (15)

28 Nov 1808 (2)
7 July 1809 (34)
14 July 1809 (7)
25 July 1809 (36)
27 July 1809 (10)
29 July 1809 (11)
28 Aug 1809 (15)
1 Nov 1809 (110)
13 Dec 1809 (8)
13 Feb 1810 (20)
1 May 1810 (15)
28 June 1810 (25)
27 Sep 1810 (33)
4 Nov 1810 (1)
23 Nov 1810 (40)
24 Dec 1810 (19)
4 May 1811 (10)
30 July 1811 (4)
2 Aug 1811 (9)

20 Sep 1811 (6)
4 Dec 1811 (19)
4 April 1812 (4)
1 and 18 Sep 1812 (21)
17 Sep 1812 (11)
29 Sep 1812 (25)
6 Jan 1813 (26)
21 March 1813 (3)
29 April 1813 (2)
Ap & May 1813 (57)
(29 April and 3 May 1813)
2 May 1813 (48)
8 April 1814 (24)
24 May 1814 (12)
3 and 6 Sep 1814 (1)
14 Dec 1814 (205)

## 91 *Army Gold Crosses and Medals* 1806-14 (BBM 58, 59, 60)

Approved in 1813 by the Prince Regent on behalf of King George III, awarded to commemorate the victories of the Napoleonic Wars and also the American War of 1812-14. The gold medals were issued in two sizes, the larger was 2.1in., 54mm. in diameter and was restricted to general officers commanding, and the smaller, 1.3in., 33mm. in diameter, was awarded to officers who commanded regiments and battalions. As with the Naval Gold Medal, the Army Medals were glazed.

The name of the first action was engraved in the centre of the reverse, although that for Barrosa was die struck. In addition, a small special medal was struck in 1806 for Maida, which is part of the gold medals series.

A second or a third action was commemorated by a die-struck gold bar(s) which was attached to the ribbon. Officers who were engaged in more than three actions received a gold cross in lieu. The names of the four actions appeared on the arms of the cross, with additional bars added to the ribbon for five actions or more. In all, 163 crosses, and 85 large and 596 small medals were issued; it therefore follows that the large gold medals are the rarest of this series. Following the successful conclusion of the Peninsular War and prior to Waterloo, these gold awards were discontinued as by then the Order of the Bath had been enlarged to three classes with a military division and it then became the normal practice to award successful officers with one of the classes of the Order of the Bath.

Unlike Naval officers who received the Naval Gold Medal *and* also the silver Naval General Service Medal in 1848, Army officers did not receive the equivalent silver Military General Service Medal if they had been awarded the Gold Cross or Medal.

| | | | |
|---|---|---|---|
| Maida 1806 | £20,000 | | |
| Small gold medal (field officers) 1.3in. dia. | £3200 | (W.Indies) | £2500 |
| Small gold medal with 1 bar (field officers) | £3600 | | |
| Small gold medal with 2 bars (field officer) | £4000 | | |
| Small gold medal for Barrosa (die-struck reverse) (11 issued) | £4500 | | |
| Large gold medal (general officers) 2.1in. dia. | £10,000 | (W.Indies) | £8000 |
| Large gold medal (general officers) 2.1in. with 1 bar | £12,000 | | |
| Large gold medal (general officers) 2.1in. with 2 bars | £15,000 | | |
| Gold cross | £12,000 | | |
| Gold cross with 1 bar | £13,000 | | |
| Gold cross with 2 bars | £15,000 | | |
| Gold cross with 3 bars | £18,000 | | |
| Gold cross with 4 bars | £22,000 | | |
| Gold cross with 5 bars | £25,000 | | |

*(163 Crosses + 237 bars, 85 large + 43 bars and 596 small gold medals + 237 bars issued.)*
*All prices are for Peninsular actions unless otherwise stated.*

## 92 *Military General Service Medal* 1793-1814 (BBM 61)

As with the Naval General Service Medal of the same period, this medal was not authorized until 1847 and then issued only to the survivors living at that time. Some 25,650 applications were made for the medal, which was awarded with a variety of 29 different bars; the maximum number issued with any one medal was 15, and only two were issued; eleven medals were issued with 14 bars.

The principal reason for the issue of this medal was to reward Wellington's troops for their victories in Spain and Portugal, although bars were issued for places as far afield as Egypt in 1801, the East and West Indies, Italy and also for the 1812-14 war with America. Three bars were issued for the North American War, two of the place-names being in Canada, one in America—Fort Detroit, which is the only American place-name to appear on a British military medal. Although the medal carries the date 1793, the first action commemorated by the medal was for Egypt 1801, this bar being issued after the other twenty-eight bars had been authorized. It has been said that the delay in the issue of the medal, some forty-six years lapsing between the first action and the issue, was due to the reluctance of the Duke of Wellington who was opposed to the issue of a standard medal to all ranks. However, when the medal was finally designed it incorporated in the reverse a likeness of the Duke, kneeling before the Queen (Victoria had come to the throne in the meantime) who is about to place a laurel wreath of victory on him.

Unlike the Naval G.S. (no. 91) this medal is far more frequently found with multiple bars although it was issued with a selection of only twenty-nine different bars. *Prices below are for single bar medals* and again, as with the Naval G.S., the addition of extra bars would normally only add a small proportion to the value. *In a number of cases, single-bar medals are more valuable than two- or three-bar medals.* The valuations for the multiple-bar medals are based on regiments where more than about a hundred bars were issued. However, one must bear in mind that one can expect prices to be higher where one or more of the bars is rare to a particular regiment, or of course if awarded to an officer.

| | | | |
|---|---|---|---|
| Egypt | £280 | Chateauguay | £1200 |
| Maida | £280 | Chrystler's Farm | £1500 |
| Roleia | £600 | Vittoria | £190 |
| Vimiera | £275 | Pyrenees | £200 |
| Sahagun | £700 | St Sebastian | £220 |
| Benevente | £2000 | Nivelle | £240 |
| Sahagun and Benevente | £375 | Nive | £260 |
| Corunna | £225 | Orthes | £200 |
| Martinique (RN/RM | | Toulouse | £180 |
| £1200) | £240 | 2 bar medal | £260 |
| Talavera | £220 | 3 bar medal | £280 |
| Guadaloupe (RN/RM | | 4 bar medal | £300 |
| £1300) | £200 | 5 bar medal | £320 |
| Busaco | £250 | 6 bar medal | £360 |
| Barrosa | £220 | 7 bar medal | £410 |
| Fuentes D'Onor | £220 | 8 bar medal | £460 |
| Albuhera | £300 | 9 bar medal | £500 |
| Java (RN/RM £1100) | £240 | 10 bar medal | £650 |
| Ciudad Rodrigo | £350 | 11 bar medal | £900 |
| Badajoz | £240 | 12 bar medal | £1100 |
| Salamanca | £260 | 13 bar medal | £2200 |
| Fort Detroit | £1500 | 14 bar medal | £3000 |

*Prices are based on medals to the most common units, however, medals to the King's German Legion are 25% lower in value.*

## 93 *Waterloo Medals* 1815 *(British and Allied)* (BBM 64-71)

This was the very first of the medals as we know them today, being awarded by the British Government to officers and other ranks alike. For the first time, the medals were officially named, thus making it possible for the recipient's service record and, frequently, biographical details, to be checked, an aspect which always fascinates collectors. Although entitled 'The Waterloo Medal', the medal was issued to those that took part in one or more of the following battles; Ligny 16th June, Quatre Bras 16th June as well as Waterloo 18th June. In addition to receiving the medals, every soldier present was credited with two years' extra service.

Medals to those regiments that suffered casualties are more sought after and consequently a little more expensive than those to regiments which suffered lightly, or indeed than those who were in General Colville's Reserve Division and did not see any action. In addition to the British troops, medals were also issued to the King's German Legion. Details of casualties suffered by the various regiments can be found in *British Battles and Medals,* published by Spink & Son Ltd.

Unlike the Naval and Military General Service Medals issued in 1848 for the earlier Napoleonic campaigns, the Waterloo Medal was issued soon after the action, early in 1816; consequently, they were more frequently worn with the result that this medal is more difficult to find in really fine condition. Whether a medal is fitted with its original steel clip-ring, or with a fancy silver attachment at the recipient's expense, does not have any marked effect on the value.

The allies also issued medals of various designs to their own troops.

| | | | |
|---|---|---|---|
| Heavy cavalry | £400 | King's German Legion | £250 |
| Light cavalry | £350 | Allies Waterloo medals: | |
| Foot guards | £300 | Hanovarian | £120 |
| Foot regiments | £300 | Brunswick | £160 |
| RA etc | £250 | Dutch Silver Cross | £100 |
| General Colville's reserve | | Saxe-Gotha-Altenberg | £180 |
| division 2/35th, 1/54th | | Nassau | £110 |
| 2/59th and 1/91st Foot | £250 | Prussian | £25 |

## 94 *Army of India Medal* 1799-1826 (BBM 72)

This was the fourth and last medal to cover events connected directly or indirectly with the Napoleonic Wars. The Naval and Military General Service Medals, the Waterloo Medal and the Army of India Medal are considered by collectors as the 'classics' of a medal collection.

As with the two general service medals just referred to, the medal was not authorized until 1851, and again was only issued to the survivors *living* at that time. It was awarded for the various battles and campaigns in India and Burma between 1803 and 1826; the medal carried on the obverse the effigy of Queen Victoria, who had not been born when many of the actions were fought.

The medal is unusual in that the last bar awarded is placed nearest the medal, so that the correct sequence reads downwards. One medal was awarded with as many as 7 bars, and two received 6 bars and ten medals were issued with 5 bars.

The medal was issued to those that took part in many very arduous campaigns and, if one takes into account the hardships and conditions of service against very determined enemies in an alien climate, one can more readily appreciate the award. The medal covered three separate wars, namely the Second Maharata War 1803-04 (the first took place in 1778-84), the Nepal War of 1814-16 and the Pindaree, or Third Maharata War, 1817-18. Major General Arthur Wellesley, later the Duke of Wellington, 'earned his spurs' in the Second Maharata War and was often referred to later on as 'The Sepoy General'.

The medal is more sought after when issued to the Sovereign's troops or to European officers and other ranks serving with the H.E.I.C. as opposed to those awarded to natives. The drawback to the medals awarded to natives is the difficulty of confirming the medal in the records, in addition to which they were frequently issued engraved as opposed to the European medals, invariably issued with impressed lettering. It follows that engraved medals are easier to fake.

In spite of the fact that, of the 4500 medals awarded, nearly 4000 were issued with single bars, a number of the scarcer bars are more common when found in combination with others. Consequently, when considering the price of a particularly rare bar we have chosen the more numerous issue, ie possibly a two- or three-bar combination; in cases such as these, the number of bars is shown in brackets, therefore, Assye is the price of a medal with three different bars:

| | *Imperial Regiments*★ |
|---|---|
| Allighur (3 bar medal) | £3000 |
| Battle of Delhi (3 bar medal) | £3000 |
| Assye (3 bar medal) | £2750 |
| Asseerghur (3 bar medal) | £3000 |
| Laswarree | £1200 |
| Gawilghur (3 bar medal) | £2750 |
| Argaum (3 bar medal) | £2750 |
| Defence of Delhi | £15,000 |
| Battle of Deig (2 bar medal) | £3400 |
| Capture of Deig (2 bar medal) | £2250 |
| Nepaul | £550 |
| Kirkee | £15,000 |

| | |
|---|---|
| Poona | £1500 |
| Kirkee & Poona | £1250 |
| Seetabuldee | rare |
| Nagpore | £850 |
| Seetabuldee & Nagpore | £10,000 |
| Maheidpoor | £1000 |
| Corygaum | rare |
| Ava (RN £375) | £275 |
| Bhurtpoor | £350 |
| Gilt *specimen* with the Duke of Wellington's bars. Gawilghur, Argaum, Assye | £325 |
| Indian recipients | from £200 |
| 2 bar medal | £600 |
| 3 bar medal | £2750 |
| 4 bar medal | £6500 |
| 5 bar medal | £12,000 |

*The above prices apply to either single or multiple bars, whichever is the most common.*

★*These prices also apply to officers in the H.E.I.C's service.*

## 95 *Ghuznee Medal* 1839 (BBM79)

This was the first of many medals to be awarded for actions in connection with Afghanistan, an area which was to be a regular battleground for the armies in India during the next one hundred years. This was the second campaign medal to be issued to British troops, the first being for Waterloo 1815. The medal was awarded to both British and Indian troops who were present at the storming of and fighting around the fortress of Ghuznee between the 21st and 23rd July 1839. The purpose of the British presence in Afghanistan was to remove the anti-British King, Dost Mahomed, who had exiled his predecessor Shah Shojaah, and it appeared to the British that there was a distinct possibility that the regime of Dost Mahomed might associate itself with the Russians, in which case the presence of Russian troops would have endangered the whole of the Indian subcontinent.

The forces under the command of Dost Mahomed were defeated and Shah

Shojaah was reinstated. To record his appreciation, the Shah instituted the Order of the Dooranie Empire (No. 24) which was awarded in three different classes to British officers of field rank and above. The medal itself was issued at the expense of the Indian Government and was issued unnamed, although it is frequently found privately named in various styles.

| British troops | £230 | Unnamed | £150 |
|---|---|---|---|
| Indian troops | £150 | | |

### 96 *St Jean d'Acre Medal* 1840 (BBM 56)

Awarded by the Sultan of Turkey for the capture of Acre on the Syrian coast in 1840. This special medal was awarded in gold to naval captains, field officers and above, in silver to all other officers and warrant officers, and bronze to the remainder of the seamen, marines and soldiers. It was awarded to all who received the Naval General Service Medal with bar Syria (No. 90), and is often found in a pair or group with British Service Medals.

| Gold | £600 | Silver | £90 | Bronze | £50 |
|---|---|---|---|---|---|

### 97 *Candahar, Ghuznee and Cabul Medals* 1841-42

(BBM 80)

There were four main varieties of this medal, bearing on the obverse the diadem head of Queen Victoria with the legend 'Victoria Vindex', while the reverses bore the name of the action or actions in cases where the recipient was involved in more than one of the battles. The different reverses read 'Candahar', 'Cabul', 'Ghuznee and Cabul', 'Candahar, Ghuznee and Cabul'. The Cabul reverse was either spelt Cabul or Cabvl, the latter being very scarce.

The medals were issued to both the Queen's forces and those of the Company at the expense of the Honourable East India Company. These actions were at the commencement of almost one hundred years of activity against the mobile and warlike Afghans, which involved a succession of marches and counter-marches, defences and reliefs of fortresses, through hard winters and hot summers, when many regiments particularly distinguished themselves. The event which caused shock to the public was the virtual annihilation of the 44th Foot (the Essex Regiment)—only the doctor, Dr Bryden, managed to reach Jellalabad alive. The number of men killed in the Essex Regiment was 565, while 3 officers and 51 men were taken prisoner, 36 of them later being released by British troops.

| | Imperial Regiments | Europeans in H.E.I.C. units | Indian units | Unnamed |
|---|---|---|---|---|
| Candahar | £500 | £400 | £200 | £175 |
| Cabul | £260 | £200 | £110 | £120 |
| Cabvl ('Victoria Regina' legend) | £1100 | £950 | £800 | £250 |
| Ghuznee/Cabul | £485 | £300 | £225 | £170 |
| Candahar/Ghuznee/ Cabul | £280 | £200 | £145 | £130 |

## 98 *Jellalabad Medals* 1841-42 (BBM 81)

This medal was issued as one of the First Afghan War series, being presented by the Honourable East India Company. The medals were awarded to the surviving members of the garrison of Jellalabad which gallantly defended the fortress from the 12th November 1841 until 7th April 1842. There were two different types, one with a mural crown which was exchanged for the one with a flying figure of Victory. Most of the next of kin of those killed received the flying Victory type.

|  | Imperial Regiments | Europeans in H.E.I.C. units | Indian units | Unnamed |
|---|---|---|---|---|
| *1st type:*<br>Obverse—mural crown 'Jellalabad' Reverse—'VII April 1842' | £300 | £260 | £150 | £100 |
| *2nd type:*<br>Obverse—bust of Victoria 'Victoria Vindex' legend Reverse—a winged figure of Victory 'Jellalabad VII April MDCCCXLII | £600 | £500 | £275 | £175 |
| 'Victoria Regina' legend | £1200 | £900 | £600 | £400 |

## 99 *Defence of Kelat-i-Ghilzie Medal* 1842 (BBM 82)

This is the last of the medals issued by the Company to commemorate an action during the First Afghan War. This was for the defence of the fortress of Kelat-i-Ghilzie, and the medal is particularly rare. None of the Queen's regiments were present, but fifty-five Europeans of the Company's forces received the medal. In addition to these Europeans, the medal was awarded to 877 native troops, and few of these medals have survived.

European recipients £3500   Indian recipients £850   Unnamed £450

## 100 *China War Medal* 1842 (BBM 83)

The issue of such a medal, originally suggested by the Governor General of India, was for presentation to all ranks of the Honourable East India Company. However, it was subsequently awarded by the British Government in 1843 and presented to those who had taken part in the operations in China during 1841 and 1842. The campaign ended with the capture of Nanking and, as one result of the war, the British took possession of Hong Kong. The medal originally had a different design to that actually issued, the original reverse depicted a lion with its forepaws on a dragon with 'Nanking 1842' in the exergue, but upon

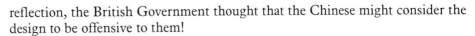

reflection, the British Government thought that the Chinese might consider the design to be offensive to them!

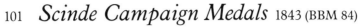

| Royal Navy | £180 |
| Indian and Bengal Marine Ships | £300 |
| Imperial Regiments | £180 |
| Indian Army | £110 |
| Original Design, specimen | £350 |

## 101 *Scinde Campaign Medals* 1843 (BBM 84)

The medal was issued with three different reverses which read either 'Meeanee', 'Hyderabad' or 'Meeanee-Hyderabad', with all three versions having the date 1843 below the name of the battle(s). The medal was only issued to the 22nd Foot (the Cheshire Regiment) of the Queen's regiments, the remainder being awarded to the Hon. East India Company's forces, including four ships of the Indian Navy.

Following the end of the First Afghan War and the withdrawal of British and Indian troops, the Amirs of Scinde opened hostilities against the allied forces. The first task of the force, assembled under Major-General Sir Charles Napier, was the destruction of the fort of Emaum Gur, situated in the desert. The action was described by that past master of military tactics, the Duke of Wellington, 'as one of the most curious military feats I have ever known to be performed.' General Napier set an example which has since been continuously followed, of naming in his official despatches N.C.Os and men who had specially distinguished themselves. These days such a 'mention' entitles one to wear a 'Mention in Despatches' emblem.

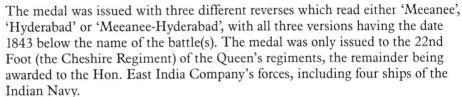

| | European Members Indus Flotilla | Natives Indus Flotilla | Imperial Regiments | Europeans in Indian Regiments | Indian units | Unnamed |
| --- | --- | --- | --- | --- | --- | --- |
| Meeanee | £1000 | £600 | £600 | £500 | £250 | £120 |
| Hyderabad | £800 | £400 | £600 | £400 | £150 | £120 |
| Meeanee-Hyderabad | — | — | £500 | £400 | £150 | £120 |

## 102 *Gwalior Campaign Stars* 1843 (BBM 85)

These were issued in bronze, each having a silver centre struck with the name of the action, which was either 'Maharajpoor' or 'Punniar' together with the date. The bronze stars were struck from guns captured from the enemy, thus preceding the policy of casting Victoria Crosses from captured Russian cannon. Both actions were fought on the same day, 29th December, and it was probably the shortest campaign for which medals were ever issued.

In spite of the very short duration of the actions, British losses were substantial.

At the time, peace manoeuvres were being carried out so as to overawe the population, but events soon changed to a war operation, and moved so quickly

that four ladies who were spectators came under the fire of the Maharatta guns. Lord Ellenborough, the Governor General, presented these four ladies with gold and enamel stars bearing the effigy of Queen Victoria. The regiments that particularly distinguished themselves were Her Majesty's 16th Lancers, the 39th (the Dorsetshire Regiment) and the 40th Regiment (South Lancashire Regiment). The star issued for Punniar is scarcer than that issued for Maharajpoor.

|  | Imperial Regiments | Indian Units |
|---|---|---|
| Maharajpoor Star | £180 | £140 |
| Punniar Star | £200 | £150 |

## 103 *Sutlej Campaign Medal* 1845-46 (BBM 86)

This was the first of the campaign medals which were issued with different bars and awarded to both officers and men alike (the medals for the earlier Napoleonic Wars which were issued with bars were not authorized until 1847). An unusual aspect of this medal is that the first action is mentioned in the reverse exergue of the medal, and those that were engaged in more than one action had a bar(s) placed above the medal suspender. The medal was issued to both the Queen's regiments and those of the Hon. East India Company. The 31st Regiment (East Surreys) and the 50th Foot (Royal Queen's West Kent Regiment) were the only British units that qualified for all four actions, consequently many of them received the medal with three bars which of course covered the four actions. The campaign was caused by a state of anarchy which ruled in the Sutlej following the death of the ruler Ranjit Singh in 1839, and which culminated in the Sikh army crossing the River Sutlej into the East India Company's territory. The casualties were particularly severe, an aspect which was expected as the fighting qualities of the Sikh nation were renowned, in fact, the officers of the British regiments suffered some fifty per cent casualties and forty per cent to other ranks in a period of less than two months. To illustrate the fact that commanding officers did not command from the rear, three major-generals and four brigadiers were killed, while one major-general and seven brigadiers were wounded.

|  | Imperial Regiments | Europeans in H.E.I.Co. units | Indian units |
|---|---|---|---|
| Moodkee (18th December 1845) |  |  |  |
| *Reverse* (no bar) | £185 | £130 | £105 |
| Moodkee *Reverse* with 1 bar | £220 | £180 | £135 |
| Moodkee *Reverse* with 2 bars | £280 | £220 | £175 |
| Moodkee *Reverse* with 3 bars | £425 | £300 | £240 |
| Ferozeshuhur (21st December 1845) |  |  |  |
| *Reverse* no bar | £175 | £120 | £100 |
| Ferozeshuhur *Reverse* with 1 bar | £215 | £170 | £165 |
| Ferozeshuhur *Reverse* with 2 bars | £375 | £300 | £220 |
| Aliwal (28th January 1846) *Reverse* no bar | £165 | £120 | £100 |
| Aliwal *Reverse* with 1 bar | £200 | £180 | £170 |
| Sobraon (10th February 1846) |  |  |  |
| *Reverse* no bar | £145 | £130 | £100 |
| 3 bar glazed gilt specimen | £250 |  |  |

## 104 *Punjab Campaign Medal* 1848-49 (BBM 87)

The actions for which this medal was awarded were really an extension to the Sikh War of 1845-46 (No. 103). The medal was issued with three different bars, the maximum to any one medal being two bars, the last bar being nearest the medal. As with the Sutlej Medal, this was awarded to both Europeans and to Indian troops. Medals to the South Wales Borderers (24th Foot) are eagerly sought after as about half the regiment became casualties at Chilianwala, while medals to the supporting Indus flotilla are also scarce. The reverse of the medal is thought to be one of the most attractive ever designed, showing General Sir Walter Gilbert on horseback receiving the surrender of the Sikh army, with a palm tree on a hill and inscription in the background. The fantastic diamond Koh-i-Noor, or Mountain of Light, was captured during the campaign and was later presented to Queen Victoria. The stone is now set in the crown to be worn by a queen consort and which is permanently on display in the Jewel House in the Tower of London.

The 3 bars awarded were Mooltan, Chilianwala, Goojerat

|  | Imperial Regiments | Europeans in H.E.I.Co units | Indian units |
|---|---|---|---|
| No bar | £120 | £90 | £70 |
| 1 bar | £225 | £150 | £100 |
| 2 bars | £170 | £130 | £85 |
| Medals to casualties of the 24th Foot and other units at Chilianwala | £275 | | £200 |
| Medals to the Indus flotilla (154)   Europeans | £345 | | £175 |
| 3 bar glazed gilt specimen | £250 | | |

## 105 *South African Campaign Medal* 1834-53 (BBM 88)

This medal was awarded for three different campaigns in southern Africa, namely 1834-35, 1846-47 and 1850-53. All received the same medal without bars and carrying the date 1853 on the reverse, consequently, it is impossible to tell which campaign or indeed campaigns the recipient had served in without referring to the medal rolls. The majority of the recipients were British troops although several hundred were issued to Navy personnel who had served on five different ships. In addition, a few medals were awarded to local troops and officers.

The campaigns resulted from the aggressive warlike nature of the Kaffir tribes. These tribes made frequent raids on the settlers, making it necessary for military action to be undertaken. The Commanders-in-Chief were Major-General Sir Benjamin D'Uban, after whom Durban was named, and Sir Harry Smith, who was later Governor of Cape Province (the town of Ladysmith was named after his wife). The second campaign of 1846-47 was rather more hazardous, as by then many of the natives had acquired up-to-date firearms. The third and last campaign occured because the natives blockaded Sir Harry Smith's troops in Fort Cox. Severe fighting subsequently took place with unexpected setbacks to the British troops.

An interesting sideline to this campaign was the sinking of the troopship

*Birkenhead* off South Africa while on its way with reinforcements. The epic gallantry and outstanding discipline of the troops on board so impressed King William of Prussia that he had the full story read out at parades at every barracks in Germany.

| Royal Navy | £225 | Colonial Regiments | £185 |
| Imperial Regiments | £200 | H.M.S. Birkenhead survivor | £600 |

Add £100 if proved to have been for 1834-35 campaign and £75 for 1846-47 campaign.

## 106 *Sir Harry Smiths' Medal for Gallantry* 1851

When the Eighth Kaffir War commenced at the end of 1850, Sir Harry Smith was Governor and Commander-in-Chief at the Cape. During the early part of the war Sir Harry was blockaded in Fort Cox in the vicinity of King Williamstown by the Gaikas under Chief Sandilli. Eventually the C-in-C with 250 men of the Cape Mounted Riflemen broke out. Being impressed with his men for this and other actions in the campaign Sir Harry ordered and presented a special silver medal. At least 30 medals were struck and 22 are known to survive. The medal was issued unnamed but is found privately engraved. It is worn suspended from the Sutlej Medal ribbon.

| Unnamed | Named |
| £1400 | £2500 |

## 107 *India General Service Medal* 1854-95 (BBM 89)

This was the first of several general service medals issued to cover minor campaigns in India and, unlike previous medals which were frequently awarded very many years or even decades after the actions; it was instituted as early as January 1854. The medal is found with numerous bars, and was never issued without at least one; twenty-four different bars were issued during the forty-year period. The majority were awarded for services on the Nothern Frontiers of India, particularly the NW Frontier, others being issued for expeditions to Persia and Burma. As with most of the previous medals, this was issued in silver but, for the first time, the later medals from 1885 onwards were also issued in bronze, these being awarded to native support personal such as transport drivers, servants and sweepers. The medal itself is very common, but some of the bars are rare, such as Kachin Hills 1892-93, Hunza 1891 and Chin Hills 1892-93. Kachin Hills was awarded to the Yorkshire Regiment and Chin Hills to the Norfolk Regiment, these being the rarest of the whole series. The maximum numbers of bars to one medal appears to be seven.

Medals to European Privates in Indian regiments are assessed at 25% less value than to Imperial regiments

| | Royal & Indian Navies (Europeans) | Indian Navy (Natives) | Imperial Regiments | Indian Regiments (Natives) | Bronze |
|---|---|---|---|---|---|
| Pegu | £70 | £70 | £55 | £40 | — |
| Persia | £100 | £80 | £55 | £45 | — |
| North West Frontier | — | — | £55 | £40 | — |
| Umbeyla | — | — | £80 | £60 | — |
| Bhootan | — | — | £60 | £40 | — |
| Looshai | — | — | — | £85 | — |
| Perak | £80 | £70 | £60 | £40 | — |
| Jowaki 1877-8 | — | — | £60 | £40 | — |
| Naga 1879-80 | — | — | — | £145 | — |
| Burma 1885-7 | £75 | £65 | £50 | £35 | £45 |
| Sikkim 1888 | — | — | £100 | £85 | £60 |
| Hazara 1888 | — | — | £60 | £45 | £55 |
| Burma 1887-89 | £85 | £65 | £50 | £30 | £50 |
| Burma 1887-9 | £200 | — | £180 | — | — |
| Chin Lushai 1889-90 | £150 | £120 | £70 | £70 | £80 |
| Lushai 1889-92 | — | — | £175 | £100 | £150 |
| Samana 1891 | — | — | £60 | £50 | £60 |
| Hazara 1891 | — | — | £60 | £45 | £40 |
| NE Frontier 1891 | — | — | £80 | £65 | £45 |
| Hunza 1891 | — | — | — | £190 | £250 |
| Burma 1889-92 | — | — | £50 | £45 | £60 |
| Chin Hills 1892-93 | — | — | £260 | £120 | £100 |
| Kachin Hills 1892-93 | — | — | £450 | £150 | £125 |
| Waziristan 1894-95 | — | — | £80 | £40 | £45 |

## 108 *Baltic Medal* 1854-55 (BBM 90)

This medal is associated with the Crimean War as the operations conducted in the Baltic against the Russian fleet were in general support of the Naval and Army operations in the Crimea. It was principally awarded to the Royal Navy and Royal Marines, but also awarded to approximately one hundred members of the Royal Sappers and Miners who were with the fleet for demolition purposes. The British fleet consisted of about one hundred ships, including floats and mortar ships and was reinforced by a French fleet. Russian merchant ships were destroyed in the Gulfs of Bothnia and Riga, while the fortress of Bomarsund was attacked and later the fortress of Sveaborg.

The medals were issued unnamed but are found privately engraved, the exception being those issued to the Royal Sappers and Miners, which were officially impressed in the same style of lettering as the Crimea Medal.

| | | | |
|---|---|---|---|
| Unnamed | £55 | Officially impressed medals | |
| Engraved | £75 | to the Sappers and Miners | £475 |
| Impressed | £145 | | |

## 109 *Crimea Medals* 1854-56 (BBM 91)

From Waterloo 1815 to the commencement of the First World War, very many campaign medals were issued, but this was the only one awarded for services against a major power.

Queen Victoria was so impressed by the deeds performed by her Army in the Crimea that she directed, as early as 1854, a medal be issued with the bars for Alma and Inkermann, which explains why the single date 1854 is to be found on the medal—the bars for Balaklava and Sebastopol were sanctioned in 1855. In addition to a considerable number of medals awarded to the Navy and the Army, a few were also awarded to our French allies.

The war was due to Russian expansionist policies, principally directed at Turkey, known at the time as 'The Sick Man of Europe'. War was declared by both Britain and France at the same time, namely 28th May 1854 and the allies were later joined by the Italian kingdom of Sardinia.

The outstanding gallantry and extreme suffering of the troops during the campaign are now part and parcel of our history, and reflect the fact that the armed forces were ill-prepared to combat the hardships and climate that prevailed. The Army was led by many generals whose last service was under Wellington during the Napoleonic Wars, and it is recorded that Lord Raglan, the C-in-C, often unthinkingly referred to the French as 'The Enemy'. Medals awarded to those that participated in the charges of the Light and Heavy Brigades are particularly sought after, as indeed are those who manned 'The Thin Red Line', namely the 93rd Highlanders.

5 bars were issued, but not more than 4 to a medal

|  | Unnamed | Engraved or privately impressed to Army | Officially impressed to Army | Engraved or privately impressed to R.N. | Officially impressed to RN/RM |
|---|---|---|---|---|---|
| No bar | £45 | £45 | £55 | £50 | £100 |
| 1 bar Alma | £75 | £85 | £140 | — | — |
| 1 bar Inkermann | £65 | £75 | £160 | £90 | £180 |
| 1 bar Azoff | £95 | — | — | £130 | £190 |
| 1 bar Balaklava | £60 | £75 | £110 | £100 | — |
| 1 bar Sebastopol | £45 | £50 | £80 | £75 | £100 |
| 2 bars | £70 | £75 | £150 | £140 | £180 |
| 3 bars | £90 | £110 | £170 | £200 | £250 |
| 4 bars | £140 | £200 | £320 | — | — |

|  | Engraved, regimentally or privately impressed | Officially impressed |
|---|---|---|
| bar Balaklava Heavy Brigade (4th & 5th Dragoons Gds, 1st, 2nd and 6th Dragoons) | £325 | £500 |
| Light Brigade (4th Light Dragoons, 8th and 11th Hussars, 13th Light Dragoons and 17th Lancers) | £1000 | £2500 |
| 'Thin Red Line' (93rd Foot) | £250 | £450 |

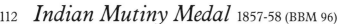

## 110 *Turkish Crimea Medals* 1855 (BBM 92)

The Turkish Government also awarded a service medal for the Crimean campaign, which was issued to the French and British troops—approval was given by the British Government for this to be worn in uniform. There were three types and they seemed to have been issued indiscriminately; one had the wording 'Crimea 1855', supposedly for the British troops, 'La Crimée 1855' the French issue, or 'La Crimea 1855' the Italian/Sardinian issue.

| British, unnamed | £40 | Sardinian, unnamed | £25 |
|---|---|---|---|
| British, named | £60 | Sardinian, named | £35 |
| French | £100 | | |

## 111 *Sardinian Medal for Valour*

For the Crimean campaign the Italian/Sardinian Government also awarded a medal for valour to selected officers and men which was issued engraved.

| Silver (named) | £350 |
|---|---|

## 112 *Indian Mutiny Medal* 1857-58 (BBM 96)

This medal was awarded to those who had taken part in quelling the mutiny of the Hon East India Company's troops. The mutiny resulted from unrest among some of the Indian princes and the population in general, trouble having been fermenting for many years. The final breaking point was caused as a result of the actions of the Indian Government who had annexed Oudh, thus diminishing the power of the King. The Indian Medal was issued with five different bars, although the maximum number issued to one medal was four; fewer than 200 four-bar medals were awarded which were issued to the Bengal Artillery. The maximum number of bars that could be earned by the Queen's troops was three and these were awarded to those who qualified in the 9th Lancers. The most desirable medals are those issued for the *original* Defence of Lucknow, the Queen's regiment involved being the 32nd (Duke of Cornwall's) Light Infantry. Those awarded to the Naval Brigade are also sought after as the Brigade took part in no fewer than ten battles throughout the whole of India in its fifteen months of existence.

| | Navy | †Imperial Troops | Native Troops |
|---|---|---|---|
| No bar | £300 | £70 | £50 |
| 1 bar Delhi | — | £120 | £65 |
| 1 bar Defence of Lucknow | — | — | — |
| 1 bar Relief of Lucknow | £350 | £110 | £85 |
| 1 bar Lucknow | £350 | £110 | £85 |
| 1 bar Central India | — | £100 | £80 |
| 2 bars★ | £500 | £200 | £150 |
| 3 bars★ | — | £400 | £400 |
| 4 bars★ | — | £1200 | £1200 |

"Sarah Sands" survivor £500
4 bar glazed gilt specimen £250

★The multiple bars exclude the Defence of Lucknow bar (see below) which is particularly sought after, the value depending whether the recipient was:

| | †Imperial Troops |
|---|---|
| an original defender | £500 |
| part of the 1st relief force | £250 |

†includes Europeans serving with Indian regiments and the H.E.I.C.

## 113 *Second China War Medal* 1857-60 (BBM 97)

Like the Crimean War, this was another campaign in which the British and French forces co-ordinated, some 10,000 British and 7000 French servicemen participating.

The Second China War (the first was fought between 1840-42) was caused due to various aggressive acts by the Chinese, among which was the seizure of the crew of the *Arrow,* sailing under British colours. During the first operations, the Navy and Marines only, under Admiral Sir Michael Seymour were involved. 11 British gunboats and about 50 ships defeated some 80 junks armed with 800 guns and manned by 6000 seamen at Fatshan Creek. Having destroyed the fleet, the British undertook the capture of Canton, which involved the Navy and the only British regiment there, the 59th (East Lancashire) Regiment. This ended the first phase of the war, peace being signed on the 26th June 1858.

In the meantime, troops had been sent out from the U.K. but they were diverted to quell the mutiny in India. The peace treaty, however, was not ratified, and consequently hostilities reopened which involved considerable British land forces. The forts at the mouth of the River Peiho were captured, the occupation of Pekin took place and the summer palace at Pekin was destroyed by fire which took almost two days to burn out. Indiscriminate looting took place and many of the superb works of art are in western collections today.

| | | Engraved | | Impressed | |
| --- | --- | --- | --- | --- | --- |
| | Unnamed | Army | Navy | Army | Navy |
| No bar | £45 | £55 | £60 | £75 | £100 |
| 1 bar China 1842 | £200 | — | — | — | £300 |
| 1 bar Fatshan 1857 | £80 | — | £95 | — | £200 |
| 1 bar Canton 1857 | £85 | £95 | £85 | £150 | £200 |
| 1 bar Taku Forts 1858 | £90 | — | £95 | — | £200 |
| 1 bar Taku Forts 1860 | £55 | £70 | £90 | £120 | £200 |
| 1 bar Pekin 1860 | £60 | £70 | £80 | £130 | £200 |
| 2 bars | £70 | £85 | £90 | £130 | £240 |
| 3 bars | £90 | £110 | £110 | £180 | £300 |
| 4 bars | £135 | — | £175 | — | £400 |
| 5 bars (specimen) | £250 | — | — | — | — |
| China Medal 1842 with China 1842 bar with or without other China 1857 bars | | | | | £1250 |

## 114 *New Zealand Medal* 1845-47 and 1860-66 (BBM 98)

The reverse of this medal differs from all others in the series in that the recipient's dates of service are die struck in the centre. In addition, medals were issued without dates signifying service in either the first or second war. The medal was authorized in 1869, consequently some of the recipients had to wait twenty-four years before receiving their medals (the medal was only issued to those that survived to 1869). Many of the dates are rare, particularly those issued to naval ships for the first of the wars.

It was not until about 1839 that the first British settlers arrived in New Zealand and a treaty was agreed with the Maoris regarding the purchase of lands.

Not surprisingly, it was not very long before the increase in the number of settlers placed considerable strain on relations with the Maori tribes, with the result that fighting broke out. The second war came about due to the same reasons as the first, and it was in this war that the Maori tribes proved themselves to be quite remarkable antagonists, their bravery causing considerable British casualties. Peace was declared in 1866, and from that time onwards, relationships between the proud Maoris and the settlers improved.

It was during the latter part of the wars that the New Zealand Cross (No 26) was introduced (without the approval of Queen Victoria) as local volunteer forces did not qualify for the Victoria Cross.

The period of service is contained on the reverse in raised digits. Those issued undated could be awarded for either the first or the second of the Maori uprisings.

| First war | Navy | Army | Local volunteers | Second War | Navy | Army | Local volunteers |
|---|---|---|---|---|---|---|---|
| Undated | £100 | £135 | £130 | 1861 | — | £1800 | — |
| 1845-46 | £250 | £300 | — | 1861-63 | — | — | — |
| 1845-47 | £300 | £300 | — | 1861-64 | — | £250 | — |
| 1846-47 | £300 | — | — | 1861-65 | — | £2500 | — |
| 1846 | £600 | — | — | 1861-66 | — | £200 | £200 |
| 1847 | £500 | £2500 | — | 1862-66 | — | £2500 | — |
| 1848 | — | £2500 | — | 1863 | — | £450 | £150 |
| | | | | 1863-64 | £200 | £220 | — |
| *Second war* | | | | 1863-65 | £220 | £200 | — |
| Undated | £100 | £100 | £110 | 1863-66 | — | £180 | — |
| 1860 | £1000 | £1500 | — | 1864 | £600 | £225 | £275 |
| 1860-61 | £150 | £600 | — | 1864-65 | — | £180 | — |
| 1860-63 | — | £1800 | — | 1864-66 | — | £150 | — |
| 1860-64 | — | £200 | — | 1865 | £600 | £400 | — |
| 1860-65 | — | £200 | — | 1865-66 | — | £155 | — |
| 1860-66 | — | £200 | — | 1866 | — | £170 | — |

## 115 *Abyssinian War Medal* 1867-68 (BBM 99)

This campaign resulted from King Theodore of Abyssinia imprisoning the British Consul and other British subjects as well as a number of foreigners. After negotiations, the prisoners were released, but in a short time they were rearrested together with the negotiators! As a result of the campaign, the capital of those days, Magdala, was captured and razed to the ground, the King committed suicide and peace terms were concluded.

The medal was sanctioned in 1869 and was probably the most expensive of the campaign medals ever to be produced as the recipient's name and unit, etc were embossed in the centre of the reverse which necessitated an expensive manufacturing operation. Those awarded to the Indian troops had their names impressed or engraved in the more normal way. 12,000 were awarded to the British Army and 2000 to the Royal Navy, who were under the general command of Lieutenant-General Sir Robert Napier (later Lord Napier of Magdala). The Navy landed a small brigade of one hundred to man the rockets. Casualties amounted to only two killed and twenty-seven wounded, this was probably one

of the most successful of the Victorian campaigns. As a result of the lack of casualties and blood and thunder generally, the medal does not attract the attention of collectors to the same extent as medals for, say, the Crimea or the Indian Mutiny. Later on, in 1896, the Italians attempted a similar expedition, but their forces suffered almost total annihilation at Adowa.

| British regiments | £140 | Indian troops | £95 |
| Royal Navy | £150 | RN Rocket Brigade | £250 |

### 116 *Canada General Service Medal* 1866-70 (BBM 100)

This medal was not approved until as late as January 1899, some thirty years after the event. The medal was issued by the Canadian Government to both British forces and the Canadian local forces for participation in quelling the rebellions of 1866 and 1870. Approximately 16,100 medals were awarded, the vast majority, over 15,000, being given to Canadians, the remainder going to the British Army and Navy.

The campaign took place following the end of the American Civil War, when large numbers of soldiers were available for recruitment by the Fenians. Their aim was to cause embarrassment to Britain so as to endeavour to establish a united Irish Republic, and they therefore organized an invasion of Canada from the United States.

Less than two dozen medals were issued with three bars, while 1600 were awarded with two bars, and a few medals were issued to the Royal Navy, which command higher prices than those awarded to the Army.

| | Canadian Units | Imperial Regiments | Royal Navy |
| --- | --- | --- | --- |
| Fenian Raid 1866 | £90 | £130 | £180 |
| Fenian Raid 1870 | £100 | £150 | — |
| Red River 1870 | £500 | £600 | — |
| 2 bars Fenian Raid 1866 and 1870 | £150 | £250 | — |
| 3 bars | £2500 | — | — |

*Multiple bars should be verified*

### 117 *Ashantee Medal* 1873-74 (BBM 101)

The Port of Elmina in the Ashanti was Dutch territory but this was then transferred to the British. The Dutch had made a practice of giving King Kofi an annual payment for the use of the port but this ceased when the British took over and, as a result, hostilities broke out. During the early part of the campaign, the fighting was on the coast and this was largely undertaken by a small force of Marines and the Royal Navy. The advance on, and the capture of Kumasi the capital was undertaken in a period lasting one month only, but during this short period four Victoria Crosses were awarded. A small Naval detachment under Captain Glover, known as 'Glover's Force', was ordered to attack Kumasi the rear, which caused the King to sue for peace, whereupon he had to pay an indemnity demanded by the British C-in-C General Wolseley. The rate of sickness during the campaign was extremely high, some ninety-eight per cent of the Naval forces engaged on land reported sick during the period. The medal was issued with bar 'Coomassie', this being awarded to those who took part in the attack on the capital. Silver medals were also awarded to natives and a few bronze medals may have been issued. These natives were recruited locally by the Navy and their medals are sometimes found officially inscribed with the very amusing names given to them by the crews of the ships, such as Pea Soup, Bottle of Beer, Prince of Wales and Tom Twoglass, etc.

|  | Royal Navy | Army | Natives | Bronze |
|---|---|---|---|---|
| No bar | £95 | £100 | £80 | — |
| Bar Coomassie | £200 | £150 | £100 | £500 |

### 118 *South Africa Medal* 1877-79 (BBM 102)

This medal was of the same design as that for the earlier wars fought between 1835-53, except that the reverse date '1853' in the exergue is replaced by a Zulu shield and four crossed assegais. While the earlier medal was issued without a bar, this was issued either with or without one of the bars listed below.

The campaign came about largely due to tribal conflicts, principally the attack by the Galeka and Gaikas tribes on the Fingoes, the latter being under British protection. The disturbances spread which made it necessary for fairly large contingents from the Army, Navy and local units to become involved. Possibly the most notable and disastrous event from the British point of view was the Zulu nation's attack on Lord Chelmsford's columns near the border at Isandhlwana, where more than 1300 British troops, including the 24th Foot (South of Wales Borderers) and native followers were annihilated. After that, the Zulus moved on some ten miles to the post at Rorke's Drift, and here the small garrison of 139 men who were guarding the sick and wounded were attacked by 3000 Zulus. During the defence, no fewer than eleven Victoria Crosses were awarded. The campaign eventually ended successfully, after the defeat of the Zulus at Ulundi.

|  | Royal Navy | Army | Colonial |
|---|---|---|---|
| Without bar | £100 | £95 | £80 |
| 1877 | — | — | £650 |
| 1877-8 | £350 | £150 | £160 |
| 1877-8-9 | £400 | £150 | £160 |
| 1878 | — | £170 | £180 |
| 1878-9 | £325 | £180 | £200 |
| 1879 | £120 | £120 | £110 |
| Rorke's Drift participant | — | £5500 | — |
| Isandhlwana participant | — | £1200 | — |
| Ulundi participant | — | £250 | — |

*A very small number were issued to colonial troops with 2 bars*

## 119 *Afghanistan War Medal* 1878-80 (BBM 103)

This medal commemorates the Second Afghan War, the first wars having been fought in the early 1840s for which medals were issued by the Hon. East India Company. The campaign came about due to the same basic reasons as the first war, namely British suspicion of the intentions of the Afghans towards Russia. In 1873, the Amir of Afghanistan agreed on the question of boundaries between Afghanistan and India which was always a contentious subject, and also the maintenance of peace, and it was agreed that the Amir would be paid a subsidy. In 1877, the Amir refused to accept a British resident at Kabul and he raised an army to antagonize the British forces stationed on the border, and in 1878 he went further and signed a treaty with Russia, giving Russia the right to protect Afghanistan. The campaign that resulted was a particularly ardous one, due to the nature of the country, as well as the warlike attitude of the Afghans. Many notable actions were fought, the most outstanding being that at Maiwand by the 66th Regiment (2nd Battalion, The Royal Berkshires) and E. Battery, B. Brigade of the Royal Horse Artillery. In fact, almost half the casualties in the whole war took place at the battle of Maiwand, namely 1150.

*Six bars were issued but the maximum number attached to any one medal was four*

|  | Imperial Regiments | Indian Regiments |
|---|---|---|
| No bar bronze | — | £150 |
| No bar silver | £35 | £30 |
| 1 bar Ali Musjid | £60 | £40 |
| 1 bar Peiwar Kotal | £60 | £40 |
| 1 bar Charasia | £55 | £40 |
| 1 bar Kabul | £55 | £40 |
| 1 bar Ahmed Khel | £60 | £40 |
| 1 bar Kandahar | £50 | £40 |
| 2 bars | £65 | £45 |
| 3 bars | £130 | £60 |
| 4 bars | £350 | £95 |
| Killed at Maiwand | | — |
| 66th Foot | | |
| (Berkshires) | £500 | |
| E. Bty B. Bde RA | £400 | — |

### 120 *Kabul to Kandahar Star* 1880 (BBM 104)

The design of this star, which was manufactured in bronze from captured guns, shows a total departure from the normal circular medal. The stars were struck by a private company in Birmingham. H. Jenkins & Sons, and were awarded together with the silver medal with bar Kandahar. These were presented to those who had taken part in the famous march by General Roberts of just over 300 miles from the capital Kabul to relieve the garrison at Kandahar; both British and Indian troops were involved. The relief of the garrison at Kandahar and the action that took place soon afterwards in the vicinity effectively ended the war, although the border area could never be described as being particularly peaceful.

| | |
|---|---|
| Impressed naming on reverse to British troops | £80 |
| Engraved naming on reverse to Indian troops | £55 |
| Unnamed | £40 |

### 121 *Cape of Good Hope General Service Medal* 1880-97
(BBM 105)

Awarded in silver by the Cape Government in 1900 for services in suppressing small uprisings in the Transkei, Basutoland and Bechuanaland. Basically, the disturbances were caused due to resentment by the natives to the peace terms, which followed the defeat of Chief Moirosi, that dictated that all arms were to be handed in. Another resentment was the fact that serious outbreaks of cattle disease occurred in Bechuanaland which led to the slaughter of large numbers of the natives' cattle.

The medals were awarded to local, and volunteer regiments and were issued with up to three bars, but only twenty-three were awarded with the maximum number.

| | | | |
|---|---|---|---|
| Transkei | £250 | 2 bars | £250 |
| Basutoland | £140 | 3 bars (23) | £900 |
| Bechuanaland | £120 | | |

### 122 *Egypt Medal* 1882-89 (BBM 106)

The Suez Canal was opened in 1869 which made the strategic position of Egypt important from the British point of view. Due to the general financial chaos that prevailed in Egypt, the Egyptian Army was not paid and, as a result, mutinied. Events then took a turn for the worse, and the Arabs attacked the Europeans. Early in 1882, a combined British and French squadron of ships arrived off Alexandria and sent ultimatums ashore which were ignored. As a result, the forts at Alexandria were attacked and destroyed and the canal seized by a combined British force consisting of Naval and Army units. The French, although they arrived with the British off Alexandria, took no part in the conflict and withdrew.

A second phase opened in 1884, much further south in the Sudan, where a new leader who was proclaimed 'The Mahdi' raised a force which annihilated the British and Egyptian troops; this caused the need for another combined British Army and Navy operation. General Gordon was in command with a besieged garrison at Khartoum the capital of Sudan, but unfortunately the British forces failed to relieve him and he and his garrison were overwhelmed. Further events caused other actions up until as late as August 1889, but it was not until the battle of Toski had taken place that the general area was made more peaceful. The operation caused considerable problems of transportation on the River Nile, and to overcome these problems boatmen were recruited from as far away as Canada, who were employed for their particular skill and experience in shooting rapids which were of particular value in the taking of supplies up and down the Nile. Thomas Cook the travel agent was also employed by the Government to convey personnel and stores up and down the Nile.

The maximum number of bars that were issued on a medal was 7, but only one was awarded, six were awarded with 6 bars, while those with 5 bars are far from common. The blue and white ribbon represents the Blue and White Niles with the major river, the Blue Nile, being represented by three blue stripes and the lesser Nile, the White, by two white stripes.

| | *Royal Navy | Army | | *Royal Navy | Army |
|---|---|---|---|---|---|
| No bar | £30 | £30 | Gemaizah 1888 | £120 | £100 |
| Alexandria 11th July, | £50 | — | Toski 1889 | £300 | £200 |
| Tel-el-Kebir | £50 | £45 | 2 bars | £70 | £50 |
| El-Teb | £100 | £95 | 3 bars | £120 | £100 |
| Tamaai | £80 | £65 | 4 bars | £200 | £180 |
| El-Teb-Tamaai | £70 | £55 | 5 bars | £300 | £350 |
| Suakin 1884 | £50 | £40 | | | |
| The Nile 1884-85 | £50 | £40 | *including Royal Marines where medal is named to one of HM ships | | |
| Abu Klea (not awarded singly, with 'The Nile 1884-85') | £300 | £150 | *Multiple bars based on the most common combination, odd detached men have been ignored* | | |
| Kirbekan (not awarded singly, with 'The Nile 1884-85') | £300 | £150 | Medals to Canadian boatmen | | £550 |
| Suakin 1885 | £50 | £40 | Medals to New South Wales Units. (Suakin 1885) | | £500 |
| Tofrek (generally not awarded singly, with Suakin 1885) | £150 | £100 | Medals to Indian natives, prices at less than those for 'Army' Medals to Egyptians, prices at less than those for 'Army' | | |

## 123 *Egypt, Khedive's Stars* 1882-91 (BBM 107)

Issued by the Khedive of Egypt having been authorized by the Sultan of the Ottoman Empire. It was presented in appreciation of the services rendered by the British Army and Navy, etc and was awarded to all those who received the British Medal (See No. 122). The medal was privately struck by H. Jenkins of Birmingham and awarded with three different dates. There was also an undated type with or without a bar for Tokar, which was issued in 1891. All were issued unnamed.

| | | | |
|---|---|---|---|
| Undated | £25 | 1884 | £25 |
| Undated with Tokar clasp | £100 | 1884-86 | £25 |
| 1882 | £20 | | |

## 124 *North West Canada Medal* 1885 (BBM 108)

It is rather strange that the earlier campaign medal for services in Canada against the Fenians 1866-70 (No. 116) was not authorized until 1899, and yet this one for 1885 was authorized immediately by the Canadian Government. British troops were not engaged except for sixteen officers who were on the staff in Canada at the time. Some 5600 medals were awarded, these being issued unnamed, although some are found privately named. The medal was awarded with or without one bar, namely Saskatchewan. Just occasionally, an unofficial bar is found reading Batouche. Medals to the Steamer *Northcote* are eagerly sought after as they were awarded for an interesting boat action.

Medals were issued unnamed to the units who named them in their particular style. Medals to the N.W.M.P. are impressed in the same style as per the Canada General Service Medal.

The campaign came about due to the reaction of the local population to new settlers. In this case, the construction of the Canadian Pacific Railway was taking place which opened the prairies to white settlers, thus presenting a threat to the Metis, or half-breeds, who were squatters on the land likely to be granted to the new settlers. In spite of representations to the Government by the half-breeds, no agreement was reached, and Riel, who had been involved in the rising of 1866-70, led an uprising. This was his last rebellion as he was hung upon his capture in 1885.

|  | *Named* | *Unnamed* |
|---|---|---|
| No bar | £150 | £100 |
| Bar Saskatchewan | £280 | £165 |
| To the steamer *Northcote* | £600 | — |

## 125 *Royal Niger Company's Medal* 1886-97 (BBM 109)

Nigeria was administered by the Royal Niger Company in a similar manner to the East India Company's rule of India prior to the Indian Mutiny. In 1899, the Company's charter was revoked and the administration of the territory which is present-day Nigeria was then taken over by the Imperial Government.

The medals were struck on behalf of the Company, being designed and produced by Spink & Son Ltd of London.

The medal is scarce since only 100 silver medals were awarded to officers and NCOs for participation in numerous small expeditions against the tribes in Nigeria. Approximately 1000 medals were produced in bronze for natives. They were issued in both silver (named) and bronze (numbered). Later marked specimens from the original dies appear on the market—details appear in *British Battles & Medals*.

| | | | |
|---|---|---|---|
| Silver with bar | | Bronze with bar Nigeria | |
| Nigeria 1886-1897 *(named)* | £950 | *(numbered)* | £350 |
| Silver with bar | | Bronze with bar Nigeria | |
| Nigeria 1886-1897 | | *(Unnumbered specimen)* | £95 |
| *(specimen)* | £100 | Later unnamed specimen | £45 |
| Later unnamed specimen | £65 | | |

### 126 *Imperial British East Africa Company's Medal*

1888-95 (BBM 110)

This is the rarest of medals awarded by the trading companies, such as the British South Africa, Royal Niger and the British North Borneo Company. The medals were frequently named, and in the main were awarded for active services in the general area of Uganda at the turn of the nineteenth century. The medals, in silver were awarded with an ornamental scroll or a simple ring suspender.

£400

### 127 *East and West Africa Medal* 1887-1900 (BBM 111)

This medal is another in the 'general' series being issued for numerous small campaigns and expeditions during the period 1887-1900. Twenty-one different bars were awarded, but the action for Mwele, 1895-96, was engraved on the rim of the medal instead of a bar being awarded. The medal was issued in silver but is occasionally found in bronze, the latter being awarded to native servants, etc. Medals were not awarded to British regiments as a whole, although officers and N.C.Os seconded to native regiments, for example, as instructors, had their parent regiment impressed on the rim of the medal. Many of the bars were awarded to the personnel of Royal Naval ships which were very active off the coast and on the rivers. Of the bars issued, those of Liwondi 1893, Juba River 1893, Dawkita 1897 and Lake Nyassa are the rarest. The campaign on Lake Nyassa was only accomplished by the assistance of the ships *Adventure* and *Pioneer* which had to be hauled in sections over two hundred miles of virgin country and then assembled on the shore of Lake Nyassa.

| | Royal Navy | Europeans | Natives | | Royal Navy | Europeans | Natives |
|---|---|---|---|---|---|---|---|
| 1887-8 | £200 | £150 | £120 | Bronze Mwele 1895-96 *(on the edge* | | | |
| Witu 1890 | £100 | £130 | £130 | *of the medal)* | — | — | £250 |
| 1891-2 | £120 | £150 | £150 | 1896-98 | — | £300 | £200 |
| 1892 | £150 | £140 | £140 | Niger 1897 | — | £350 | £300 |
| Witu August 1893 | £150 | — | £160 | Benin 1897 | £100 | £100 | — |
| Liwondi 1893 | £1800 | — | — | Dawkita 1897 | — | £2000 | £1800 |
| Lake Nyassa 1893 | £1800 | — | — | 1897-98 | — | £130 | £100 |
| Juba River 1893 | £1800 | — | — | 1898 | £900 | £150 | £130 |
| 1893-94 *(Colonial Steamer)* | £130 | £130 | £130 | Sierra Leone 1898-99 | £100 | £100 | £100 |
| Gambia 1894 | £150 | — | £150 | 1899 | £900 | £350 | £200 |
| Benin River 1894 | £150 | £130 | £130 | 1900 | — | £300 | £200 |
| Brass River 1895 | £150 | — | — | | | | |
| Mwele 1895-96 *(on the edge of the medal)* | £100 | £100 | £80 | | | | |

*In the case of a multiple-bar medal, consider the basic value of the rarer bar and add 25% of the value of the more common bars.*

## 128 *British South Africa Company's Medal* 1890-97

(BBM 112)

This was another of the semi-private issues, being awarded by the Company for services in the campaigns in Mashonaland, Matabeleland and Rhodesia and unlike some private issues, Queen Victoria sanctioned that they be allowed to be worn in uniform.

The reverse of the medal is particularly striking as it depicts a charging lion with a spear sticking in its chest, in the background is a mimosa bush and in the foreground a native shield and spears. Ten recipients were entitled to the medal with 4 bars, but only one was known to be issued; fifteen medals were awarded with 3 bars. The medal was issued to both Imperial troops and to local units. That with the reverse reading 'Rhodesia 1896' was the commonest issue,

The name of the first campaign is continued on the reverse of this medal (with the exception of Mashonaland 1890), with a bar(s) to denote subsequent engagements. The Mashonaland 1890 campaign was not recognized until 1927 when a similar medal was issued but without place, name or date on the reverse, the medal being issued with a bar for the campaign.

The 4 bars awarded were Mashonaland 1890, Matabeleland 1893, Rhodesia 1896 and Mashonaland 1897.

|  | British Regiments | Colonial Units |
|---|---|---|
| Mashonaland 1890 (bar) | — | £500 |
| Matabeleland 1893 (reverse) | £150 | £120 |
| Matabeleland 1893 (reverse) with 1 bar | £200 | £160 |
| Rhodesia 1896 (reverse) | £120 | £95 |
| Rhodesia 1896 (reverse) with 1 bar | £150 | £130 |
| Mashonaland 1897 (reverse) | £200 | £120 |

## 129 *Hunza Naga Badge* 1891 (BBM 113)

This is in the form of a plaque, being produced in London upon the instruction of the Maharajah of Jummoo (Jammu) and Kashmir for awarding to his own troops who also received the I.G.S. 1854 medal (No. 107) with bar Hunza 1891. The badge was originally intended to be worn as a brooch at the neck but it was later decided that it should be worn as a medal and some badges are therefore seen converted for wear from a ribbon.

£250

### 130 *Central Africa Medal* 1891-98 (BBM 114)

Awarded for participation in a number of small expeditions in Central Africa in the general area of what is now Uganda. British troops were not entitled to this medal, although a few officers and N.C.Os who were attached as instructors were awarded the medal in silver. A few were issued to native servants in bronze. The ribbon is divided into three equal stripes of black, white and terracotta, representing the Africans, Europeans and Indians.

| | |
|---|---|
| Without bar with ring suspender | £200 |
| With bar Central Africa 1894-98 with ring suspender | £280 |
| With bar Central Africa 1894-98 and straight bar suspender | £350 |
| With bar Central Africa 1894-98 and straight bar suspender in bronze | £750 |

*Prices based on medals to natives*

### 131 *Hong Kong Plague Medal* 1894 (BBM 115)

This medal was awarded by the community of Hong Kong to three hundred men of the King's Shropshire Light Infantry and fifty members of the Navy and Royal Engineers as well as to a few members of the local police. The medal was not authorized to be worn on uniform, but it is more than likely, due to the very lax regulations of the period, that the medals were worn from time to time. In addition to the silver medals, forty were awarded in gold to officers, nursing sisters, and a few civilian officials.

The medal was awarded for service in 1894 during the severe epidemic of bubonic plague. The epidemic broke out near Canton and then in May, gained a foothold in Hong Kong; over 2500 people died during a three-month period.

The obverse design is very symbolic, showing a Chinese lying on a trestle table leaning against a man who is fending off a winged figure of death with his left hand, while a woman is bending over the sick man. On a scroll in the exergue is the date 1894, and to the left is a Chinese inscription.

| | Royal Navy | Royal Engineers | King's Shropshire Light Infantry |
|---|---|---|---|
| Gold | £2000 | £2000 | £2000 |
| Silver | £500 | £450 | £420 |

### 132 *India Medal* 1895-1902 (BBM 116)

This medal was introduced to replace the India General Service Medal, 1854-95 which had been awarded for the previous forty years, had twenty-four different bars, and was consequently in need of replacing.

The medal was issued with two different obverses, the first bore the crowned head of Queen Victoria, and the second the head and shoulders of Edward VII in field marshal's uniform.

As with the previous medal, this was issued for services mostly on the North-West Frontier over a six-year period. Seven different bars were awarded, the rarest being that for the Defence of Chitral followed by Malakand. Unlike the earlier medal, all issues were awarded in silver *and* bronze; they were issued to British and Indian regiments but not to the Royal Navy.

|  | British Regiments (Silver) | Indian Regiments (Silver) | Bronze |
|---|---|---|---|
| Defence of Chitral 1895 | — | £500 | £950 |
| Relief of Chitral 1895 | £45 | £35 | £40 |
| Punjab Frontier 1897-98 | £40 | £30 | £40 |
| Malakand 1897 | £100 | £60 | £70 |
| Samana 1897* | £100 | £60 | £60 |
| Tirah 1897-98* | £60 | £50 | £60 |
| Waziristan 1901-2 (Edward VII obverse) | — | £50 | £45 |

*Not awarded as single bars, prices are for 2 bar combination.

Multiple bars (excluding Defence of Chitral and Malakand)

|  | British Regiments (Silver) | Indian Regiments (Silver) | Bronze |
|---|---|---|---|
| 2 bars | £60 | £40 | £60 |
| 3 bars | £85 | £60 | £70 |
| 4 bars | — | £85 | £95 |
| 5 bars | — | £125 | £125 |

## 133 *Jummoo and Kashmir Medal* 1895 (BBM 117)

Awarded by the Maharajah of Jummoo (Jammu) and Kashmir to the native levies who took part in the Defence of Chitral 1895, an event covered by a bar to the India Medal 1895 (No. 132). The bronze medal, which was produced in London, is unusual in that it is kidney-shaped.

| named | £180 |
|---|---|
| unnamed | £120 |

## 134 *Ashanti Star* 1896 (BBM 118)

This unusual-looking bronze medal is in the form of a four-pointed star, together with the cross of St. Andrew. The medal was struck in bronze with a dull gun-metal finish. The recipients' names were not officially engraved on the medals, as was the case with most issues, the reverses simply reading 'From the Queen'. However, the Colonel of the West Yorkshire Regiment, which was the only regiment present in force, had the medals of his 2nd Battalion named at his own expense. It is said that the star was designed by Princess Henry of Battenburg whose husband died of fever in the campaign. The star was awarded to some 2000 troops who took part in the Ashanti expedition under Major-General F. C. Scott against King Prempeh, who had been indulging in cannibalism and human sacrifices. The campaign culminated in the capture of the capital Kumassi, which is now part of Ghana.

| Unnamed as issued | £90 | Regimentally named (West Yorks) | £150 |
|---|---|---|---|

## 135 *Queen's Sudan Medal* 1896-97 (BBM 119)

Issued in 1899 in silver and bronze, the latter being scarce. Unlike many other issues, the medal was issued without bars. The medal was awarded to all the forces engaged in the reconquest of Sudan between 1896-98, the principal actions being Firket, Hafir, Abu Hamed, the Atbara and Khartoum. The bar Khartoum was awarded for the Battle of Omdurman, where the British 21st Lancers made their gallant charge against a very large and determined enemy force. Some five hundred casualties were incurred by the British before Khartoum.

The medal was awarded to commemorate the reconquest of the Sudan, which followed Britain's departure some years before. The half-yellow and half-black colours on the ribbon represent the desert and the Sudanese nation while the narrow red stripe in the centre is symbolic of the British Army and Navy.

| | | | |
|---|---|---|---|
| Silver | £75 | Bronze (unnamed) | £120 |
| Silver 21st Lancers | £250 | Bronze (named) | £200 |
| Silver 21st Lancers (confirmed charger) | from £1000 | | |
| Silver (unnamed) | £50 | | |

## 136 *Khedive's Sudan Medal* 1896-1908 (BBM 120)

The medal was authorized by a special Egyptian Army order on 12th February 1897 to commemorate the reconquest of the Dongola province. The medal was issued with as many as fifteen different bars, but is rare with more than the two bars 'The Atbara' and 'Khartoum', to British troops. Approval was given for the medal to be worn in uniform. The medal was issued in both silver and bronze but is very scarce in the latter metal.

It was awarded to both British and Egyptian Armies as well as to the Royal Navy who manned the river steamers on the Nile. The yellow of the ribbon represents the deserts, while the central blue stripe the Blue Nile which, with the specially built railway, was the main supply artery.

| | | | |
|---|---|---|---|
| No bar (silver) | £40 | Gederef | £60 |
| No bar (bronze) | £60 | Gedid | £60 |
| Firket | £60 | Sudan 1899 | £50 |
| Hafir | £65 | Bahr-el-Ghazal 1900-02 | £90 |
| Abu Hamed | £60 | Jerok | £90 |
| Sudan 1897 | £60 | Nyam-Nyam | £90 |
| The Atbara *(as a single bar to British troops)* | £80 | Talodi | £100 |
| | | Katfia | £90 |
| Khartoum (British Regt.) | £40 | Nyima | £90 |
| Multiple bars, unnamed to natives | | | |
| 2 bars | £60 | 6 bars | £120 |
| 3 bars | £70 | 7 bars | £140 |
| 4 bars | £100 | 8 bars | £160 |
| 5 bars | £110 | | |

*Prices are based on named medals to Indians and Arabs with the exception of The Atbara and Khartoum as they were mostly awarded to British regiments.*

## 137 *General Gordon's Star for Khartoum* (BBM 121)

During the time General Gordon was besieged in Khartoum, he had cast a star for distribution to his officers and troops with the idea of raising morale. Recipients had to buy the award and the funds went to relieve the poor. The design was based on the Turkish Order of Medjidie and the stars were crudely cast in sand. They are found in pewter, in gold-plated pewter and possibly a few exist in silver.

| Pewter | £250 | Silver | £300 | Gilt pewter | £300 |
|--------|------|--------|------|-------------|------|

## 138 *East and Central Africa Medal* 1897-99 (BBM 122)

Mainly awarded in silver, but a few were issued in bronze to camp followers. The medal was awarded for operations in Uganda and Southern Sudan and was issued to local units such as the Uganda Rifles and various regiments from India. British recipients were mostly officers in command of these regiments.

| | | | |
|---|---|---|---|
| No bar | £200 | 1 bar 1898 (silver) | £200 |
| 1 bar Lubwa's | £350 | 1 bar 1898 (bronze) | £400 |
| 2 bar Lubwa's, Uganda 1897-98 | £250 | 1 bar Uganda 1899 | £200 |
| 1 bar Uganda 1897-98 | £180 | | |

*Prices are for medals named to natives*

## 139 *British North Borneo Company's Medals* 1897-1937

(BBM 123, 124, 153)

This is another in the series of medals issued by a trading company such as those awarded by the Honourable East India Company and the Royal Niger Company.

The medals were awarded for various expeditions in the areas which are now Sarawak, Brunei and Sabah, the first and last states forming part of the present-day Federation of Malay States. The medals were issued in silver and bronze (except Rundum) to both British and native officials and servants, and a small number of Sikh troops. British subjects, however, were not permitted to wear the medal except in Borneo. The medals were produced by Spink & Son Ltd of London.

| | Silver | | Bronze | |
|---|---|---|---|---|
| | Original | Specimen | Original | Specimen |
| Punitive Expedition | £400 | £60 | £220 | £40 |
| Punitive Expeditions | £400 | £60 | £220 | £40 |
| Tambunan | £400 | £60 | £220 | £40 |
| Rundum | £400 | £60 | (Not issued in bronze) | |
| General Service Medal, issued without a bar, in silver only | £450 | £120 | — | — |

*Specimens are struck from heavy gauge blanks or with 'S' of Spink or 'S' of Son on the reverse deleted. The G.S. specimen has the tip of the wreath in the exergue stamped out.*

## 140 *The Sultan of Zanzibar's Medal* 1896 (BBM 125)

A silver medal, the obverse bearing the bust of the Sultan and worn from a plain bright scarlet ribbon. Four bars were awarded, in arabic script, for Pumwani, Jongeni, Takaungu and Mwele. Awarded to the Sultan's forces under the command of Lieut. Lloyd-Matthew R.N. for actions in East Africa in association with British and Imperial forces.

£200

## 141 *Queen's South Africa Medal* 1899-1902 (BBM 126)

Relations between the British Government and the Boers had never been exactly cordial, however, the latter's hostility was not confined just to the British as they had rebelled against the Dutch East India Company. Prior to the British conquest of the Cape of Good Hope and from the very early stages of settlement there had been constant friction between the Boers and the natives. War finally came about due to an ultimatum handed into the British agent in Pretoria.

The Boers from the very outset assumed the offensive, while the British, owing to their numerical inferiority, were compelled to act strictly on the defensive until the arrival of reinforcements from England. Eventually, the number of troops involved increased considerably and it came about that the Queen's South Africa Medal was issued in very large numbers. It was issued with a variety of twenty-six bars, the maximum number of bars issued with any one medal was nine to the Army and eight to the Navy. Various units were involved for the first time, such as the balloon and photographic sections, cyclist units, field force canteens as well as units from Canada, Australia and New Zealand. In addition, volunteer battalions from all over the British Isles served in South Africa.

| | Royal Navy | | Imperial Regiments | | South African Units & Indian units | | Australian & New Zealand | | Canadian Regiments | |
|---|---|---|---|---|---|---|---|---|---|---|
| Without bar (bronze) | — | — | — | — | £70 | — | — | — | — | — |
| Without bar (silver) | £35 | — | £22 | — | £25 | — | £100 | — | £130 | — |
| Cape Colony | £50 | (£45) | £25 | (£25) | £30 | (£30) | £75 | (£75) | £120 | (£150) |
| Rhodesia | Rare | — | £150 | (£150) | £90 | (£80) | £250 | (£200) | £300 | (£250) |
| Relief of Mafeking | — | — | £250 | (£200) | £150 | (£95) | £300 | (£250) | £350 | (£300) |
| Defence of Kimberley | — | — | £95 | (£70) | £90 | (£50) | — | — | — | — |
| Talana | — | — | £75 | (£60) | £130 | (£200) | — | — | — | — |
| Elandslaagte | — | — | £150 | (£75) | — | (£100) | — | — | — | — |
| Defence of Ladysmith | £120 | — | £60 | (£50) | £75 | (£60) | — | — | — | — |
| Belmont | £160 | (£200) | £60 | (£40) | — | (£70) | £350 | (£300) | — | — |
| Modder River | — | (£120) | £120 | (£40) | — | (£70) | £350 | (£300) | — | — |
| Tugela Heights | — | (£100) | — | (£40) | — | — | — | — | — | — |
| Natal | £60 | (£200) | £40 | (£55) | £60 | (£50) | — | — | £200 | (£180) |

| | Royal Navy | Imperial Regiments | South African Units & Indian units | Australian & New Zealand | Canadian Regiments |
|---|---|---|---|---|---|
| Relief of Kimberley | —(£200) | £175 (£40) | £100 (£50) | £300(£250) | — — |
| Paardeberg | — (£100) | £175 (£40) | £100 (£60) | £250(£200) | £140 (£150) |
| Orange Free State | — (£120) | £45 (£25) | £80 (£50) | £150 (£75) | £120 (£150) |
| Relief of Ladysmith | £260 (£100) | £60 (£40) | £120 (£50) | — — | — — |
| Driefontein | — (£100) | £180 (£35) | — (£70) | £200 (£125) | £185 (£160) |
| Wepener | — — | £200(£220) | £200 (£180) | — — | |
| Defence of Mafeking | — — | — — | £550(£550) | — — | — — |
| Transvaal | — (£100) | £25 (£25) | £40 (£30) | £100 (£75) | £200 (£170) |
| Johannesburg | — (£100) | £150 (£40) | £100 (£45) | £125 (£75) | £140 (£150) |
| Laing's Nek | — (£120) | £100 (£40) | — — | — — | |
| Diamond Hill | — (£120) | £100 (£40) | £100 (£50) | £150 (£100) | £200 (£170) |
| Wittebergen | — — | £75 (£30) | £120 (£60) | £150 (£100) | — — |
| Belfast | — (£100) | £120 (£40) | — (£45) | £125 (£75) | £140 (£150) |
| South Africa 1901 | — (£45) | £75 (£25) | £140 (£30) | £120 (£75) | £180 (£150) |
| South Africa 1902 | — (£150) | £75 (£25) | £140 (£30) | £120 (£75) | £140 (£150) |
| | | | | | |
| 2 bars | £45 | £25 | £30 | £75 | £150 |
| 3 bars | £100 | £30 | £35 | £100 | £175 |
| 4 bars | £100 | £35 | £40 | £130 | £200 |
| 5 bars | £110 | £40 | £45 | £150 | £250 |
| 6 bars | £150 | £55 | £100 | £200 | £300 |
| 7 bars | £200 | £100 | £145 | £350 | — |
| 8 bars | £400 | £260 | £375 | — | — |
| 9 bars | — | £450 | — | — | — |
| Relief dates on reverse (Canadian) | — | — | — | — | £2000 |
| Nurses | — | £90 | £100 | £500 | — |
| War correspondents | — | £400 | — | £500 | — |

It should be noted that some bars are more rare when issued singly as opposed to multiple-bar combinations, whilst in a few cases single bars were not issued. Single-bar prices are placed first with the most common multiple-bar combinations following in brackets (£x). Medals with reverse dates in relief (*not* ghost dates) are rare.

142 *Queen's Mediterranean Medal* 1899-1902 (BBM 127

This medal was awarded in silver only to men of garrisons in the Mediterranean who guarded Boer prisoners of war.

£95

### 143 *King's South Africa Medal* 1901-02 (BBM 128)

This medal was never issued without the Queen's Medal, neither was it issued without a bar, except in the case of nurses (plus a few 'odd' men), who received almost 600 medals. The medal commemorated service in South Africa during the latter part of the Boer War in 1901-02, although in actual fact the official surrender of the Boers came about in 1900. The medal commemorates the very many minor actions, which were mostly guerilla, in 1901 and 1902. Very few King's Medals were awarded to the Royal Navy as the Naval brigades had returned to their ships in 1901.

| | |
|---|---|
| No bar (Nurses) | £90 |
| 2 bars 1901 & 1902 (RN) | £400 |
| 2 bars 1901 & 1902 (Army | £20 |
| 2 bars 1901 & 1902 (Canadians) | £200 |
| 2 bars 1901 & 1902 (Australians) | £400 |
| 1 bar 1902 | £300 |

### 144 *St John Ambulance Brigade Medal for South Africa* 1899-1902 (BBM 129)

A bronze medal was issued by the Order of St John to the members of the St John Ambulance Brigade who served in South Africa during the Boer War or who took an active part in mobilization, training or despatch of comforts. A total of 1871 were issued, all were engraved on the rim with the name and unit of the recipient and often the medal is found associated with the Queen's and King's South Africa Medals. Fourteen members of the brigade who travelled to China from South Africa aboard the hospital ship USS *Maine* were awarded the China Medal.

| | |
|---|---|
| | £65 |

### 145 *Kimberley Star and Medal* 1899-1900 (BBM 130, 131)

This is one of an extensive series of private medals awarded by, individuals and towns in both South Africa and the United Kingdom. This was awarded by, or in the name of, the Mayor of Kimberley to those involved in the defence of the town against the Boers. Although a local and private issue, a number of medals were awarded as mementoes to British troops.

See *Boer War Tribute Medals* by M. G. Hibbard for a comprehensive study of the series.

| | |
|---|---|
| Star | £65 |
| Medal | £350 |

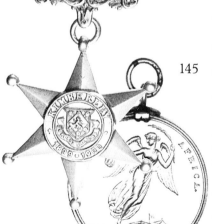

**146** *Yorkshire Imperial Yeomanry Medal* 1900-02 (BBM 132)

Many different medals were issued by towns and boroughs, etc, to local troops who served in the Boer War, which are the subject of a book entitled *Boer War Tribute Medals* by M. G. Hibbard. The medals issued to the Yorkshire Imperial Yeomanry are included in this catalogue as more were issued than any other and they often appear on dealers' lists.

The medal was awarded to the 3rd and 66th Imperial Yeomanry Battalions with different reverse dates. All were produced by Spink & Son Ltd in London.

| | |
|---|---|
| 3 Imperial Yorkshire Yeomanry S. Africa 1900-01 | £50 |
| 3 Imperial Yorkshire Yeomanry S. Africa 1901-02 | £60 |
| 66 Imperial Yorkshire Yeomanry S. Africa 1900-01 | £110 |

**147** *Cape Copper Company Ltd, Medal for the Defence of Ookiep* 1902 (BBM 133)

This medal, in silver to officers and in bronze to other ranks, was awarded for the Defence of Ookiep in Namaqualand, the siege lasting from 4th April-4th May 1902. Ookiep was the centre of the Cape Copper Mining Company's operations. When Smuts, a commando leader (later Field Marshal, Prime Minister of South Africa and a member of the Imperial War Cabinet), invaded the district, the garrison in the area retired on Ookiep, the defence of which was commanded by Major Dean, the Company's manager. The garrison consisted of 660 half-castes, 206 European miners and 44 men of the 5th Warwickshire militia, as well as 12 men of the Cape Garrison Artillery. The total strength was just over 900 officers and men.

| | |
|---|---|
| Silver £1250 | Bronze £500 |

**148** *China War Medal* 1900 (BBM 134)

This is the third and last of the medals awarded for services against China, unless we consider the Naval General Service Medal with bar for Yangtze 1949. Three bars were issued, but the maximum number of bars on any medal was two. The majority of the medals were issued in silver; native servants and followers received their medals in bronze.

The war broke out due to the persecution of European missionaries and traders by the various Chinese secret societies, commonly known as Boxers. As the Chinese Government was not able or willing to curtail their activities, the Royal Navy commenced hostilities under the command of Admiral Sir Edward Seymour. An international force was quickly raised comprising units from America, France, Japan, Russia and Germany, under the overall command of the

German Field Marshal, Count Von Waldersee. Until the relief force arrived, Pekin had to be defended by the small garrisons maintained by most of the legations. The British Legation guard comprised among others some eighty members of the Royal Marines and naturally their medals with bar 'Defence of Legations' is particularly sought after.

| | Royal Navy | Army | Native Regiments | Colonial Navy |
|---|---|---|---|---|
| No bar (bronze) | — | — | £60 | — |
| No bar (silver) | £70 | £65 | £60 | £300 |
| 1 bar Taku Forts (silver) | £265 | — | — | — |
| 1 bar Defence of Legations (silver) | £3200 | — | — | — |
| 1 bar Relief of Pekin (silver) | £130 | £185 | £75 | £450 |
| 1 bar Relief of Pekin (bronze) | — | — | £100 | — |
| 2 bars (excluding Defence of Legations) | £325 | — | — | — |

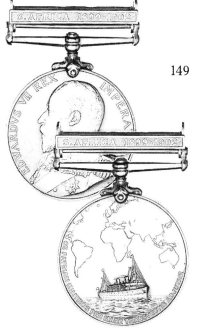

## 149 *Transport Medal* 1899-1902 (BBM 135)

This medal was introduced for award solely to the Mercantile Marine. The unusual feature of the medal is that it was restricted solely to the master, the 1st, 2nd and 3rd officers, 1st, 2nd and 3rd engineers, pursers and surgeons only. The medal was issued in silver to these officers with a bar(s) reading either South Africa and/or China, which covered the Boer and the Boxer Wars of 1900. 1219 medals were awarded with the bar South Africa 1899-1902 and 322 with the bar China 1900, while 178 only had both bars. In both cases, the medals with bars were awarded for transporting troops, etc, by sea.

| | Masters | Other Officers |
|---|---|---|
| 1 bar S. Africa 1899-1902 | £220 | £200 |
| 1 bar China 1900 | £300 | £250 |
| 2 bars | £350 | £300 |

## 150 *Ashanti Medal* 1900 (BBM 136)

This was the first campaign medal authorized during the reign of Edward VII and was issued in silver to combatants and in bronze to native transport personnel, etc. Some 4000 medals were issued in silver to native troops, with rather less than 1000 in bronze. In addition approximately 400 were issued to British officers, NCOs and civilians.

The Ashanti uprising was sparked off by the Governor's attempt to take possession of the 'Golden Stool', which was the symbol of authority in the Ashanti. As a result, the Governor was besieged in the area of the fort at Kumassi (spelt differently from that on the 1873 medal, No. 117). Owing to the shortage of food, a force, including the Governor and other civilians, broke out,

|  | Silver | Bronze |
|---|---|---|
| Without bar | £150 | £300 |
| Bar Kumassi | £220 | £500 |

*Based on awards to natives*

withdrawing to the coast. The small garrison remaining was eventually relieved after a siege of about six months. The bar Kumassi was awarded to all who had been beseiged in the fort and to the two relieving columns. British troops did not participate as a whole as they were heavily involved in events in South Africa and China.

## 151 *Africa General Service Medal* 1902-56 (BBM 137)

This medal was introduced to replace the East and West Africa Medal 1887-1990, to which twenty-one bars had already been issued. This 1902 medal was in existence for fifty-four years, the longest of any British Service Medal.

The medal was issued with the obverse effigies of King Edward VII, George V and Queen Elizabeth II, no bars being awarded during the reign of King George VI (1936-52). Thirty-four bars were awarded during the short reign of Edward VII, ten with George V and one only with Queen Elizabeth, a total of forty-five in all. The medal was normally awarded in silver, but a few were issued in bronze. The bronze issues are, therefore, scarce, as indeed are all issues with the head of George V.

| | Royal Navy | British Regiments | African & Indian Regiments | | Royal Navy | British Regiments | African & Indian Regiments |
|---|---|---|---|---|---|---|---|
| N. Nigeria | — | — | £120 | Somaliland 1902-04 | £65 | £75 | £45 |
| N. Nigeria 1902 | — | — | £120 | Somaliland 1902-04 | | | |
| N. Nigeria 1903 | — | — | £85 | (bronze) | — | — | £90 |
| N. Nigeria 1903-04 | — | — | £120 | Somaliland 1908-10 | £85 | — | £80 |
| N. Nigeria 1903-04 (bronze) | — | — | £150 | Somaliland 1908-10 | | | |
| N. Nigeria 1904 | — | — | £150 | (bronze) | — | — | £90 |
| N. Nigeria 1906 | — | — | £150 | Somaliland 1920 (RAF | | | |
| S. Nigeria | — | — | £250 | £250) | £200 | — | £120 |
| S. Nigeria 1902 | — | — | £150 | Jidballi (not awarded | | | |
| S. Nigeria 1902-03 | — | — | £150 | singly—with | | | |
| S. Nigeria 1903 | — | — | £140 | Somaliland 1902-04) | — | £150 | £100 |
| S. Nigeria 1903-04 | — | — | £250 | Uganda 1900 | — | — | £150 |
| S. Nigeria 1904 | — | — | £120 | B.C.A. 1899-1900 | — | — | £150 |
| S. Nigeria 1904-05 | — | — | £200 | Jubaland | £175 | — | £100 |
| S. Nigeria 1905 | — | — | £450 | Jubaland (bronze) | — | — | £240 |
| S. Nigeria 1905-06 | — | — | £150 | Jubaland 1917-18 | — | — | £200 |
| Nigeria 1918 | — | — | £125 | Jubaland 1917-18 | | | |
| East Africa 1902 | — | — | £450 | (bronze) | — | — | £300 |
| East Africa 1904 | — | — | £350 | Gambia | £220 | — | £150 |
| East Africa 1905 | — | — | £200 | Aro 1901-1902 | £300 | — | £150 |
| East Africa 1906 | — | — | £200 | Lango 1901 | — | — | £200 |
| East Africa 1913 | — | — | £250 | Kissi 1905 | — | — | £280 |
| East Africa 1913-14 | — | — | £200 | Nandi 1905-06 | — | — | £120 |
| East Africa 1914 | — | — | £250 | Shimber Berris 1914-15 | — | — | £180 |
| East Africa 1915 | — | — | £250 | Nyasaland 1915 | — | — | £150 |
| East Africa 1918 | — | — | £125 | Kenya (RAF £75) | £95 | £45 | £35 |
| West Africa 1906 | — | — | £175 | 2 bars | £200 | £150 | £90 |
| West Africa 1908 | — | — | £320 | 3 bars | — | — | £150 |
| West Africa 1909-10 | — | — | £240 | 4 bars | — | — | £200 |
| Somaliland 1901 | — | — | £280 | 5 bars | — | — | £250 |
| Somaliland 1901 | | | | 6 bars | — | — | £300 |
| (bronze) | — | — | £240 | | | | |

*British Regiments' values have only been placed against those bars where at least one British regiment was present in some force*

## 152 *Tibet Medal* 1903-04 (BBM 138)

It was the desire of the British Government to extend trading relations with Tibet, partly for reasons of commerce, but partly to counter the growing Russian influence in the area. A trade mission under Colonel Younghusband was sent by the Indian Government to Tibet, but its progress was barred by hostile Tibetan troops. It thus became necessary to mount a punitive expedition, which eventually reached Lhassa, where a treaty was finally signed. The majority of the silver medals were awarded to Indian regiments, those to the few British regiments present being scarce.

| | Silver British Regiments | Silver Indian Regiments | Bronze Camp Followers etc |
|---|---|---|---|
| Without bar | £150 | £70 | £35 |
| Bar Gyantse | £280 | £120 | £90 |

## 153 *Natal Rebellion Medal* 1906 (BBM 139)

The medal was issued by the Natal Government for services in operations following the Zulu uprising, which arose because of the refusal of the Zulus to pay taxes, which in turn was followed by the murder of two Natal policemen. Without the assistance of Imperial troops, the Natal Government soon organized their local units which quickly achieved the desired results. Medals to the Natal Naval Corps are particularly scarce, some two hundred only being issued. One interesting recipient was Sergeant-Major M. K. Gandhi who was later responsible for guiding India towards independence.

Some 10,000 medals were issued, 2000 only without a bar reading '1906'. The medal was only issued in silver.

| | |
|---|---|
| Without bar £95 | Bar 1906 £120 |

## 154 *India General Service Medal* 1908-35 (BBM 140)

This is the fourth of the India General Service Medal series, being sanctioned by King Edward VII. Twelve different bars were issued during the reign of Edward VII and George V. The medals with the bars North West Frontier 1908 and Abor 1911-12 were awarded both in silver and bronze, the remaining issues being in silver only.

The medals were struck both by the Royal Mint in London and by the Indian Government Mint in Calcutta, the only difference being a slight variation in the claw suspenders. Most of the bars are quite common, particularly when awarded to Indian soldiers, with the exception of Abor 1911-12, Mahsud 1919-20, Malabar 1921-22, Waziristan 1925 and Mohmand 1933.

| | British Regiments | Royal Air Force | Native Regiments |
|---|---|---|---|
| NW Frontier 1908 bronze | — | — | £55 |
| NW Frontier 1908 silver | £40 | — | £25 |
| Abor 1911-12 bronze | — | — | £300 |
| Abor 1911-12 silver | — | — | £140 |
| Afghanistan NWF 1919 | £25 | £110 | £20 |
| Mahsud 1919-20 (not awarded singly, with bar | | | |
| Waziristan 1919-21) | £85 | £150 | £40 |
| Waziristan 1919-21 | £30 | £100 | £20 |
| Malabar 1921-22 | £65 | — | £35 |
| Waziristan 1921-24 | £35 | £100 | £20 |
| Waziristan 1925 | — | £275 | — |
| NW Frontier 1930-31 | £35 | £70 | £20 |
| Burma 1930-32 | £40 | £700 | £25 |
| Mohmand 1933 | — | £150 | £30 |
| NW Frontier 1935 | £35 | £125 | £20 |

## 155 *Khedive's Sudan Medal* 1910 (BBM 141)

This medal, which is particularly scarce to British troops, was introduced by the Khedive of Egypt to replace the previous Sudan Medal (No. 136) which was awarded between 1896 and 1908. It was awarded for numerous small expeditions, mostly in the southern part of the country, between 1910 and 1922. Bars were awarded, which contained an inscription in both English and Arabic. The silver medal was issued with bars to combatant troops, and without a bar to non-combatants. The medal was also issued in bronze without a clasp to transport personnel, servants and camp followers generally.

The first issue of the medal was from 1910 until 1917, when the new Khedive changed the Arabic cypher and date.

| | | | |
|---|---|---|---|
| Silver without bar, 1st issue | £100 | Fasher | £180 |
| Silver without bar, 2nd issue | £100 | Lau Nuer | £250 |
| Bronze without bar, 1st issue | £180 | Nyima 1917-18 | £170 |
| Bronze without bar, 2nd issue | £180 | Atwot 1918 | £180 |
| Atwot | £180 | Garjak Nuer | £220 |
| S. Kordofan 1910 | £170 | Aliab Dinka | £220 |
| Sudan 1912 | £200 | Nyala | £250 |
| Zeraf 1913-14 | £250 | Darfur 1921 | £250 |
| Mandal | £250 | 2 bars | £300 |
| Miri | £220 | | |
| Mongalla 1915-16 | £250 | | |
| Darfur 1916 | £150 | | |
| *Prices based on unnamed medals.* | | | |

### 156 *1914 and 1914-15 Stars* (BBM 142 143)

These stars, of which there are three distinct issues, were the first of several medals issued to commemorate the holocaust of the First World War. The first star, approved in 1917, was the 1914 Star for award to all those who had served in France and Belgium, on the strength of a unit, between 5th August and midnight on 22nd/23rd November 1914; fewer than 400,000 were issued. In 1919, the King sanctioned the award of a bar to the previously issued 1914 Star to those who had actually been under fire during this period. This is often referred to as the 'Mons Star'.

The majority of the recipients of the 1914 Star would have been the pre-war regular Army, known as 'The Old Contemptibles', a term that the German Kaiser Wilhelm used when referring to the small but professional British Army.

The third type of star, the 1914-15 Star, is identical to the 1914 Star except that the central scroll carries the dates 1914-15 instead of 5 Aug.-22 Nov. 1914. This 1914-15 Star was awarded to those who saw service in any theatre of war between 5th August 1914 and 31st December 1915, except, of course, those who had previously qualified for the 1914 Stars. The plain reverses are all inscribed and the variety of units, both British and Commonwealth, is immense, which makes the collecting and study of these stars particularly interesting.

| | |
|---|---|
| 1914 Star | £15 |
| 1914 Star with 'Mons' bar, Army | £20 |
| 1914-15 Star | £4 |

### 157 *British War Medal* 1914-20 (BBM 144)

Issued in both silver and bronze to commemorate some of the most terrible battles ever known resulting in astronomical casualties. Some 6,500,000 medals in silver and 110,000 in bronze were issued, the latter awarded mostly to Chinese, Indian, Maltese and other native labour corps.

Originally, it was intended to award bars to commemorate participation in the different battles; seventy-nine were suggested by the Army and sixty-eight by the Navy but, due to the huge number of medals authorized, the project of issuing bars had to be abandoned on account of the immense expense. However, the Naval bars were actually authorized and, although they were not issued, some recipients had their miniatures fitted with bars.

The medal was also awarded for post-First World War service in Russia, covering the period 1919-20 and for mine clearance in the North Sea up until the end of November 1919.

| | |
|---|---|
| Silver £7 | Bronze £35 |

## 158 *Mercantile Marine War Medal* 1914-18 (BBM 145)

Awarded in bronze by the Board of Trade to members of the Mercantile Marine who had undertaken one or more voyages through a war or danger zone. Unlike the earlier Merchant Navy medals issued for the third China and Boer Wars (No.149) which were given in silver to officers only, this was awarded to all ranks in bronze; just over 133,000 medals were issued. The ribbon is interesting in that it represents the steaming lights of a ship under way.

| | £10 |
|---|---|

## 159 *Victory Medal* 1914-19 (BBM 146, 147)

Issued in bronze to all those who had received the 1914 or 1914/15 Stars, and to most of those who were awarded the British War Medal—it was never awarded by itself. Nearly six million medals were issued in all, those being Mentioned in Despatches were allowed to wear an oak leaf on the ribbon. The reverse inscription of those issued by the South African Government is in both English and Afrikaans.

The medal is often called 'the Allied Victory Medal', as the same basic design and ribbon were adopted by Belgium, Brazil (an extremely rare issue), Cuba, Czechoslovakia, France, Greece, Italy, Japan, Portugal, Roumania, Siam, the Union of South Africa and the USA. In the case of Japan, the winged figure of Victory which appeared on the obverse, was replaced by a warrior holding a spear; the USA issue often contains battle bars.

The rainbow pattern ribbon was common to all issues.

| United Kingdom | £2 | Italy | £7 |
|---|---|---|---|
| Belgium | £6 | Japan | £120 |
| Brazil | £1000 | Portugal | £80 |
| Cuba | £350 | Roumania | £150 |
| Czechoslovakia | £45 | Siam | £300 |
| France | £6 | S.Africa | £15 |
| Greece | £35 | USA (without bar) | £6 |

## 160 *Territorial Force War Medal* 1914-19 (BBM 148)

As only 34,000 medals were issued to the Territorials, this makes the medal the rarest of the five medals issued to cover the First World War. The bronze medal was awarded to all members of the Territorial Force, including nursing sisters, who were members of the service on 4th August 1914 and who had completed four years' service before that date. In addition, they must have:

1 undertaken on or before 30th September 1914 to serve outside the UK;
2 to have actually served outside the UK between 4th August 1914 and 11th November 1918; and
3 been ineligible for either the 1914 or 1914-15 Stars.

| | £45 |
|---|---|

### 161 *H.M.A.S. Sydney S.M.S. Emden Medal* (BBM 149)

Early on in the First World War, the Australian cruiser *Sydney* located the German light cruiser *Emden* in the Cocos Islands in the vicinity of south-west Sumatra. When, after a short action the *Emden* was eventually boarded, a quantity of Mexican dollars was found. Many of these dollars were mounted as medals by the firm of W. Kerr of Sydney and given to the crew of H.M.A.S. *Sydney* to commemorate the engagement while others were sold to the general public to defray the cost of distribution to the crew. The medal, therefore, consists of a Mexican dollar piece on which a crown has been fitted, with the words '9th November 1914, H.M.A.S. *Sydney*—S.M.S. *Emden*.' Being strictly speaking mementoes, the 'medals' were not allowed to be worn on uniform.

| | |
|---|---|
| Mounted by W. Kerr | £320 |

### 162 *Naval General Service Medal* 1915-62 (BBM 150)

This is the second Naval General Service Medal to have been issued since medals were first introduced, the earlier one being predominantly for the Napoleonic Wars from 1793.

The medal was issued with the obverse effigies of Kings George V and VI and Queen Elizabeth II. The medal was instituted for the numerous operations in which the Royal Navy and Royal Marines were involved. Naval service in Africa for this period was covered by the Africa General Service Medal 1902.

The medal covers a fascinating range of different actions, some of the bars being particularly rare. The medals issued with any of the first three bars contained the name of the recipient's ship, but this lapsed until the issue of the South Atlantic Medal 1982.

The bar for Yangtze 1949 is perhaps the best-known incident for which the medal was given. H.M.S. *Amethyst* was ordered up the River Yangtze to relieve H.M.S. *Consort* and to take supplies to the British Embassy. On her way she was heavily shelled by the Chinese Communist forces and temporarily driven ashore with seventeen killed and ten wounded. The result was that the British had to send the cruiser H.M.S. *London*, the frigate *Black Swan* and HMS *Consort* to relieve her, but they failed. As the supplies on board the *Amethyst* were running

very low the relief captain, Lt-Cdr Kerans, R.N., decided to make a dash downriver past the enemy strong points, which resulted in the famous signal being sent by *Amethyst*, 'Have rejoined the fleet. No damage or casualties. God save the King.'

| | | | |
|---|---|---|---|
| Persian Gulf 1909-1914 | £60 | Yangtze 1949 (to other ships) | |
| Iraq 1919-1920 | £650 | | £350 |
| NW Persia 1920 | £1200 | Bomb and Mine Clearance | |
| NW Persia 1919-20 | £1200 | 1945-53 | £450 |
| Palestine 1936-1939 | £50 | Bomb and Mine Clearance | |
| SE Asia 1945-46 | £90 | Mediterranean | £900 |
| Minesweeping 1945-51 | £100 | Cyprus | £40 |
| Palestine 1945-48 | £40 | Near East | £55 |
| Malaya (George VI) | £45 | Arabian Peninsula | £100 |
| Malaya (Elizabeth II) | £45 | Brunei | £80 |
| Yangtze 1949 (to | | 2 bars | £80 |
| H.M.S.*Amethyst*) | £650 | 3 bars | £120 |

163 *General Service Medal* 1918-62 (BBM 151)

Awarded to the Army and Royal Air Force (the Navy's General Service Medal was already in existence, No. 162) for the numerous actions which fell short of actual war. This medal did not cover service in Africa or India, services in these areas were covered by the Africa G.S. 1902 and Indian G.S. 1908 Medals. As with the Naval equivalent, this medal covers a very wide and interesting range of actions or campaigns in many different parts of the world. In all, sixteen different bars were issued, the majority are common with the exception of Southern Desert Iraq, Northern Kurdistan, the two Bomb and Mine Clearance bars and Brunei.

| | 1 British Regiments | 2 Royal Air Force | 3 Indian & Local Regiments |
|---|---|---|---|
| S. Persia | — | £300 | £35 |
| Kurdistan | £45 | £200 | £25 |
| Iraq | £40 | £120 | £25 |
| NW Persia | £40 | £200 | £25 |
| Southern Desert, Iraq | — | £200 | £90 |
| Northern Kurdistan | — | £300 | £100 |
| Palestine (1936-39) | £25 | £30 | £20 |
| Bomb and Mine Clearance 1945-49 | £250 | £250 | — |
| Bomb and Mine Clearance 1945-56 | £300 | £300 | — |
| Palestine 1945-48 | £25 | £25 | £20 |
| Malaya (George VI) | £20 | £20 | £18 |
| Malaya (Elizabeth II) | £20 | £20 | £18 |
| SE Asia 1945-46 | £45 | £50 | £20 |
| Cyprus | £20 | £20 | £20 |
| Near East | £45 | £55 | — |
| Arabian Peninsula | £30 | £30 | £20 |
| Brunei | £80 | £80 | £60 |
| 2 bars | £35 | £35 | £30 |
| 3 bars | £75 | £75 | £50 |

### 164 *India General Service Medal* 1936-39 (BBM 154)

This medal, the fifth and last medal in the India General Service series, was introduced to replace the 1908 Medal (No. 152), the medal was terminated in 1939 by the outbreak of the Second World War. The partition of the Indian subcontinent in 1948 made further issues unnecessary.

There were two issues or strikings, one by the Royal Mint and the other by the Mint in Calcutta; the medal was never awarded without a bar.

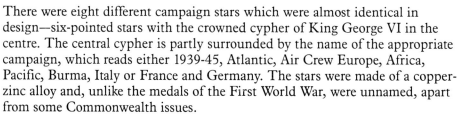

|  | Royal Mint Issue to British Troops | RAF | Calcutta Issue to Native Troops |
|---|---|---|---|
| NW Frontier 1936-37 | £50 | £75 | £20 |
| NW Frontier 1937-39 | £55 | £85 | £25 |
| 2 bars | £70 | £110 | £30 |

### 165 *Second World War Stars* 1939-45 (BBM 154-161)

There were eight different campaign stars which were almost identical in design—six-pointed stars with the crowned cypher of King George VI in the centre. The central cypher is partly surrounded by the name of the appropriate campaign, which reads either 1939-45, Atlantic, Air Crew Europe, Africa, Pacific, Burma, Italy or France and Germany. The stars were made of a copper-zinc alloy and, unlike the medals of the First World War, were unnamed, apart from some Commonwealth issues.

It was decreed that the maximum number of stars that could be earned by any one man or woman was five, and those who qualified for more received a bar to be worn on the ribbon of appropriate star. Only one bar to a ribbon was allowed. Therefore, the stars could carry the following bars:

1 1939/45 (Battle of Britain)
2 Atlantic (Air Crew Europe *or* France and Germany)
3 Air Crew Europe (Atlantic *or* France and Germany)
4 Africa (North Africa 1942-43—issue to Naval forces *or* 8th Army *or* 1st Army)
5 Pacific (Burma)
6 Burma (Pacific)
7 Italy (no bars issued)
8 France and Germany (Atlantic)

When ribands only are worn, the possession of a bar was represented by a silver rosette, the 'Battle of Britain' bar was represented by a gold-plated rosette. All the ribbons are symbolic, reputedly designed by King George VI. The ribbon of the 1939-45 Star represents the three services; the Atlantic ribbon represents the sea, incidentally the symbolism of this ribbon was also adopted for the ribbon of the South Atlantic Medal; the Air Crew Europe ribbon represents the sky by a blue stripe, yellow for the search-lights and black for night-time flying; the Africa ribbon represents the desert, the central broad stripe of red representing the major effort by the Army, flanked by lesser stripes of dark blue and light blue for the Navy and Air Force. For the Pacific ribbon, the green in the centre represents the jungle, with a narrow yellow stripe the beaches, flanked by narrow stripes of dark blue for the Navy and light blue for the Air Force, and on each edge rather wider stripes of red represent the Army. The central red stripe incorporated in the Burma ribbon represents the Commonwealth forces and the orange stripes the sun. The Italian ribbon represents the colours of the Italian State flag, while the ribbon of the France and Germany Star portrays the colours of the French and Dutch flags.

| 1939-45 Star | £6 | Africa Star | £6 |
|---|---|---|---|
| 1939-45 Star with | | Pacific Star | £18 |
| Battle of Britain bar | £100 | Burma Star | £10 |
| Atlantic Star | £20 | Italy Star | £6 |
| Air Crew Europe Star | £100 | France & Germany Star | £12 |

### 166 *Defence Medal* 1939-1945 (BBM 162)

This medal was awarded to a large number of civilians who formed part of recognized defence units, such as the Home Guard or Civil Defence. The medal was issued unnamed in cupro-nickel, although the Canadian issue was struck in silver. The ribbon is symbolic of the British Isles, which is represented by green, the orange colour represents the bombing (fires) of the UK that took place, and the black the black-out.

| Cupro-nickel | £10 | Silver | £12 |
|---|---|---|---|

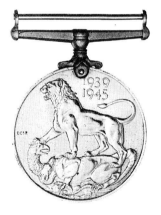

### 167 *War Medal* 1939-1945 (BBM 163)

This medal was awarded to all full-time personnel of the armed forces wherever they were serving, providing that they had served for at least twenty-eight days, irrespective of whether they were operational or non-operational. As with the Defence Medal, this was awarded unnamed in cupro-nickel, although the Canadian issues were in silver. The cupro-nickel medals issued to the South African and Australian troops were named with the recipients' number and name.

| Cupro-nickel | £6 |
|---|---|
| Cupro-nickel named to Australian & S. African forces | £6 |
| Silver | £12 |

### 168 *India Service Medal* 1939-45 (BBM 164)

Awarded to officers and men of the Indian forces for three years non-operational service in India or elsewhere and issued unnamed in cupro-nickel. It was frequently awarded in conjunction with the Campaign Stars and the War Medal, but never with the Defence Medal. This was the last of the series of medals, which covered a period of almost one hundred and fifty years, awarded in connection with India.

| | £15 |
|---|---|

### 169 *Canadian Volunteer Service Medal* 1939-47 (BBM 165)

Authorized as early as 1943 and issued unnamed in silver for eighteen months voluntary service in the Canadian forces. Those who served overseas were entitled to wear a silver bar on the ribbon which depicted a maple leaf.

| Without bar | £15 | With bar | £20 |

### 170 *Africa Service Medal* 1939-45 (BBM 166)

Instituted in 1943 for award to the armed forces of South Africa for service during the Second World War, both at home and abroad. The medals were made in silver and officially named, and issued to all full-time service members of the Union forces for a period of thirty days' service or more in South Africa. One interesting aspect is that those with the prefix 'N' indicate a native recipient, 'C' a coloured recipient and 'M' a Malay probably recruited in the Cape Town area.

£15

### 171 *Australia Service Medal* 1939-45 (BBM 167)

Awarded to members of the Australian forces, and authorized in December 1949. The medal was awarded in cupro-nickel, and named. The prefix before the number indicates the state in which the recipient enlisted. The recipients had to serve for eighteen months overseas, or three years at home.

£15

### 172 *New Zealand War Service Medal* 1939-45 (BBM 168)

Issued to all members of the New Zealand forces during the Second World War, including many reserve and home service units. Awarded in cupro-nickel and issued unnamed.

£15

### 173 *South African Medal for War Service* 1939-46 (BBM 169)

Awarded in silver to both men and women, the main qualification being two years' service in any official voluntary organization in South Africa or elsewhere—service *had* to be unpaid and voluntary. The medal could not be awarded with the previous South African War Service Medal (No. 170). Only 17,500 were awarded so the medal is scarce by Second World War standards.

£45

### 174 *Southern Rhodesian War Service Medal* 1939-45

(BBM 170)

This scarce medal was awarded to all those who served in Southern Rhodesia during the Second World War, but it was not awarded to those who qualified for an overseas campaign star or medal and, as very many Rhodesians served overseas, only 1700 medals were issued. The medals were in cupro-nickel and were issued unnamed.

£140

### 175 *Newfoundland Volunteer War Service Medal* 1939-45

(BBM 171)

Established by the Provincial Government in 1981. Awarded to servicemen of the Province who volunteered to serve in the British Imperial Forces, who served overseas and were ineligible or did not receive a voluntary service medal from any country, or for various reasons did not serve overseas. The medal may be issued to the next-of-kin of those eligible who died in or since the war.

£50

### 176 *Korea Medal* 1950-53 (BBM 172, 173)

Awarded to members of both the British and Commonwealth forces who took part in the operations in Korea.

Following the conclusion of the Second World War, the Korean peninsula was divided into two countries; the northern part was under Communist control and the southern came under American influence or protection. After a time, the controlling power in the south withdrew its forces which resulted in the north attacking the south, thus causing the United Nations to intervene with forces drawn from a great variety of different countries, but the USA, Great Britain and the Commonwealth made the most sizeable contributions. The British and Commonwealth forces were frequently very heavily engaged.

The most sought-after medals in this series are those to men of the Gloucester Regiment, who took part in the epic battle of the Imjim River. The medals were in cupro-nickel and named, those issued by Canada were struck in silver, with the obverse legend incorporating the word 'Canada'. Medals to Australian & New Zealand units may be distinguished by the style of naming; in larger capitals than the U.K. issues. The Union of South Africa issued their own special medal.

| | |
|---|---|
| British issue | £60 |
| British issue to the Gloucester Regiment present at Imjim | £200 |
| Canadian issue | £60 |
| Australian/New Zealand issue | £80 |
| S. African issue (800) | £350 |

### 177 *The United Nations Korea Medal* 1950-53 (BBM 182)

This bronze medal was awarded by the United Nations to all those who served in the UN forces during the Korean War. It was awarded to all those who held the British Medal and to those who served in Korea after the armistice in 1953. The medal was issued unnamed, except those to Canadians, which were named in small block capitals. Various types were issued to the different contingents, the reverse naming appearing in the language of the contingent concerned.

| | | | | | |
|---|---|---|---|---|---|
| English unnamed | £15 | French | £25 | Tagalog (Philippines) | £65 |
| English named to | | Greek | £45 | Thai | £150 |
| Canadians/Australians | £25 | Italian | £475 | Turkish | £110 |
| Amharic (Ethiopia) | £170 | Korean | £15 | | |
| Dutch | £65 | Spanish | £100 | | |

## 178 *Campaign Service Medal* 1962- (BBM 174)

This medal was introduced to replace the Naval General Service Medal 1915 and the General Service Medal (Army and RAF) 1918. These two medals had been issued over a long period and it was decided to issue a uniform medal to all three services when the Ministry of Defence assumed unified control. To date, ten bars have been issued: Borneo, (24th December 1962—11th August 1966) for service against rebel forces in Sabah, Sarawak and Brunei; Radfan (25th April—31st July 1964) for service in the South Arabian Federation; South Arabia (1st August 1964—30th November 1967) for supporting the local government against insurgent forces; Malay Peninsula (17th August 1964—11th August 1966) for efforts during the confrontation with Indonesia; South Vietnam (24th September 1962—29th May 1964) for award to Australian forces only, as the UK was not at war in South Vietnam; Northern Ireland (from August 1969) for participation in peace-keeping and police duties, the bar is still being awarded; Dhofar (1st October 1969-30th September 1976) for supporting the Sultan of Oman's forces in their operations against the Communist forces operating from South Yemen, Lebanon (7th February 1983-9th March 1984) for peace-keeping in Beirut; Mine Clearance-Gulf of Suez (15th August-15th October 1984) and Gulf (17th November 1986-28th February 1989) for Naval operations in the Persian Gulf and Gulf of Oman during the Iran-Iraq War.

Five bars seem to have been the maximum issued so far to any one medal and, as can be seen from the price list below, some bars are particularly scarce. In some cases medals are scarce to one force and more common to others.

| | |
|---|---|
| Borneo | £20 |
| Radfan | £45 |
| South Arabia | £25 |
| Malay Peninsula | £25 |
| South Vietnam | rare |
| Northern Ireland | £22 |
| Dhofar | £120 |
| Lebanon | £350 |
| Mine Clearance-Gulf of Suez | £450 |
| Gulf | £450 |
| 2 bars | £35 |
| 3 bars | £75 |
| 4 bars | £110 |

## 179 *The United Nations Emergency Force Medal* 1956-67
(BBM 183)

Awarded to those that served with the Emergency Force which followed the brief war between Israel and Egypt. The objective of the Force was to organize patrols and enforce peace on the Israeli/Egyptian border. The medals were issued to troops from Brazil, Canada, Colombia, Denmark, Finland, Indonesia, Norway, Sweden and Yugoslavia.

£20

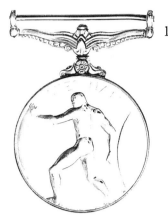

## 180 *Vietnam Medal* 1964 (BBM 175)

British forces were not involved in this war, the medals being issued to the armed forces and accredited relief societies of Australia and New Zealand, and announced in the Government of Australia's *Gazette* on 4th July 1968 and the New Zealand *Gazette* on 8th August 1968. Approximately 49,000 medals were issued to the Australian forces and 4000 to the forces of New Zealand. The ribbon represents the three services, namely dark blue, light blue and red, together with the national colours of South Vietnam.

| | |
|---|---|
| Australian recipient | £120 |
| New Zealand recipient | £140 |

## 181 *South Vietnam Campaign Medal* 1964 (BBM 176)

The Government of Vietnam also issued an award to the recipients of the previous medal (No. 180) in the same way as the United Nations issued their bronze medal for Korea. The medals issued by Vietnam were rather crudely manufactured and unnamed and, as a result, the Australian Government manufactured their own superior version, which were all named.
Medal issued with one bar '1960'.

| | |
|---|---|
| Vietnam issue | £15 |

## 182 *South Atlantic Medal* 1982 (BBM 178)

Struck in cupro-nickel with a straight bar swivel suspension and issued named. Awarded to those who were involved in regaining possession of the Falkland Islands and South Georgia from Argentina. Those that served for at least one day in the Falklands, etc., or in the South Atlantic south of sixty-five degrees south, or in any operational aircraft south of Ascension Island were awarded a distinguishing rosette worn on the ribbon of the medal or on the ribbon only when worn without the medal. Others, who served outside these areas, had to serve for thirty days and received the medal without rosette.

| | |
|---|---|
| Army | £150 |
| Royal Navy | £160 |
| Royal Air Force | £160 |
| Merchant Navy | £100 |

---

183  *United Nations Medals*  (BBM 184)

The United Nations have over a period of years issued many medals in addition to those for Korea. All the medals are of the same design but were awarded with different ribbons for the different areas where the troops were involved. Those issued to date cover:

UNTSO     United Nations Truce Supervisory Organisation (1948- ) (Israel, Syria, Egypt).

UNOGIL     United Nations Observation Group in Lebanon (1958), ribbon as for UNTSO.

ONUC     Organisations des Nationes Unies du Congo (1960-64), ribbon originally as for UNTSO with the bar 'Congo', in 1963 it was replaced by a new ribbon.

UNTEA     United Nations Temporary Executive Authority (1962) (Netherlands New Guinea).

UNMOGIP     United Nations Military Observer Group in India and Pakistan (1949- ).

UNIPOM     United Nations India/Pakistan Observation Mission (1965-66), ribbon as for UNMOGIP.

UNYOM     United Nations Yemen Observer Mission (1963-64).

UNFICYP     United Nations Force in Cyprus (1964- ).

UNEF2     United Nations Emergency Force (1973- ), to observe the Israeli-Egyptian cease-fire.

UNDOF     United Nations Disengagement Observer Force (1974- ) Golan Heights.

UNIFIL     United Nations Interim Force in Lebanon (1978- ).

UNIIMOG     United Nations Iran-Iraq Monitoring Observation Group.

UNTAG     United Nations Transitional Assistance Group (Nambia).

General Service Medal for Service in H.Q., New York.

---

£15

---

# *Miscellaneous Medals*

184 ### *King's and Queen's Messenger Badge* 1485

Although the process of using a trusted servant to carry despatches is as old as civilisation itself, the first gentleman to be formally appointed a King's messenger by King Richard III was John Norman in 1485.

Henry VIII in 1547 developed the system and formed forty men into a corps of Kings Messengers under the control of the Lord Chamberlain.

Today the Corps is under the control of the Foreign and Commonwealth Office and carries sensitive material around the world on behalf of all government departments and agencies. The emblem of the Corps is a silver greyhound which hangs from all messengers badges. Although the badge was originally worn by officers on their travels as a form of identification it is now only worn on formal occasions.

Badges can be seen engraved on the reverse with additional dates and monarchs details indicating that the badge has been re-issued to other messengers.

| | |
|---|---|
| George III type | £1300 |
| George IV type | £1200 |
| William IV type | £1000 |
| Victoria type | £800 |
| Edward VII type | £550 |
| George V type | £550 |
| George VI type | £500 |
| Elizabeth II type | £500 |

185 ## *Collar of S's*

The custom of wearing collars of S's dates back to the 14th century when they were worn by Royal and Noble families. These chains are quite distinct from Orders of Knighthood. Some reference books mention that the 'SS' originates from the shape of a swan, being the badge of the Bohun family, Marie Bohun being the wife of Henry IV. Another theory is that the chain worn by Lord Chief Justices originates from Sanctus Simplicius, an uncorrupted Judge. The collars are worn by the Lord Chief Justices, Sergeant at Arms in the Houses of Parliament and Officers of the college of Heralds.

The collars are made from alternate 'S's joined by a pair of Heraldic Badges.

| | |
|---|---|
| Collar | £2000 |

### 186 *Arctic Medal* 1818-55 (BBM 179)

This silver octagonal Medal, instituted in 1857 was awarded to all persons, regardless of rank, who had been engaged in expeditions to Arctic Regions including those involved in the search for the lost Franklin Expedition of 1845-48. These Medals were issued for extreme human endeavours against atrocious weather and conditions in the Arctic. The medals although being issued unnamed are often found privately engraved.

£240

### 187 *Arctic Medal* 1875-76 (BBM 180)

This silver medal was sanctioned on the 28th November 1876, to be awarded to the crews of the Alert (63) (Captain Sir George Nares, K.C.B.) and Discovery (57) (Captain H F Steveson) for Arctic exploration between 17th July 1875, and 2nd November 1876. At the same time authority was given for it to be awarded to the crew of the private yacht Pandora (50), which voyaged in the Arctic regions, under the command of Captain Allen Young, between 25th June and 19th October 1875, and 3rd June and 2nd November 1876. This medal was issued named in small block lettering, giving the name and rank of the recipient.

£650

## 188 *Polar Medal* 1904 (BBM 181)

This third medal for Arctic and Antarctic exploration was instituted by Edward VII in 1904 and is still issued today. It has been issued in silver and bronze and additional expeditions are represented by a bar on the medal. The medal is octagonal and is issued named.

| | |
|---|---|
| Bronze | from £600 |
| Silver | from £750 |

## 189 *Rhodesia Medal* 1980 (BBM 177)

This medal in rhodium-plated cupro-nickel was awarded by the British Government to people in the Services, Police and civilians who were part of the small multi-national force who kept the peace between guerillas and Rhodesian forces during the ceasefire run-up period to the election. The Medal was available to the Governments of Australia, New Zealand, Fiji and Kenya, whose forces participated. Recipients of this medal also received the Zimbabwe Independence Medal (No. 214).

£400

## 190 *King's Medal for Service in the Cause of Freedom* 1945

The medal was instituted by Royal Warrant dated 23rd August 1945 and together with the King's Medal for Courage in the Cause of Freedom, was the counterpart of the First World War Allied Subjects Medal. The Medal for Service was awarded to foreign civilians for furthering the British and Allied cause during the Second World War.

Approximately 2500 medals were awarded, the first issue taking place in 1947. Struck in silver, the medal was issued unnamed.

£200

## 191 *King Edward VII's Medal for Science, Art and Music* 1904

A shortlived silver medal introduced by Edward VII in 1904 but discontinued in 1906. Awarded in recognition of distinguished services in the sciences and arts. The obverse was unusual in that it displayed the conjoined busts of King Edward and Queen Alexandra. The ribbon was scarlet with a 9mm. central stripe of dark blue with 3mm. white stripes 3mm. in from the edge.

£950

## 192 *The Order of the League of Mercy*

Appointments to the Order were approved and sanctioned by the Sovereign upon the recommendation of the Grand President of the League of Mercy. Given as a reward for distinguished personal service on behalf of the League in assisting hospitals with the relief of suffering, poverty or distress. They were awarded to ladies and gentlemen who had graciously rendered services to the League.

The award was allowed to be worn in uniform.

£45

## 193 *Indian Title Badge*

Introduced by the King Emperor George V on 12th December 1911 on the occasion of the Delhi Durbar. They were awarded in three classes to civilians and the Viceroy's commissioned officers of the Indian Army for faithful service or acts of public welfare.

A recipient had to be awarded the lowest grade before progressing to a senior grade and if promoted, only the senior title could be used. The badge came in three grades, each of two types—one with wording for Hindus the other for Muslims. The badge had the name of the recipient engraved on the reverse. The class of the badge may be discerned by the wording, composition and ribbon:

1st Class: silver-gilt with a ribbon light blue edged with dark blue.
2nd Class: silver with a ribbon red edged with dark red.
3rd Class: silver with blue enamelled central surround with a ribbon dark blue edged with light blue.

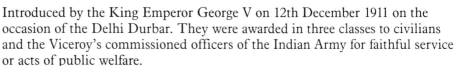

|  |  | George V | George VI |
|---|---|---|---|
| *1st Class—* 'Diwan Bahadur' for Moslems |  |  |  |
| 'Sardar Bahadur' for Hindus |  | £75 | £75 |
| *2nd Class—* 'Khan Bahadur' for Moslems |  |  |  |
| 'Rai' or 'Rao Bahadur' for Hindus |  | £50 | £50 |
| *3rd Class—* 'Khan Sahib' for Moslems |  |  |  |
| 'Rai' or 'Rao Sahib' for Hindus |  | £45 | £45 |

## 194 *The King's Medal for Native Chiefs*
## *The Queen's Medal for Native Chiefs*

This medal was instituted by a Royal Warrant of 26th April 1920 and was awarded to African Chiefs and other dignitaries for loyal and zealous service to the Crown and Empire. The oval medal was awarded in silver or in exceptional cases, in silver-gilt and worn suspended around the neck by means of a chain composed of crown, rose and cypher links. On the obverse is the bust of the sovereign, on the reverse a warship with merchant ships and hills in the background. Two George V obverse types are known; the first portrays an abbreviated bust, the second, dating from 1930, had an elongated effigy, the base of which reached the base of the medal.

In 1954 the decision was made to offer recipients the choice of either the neck badge or a smaller version for wear as a breast badge. The silver-gilt breast badge is worn from yellow ribbon with two central white stripes, the silver medal from a yellow ribbon with a single white stripe. As a breast badge the medal took precedence over all war medals.

|  | *Silver* |
|---|---|
| George V | £820 |
| George VI | £750 |
| Elizabeth II neck badge | £750 |
| Elizabeth II breast badge | £500 |

## 195 *Badge of the Certificate of Honour*

Certificates of Honour were awarded to chiefs and other non-European dignitaries of the Empire for loyal and valuable service. Recipients of the Certificate were also awarded a badge. These were of two general types:

1 African: oval bronze badge worn around the neck from a yellow ribbon 38mm. wide. In about 1954 the decision was made to offer the recipient the choice of either the neck badge or a smaller version for wear on the chest. This breast version is worn from a yellow ribbon 32mm. wide. The obverse bears the crowned bust of the sovereign, the reverse has the name of the colony or protectorate with an appropriate design: Aden, a sailing boat; Basutoland, Bechuanaland Protectorate and Swaziland, the sovereigns cypher with crown above; Gambia, Gold Coast and Sierra Leone, an elephant and palm tree; Kenya, a lion rampant; Nigeria, a crown within two entwined triangles; Northern Rhodesia, an eagle carrying a fish in its claws; Southern Rhodesia, coat-of-arms; Nyasaland Protectorate, a leopard and the rising sun; Somaliland Protectorate, head of a kudu; Tanganyika Territory, head of a giraffe; Uganda Protectorate, a golden crested crane.

2 Non-African: circular silver-gilt neck badge, the obverse bearing the crowned bust of the monarch, the reverse the coat-of-arms or design appropriate to the territory. As for the African type, a smaller version was later introduced as an alternative to the neck badge. Ribbon is 38mm. wide for the neck badge and

32mm. wide for the breast badge, the colour varies according to the territory: equal bands of red, white and blue for Hong Kong, N. Borneo, Sarawak, Singapore and Straits Settlements; yellow for British Guiana, British Solomon Islands, Cyprus, Fiji and Gilbert and Ellice Islands, and equal stripes of white, black, red and yellow for the Federated Malay States.

Both African and non-African types when worn as a breast badge take precedence over coronation and jubilee medals.

| African | |
| --- | --- |
| George V | £240 |
| George VI | £180 |
| Elizabeth II neck badge | £180 |
| Elizabeth II breast badge | £90 |
| | |
| Non-African | |
| George V | £550 |
| George VI | £480 |
| Elizabeth II neck badge | £450 |
| Elizabeth II breast badge | £380 |

## 196 *Naval Engineer's Good Conduct Medal*

The medal was introduced in 1842 to reward 1st Class Engineers of the Royal Navy for their skill and conduct.

With the increase in the number of steam vessels by the 1840s Naval Engineers became a valued commodity to the Navy. However, at the time Naval Engineers were only rated as warrant officers and their service in the Royal Navy rarely exceeded one or two full commissions. It was in the hope of inducing men to continue in the Navy that the medal was introduced. The medal became obsolete in February 1847 when commissioned rank was granted to Naval engineers.

A total of 7 medals are definitely known to have been awarded between 1842 and 1847, these being to 1st Cl.Eng. William Shaw (1842), William Dunkin (1842), William Johnstone (1843), John Langley (1843), J. P. Rundle (1845), George Roberts (1845) and Actg. 2nd Cl.Eng. Samuel B. Meredith (1846).

The medal was designed by William Wyon and struck in silver. The obverse depicted a two masted paddle steamer with a trident in the exergue; the reverse has within a rope circle a fouled anchor with crown above, with the legend 'FOR ABILITY & GOOD CONDUCT'. Between the rope circle and the outer circumference the medal was engraved with the name and rank of the recipient.

The first medal awarded to Shaw had in the obverse exergue oak leaves to either side of the trident; this embellishment was removed in time for the second and subsequent awards. The second medal, to Dunkin was suspended by means of a steel clip and ring with straight bar suspension. The medal would appear to have been worn from the Naval L.S. & G.C. Medal ribbon; initially plain blue, later the wide type blue with white edges.

Further strikings of this medal were made, firstly in 1875 and again at a later date. Restrikes were produced with a fixed ring suspension, connected to the ribbon by means of two loose rings. Original medals may be distinguished by a grooved rim, 1875 restrikes by a diagonal grained rim, later restrikes by a plain flat rim.

| | |
| --- | --- |
| Original | Rare |
| 1875 restrike | £400 |
| Later restrike | £200 |

## 197 *Indian Recruiting Badge*

Late in both the First and Second World Wars, badges were introduced as a reward to those involved in recruiting work. The First World War issue was awarded to selected Indian officers and men serving or having served during the war as a reward for their services in recruiting. In the Second World War it was awarded to selected civil and military pensioners, full-time members of the Indian Recruiting Organisation for conspicuous service and to fathers or mothers having at least three children and wives having a husband and at least two children serving in the defence forces.

The George V issue was a bronze five-pointed star with a central gilt plaque bearing the crowned bust of the King. It was worn around the neck from a ribbon of plain dark green.

The George VI issue was a multi-rayed breast badge in silver with a bronze centre bearing the crowned head of the King. It was worn from a ribbon of emerald green divided into three bands by one red and one orange stripe.

Badges could only be worn on uniform when attending Durbars or state functions, but at any time when in plain clothes.

| | |
|---|---|
| George V | £95 |
| George VI | £45 |

## 198 *Naval Good Shooting Medal* 1903

A silver medal with a straight bar swivelling suspender, issued named with the recipient's number, name, rank, ship, year of award and calibre of gun impressed in block capitals on the edge.

The medal was instituted in 1903 with the object of encouraging good performances in gunnery at the Annual Fleet Competitions. Awards were made to seamen and marines who scored a very high percentage of hits with their particular weapon. Medals were awarded for every type of gun used by the Royal Navy. A bar was awarded for further success; upon which was the name of the ship, year of award and calibre of gun. The award was discontinued in 1914.

A total of 974 medals and 62 bars were awarded, 53 men received one bar, 3 two bars and 1 three bars.

| | |
|---|---|
| Edward VII | £200 |
| George V | £230 |

## 199 *Army Best Shot Medal*

The medal, known as The Queen's Medal, was instituted by a Royal Warrant dated 30th April 1869. It was awarded annually to the best shot in the British Army.

The medal was originally to be issued in bronze but was changed to silver in 1872. It was issued with a straight bar swivelling suspender and was named in block letters on the edge, giving the recipient's rank, name and regiment followed by the words 'BEST SHOT MEDAL' and the year of award. For further success in the competition a second medal was awarded. Only one second award medal was given between 1869 and 1882. The competitions were ended and the medal discontinued in 1882.

In 1923 the competition was revived and the medal, known as The King's Medal was awarded. The medal was similar to the earlier issue and differed by being fitted with a straight bar non-swivelling suspender and a bar bearing the year of award. An additional year bar was awarded for further success in the competition. With the accession of Queen Elizabeth II in 1952 the medal again became known as The Queen's Medal.

A single medal was awarded annually to UK Military Forces at Home between 1923 and 1934. In 1935 two medals were granted; one to the Regular Army and one to the Territorial Army. A medal was awarded to forces in India, Canada (Regular Army 1923-67, Militia and R.C.M.P. from 1964, Regular Forces from 1968), Australia, Union of South Africa (1924-1961), New Zealand, S. Rhodesia (1926-54), Rhodesia, Nyasaland and B.S.A. Police (1956-59), Rhodesia and B.S.A.P. (1962-?), Ceylon, Pakistan, Ghana and Jamaica.

| | |
|---|---|
| Victoria silver 1869-82 | £500 |
| George V | £400 |
| George VI 1937-51 | £450 |
| Elizabeth II 1952- | £450 |

## 200 *Queen's Medal for Champion Shots of the Royal Navy and Royal Marines*

The medal is the R.N. and R.M. equivalent of the Army Best Shot Medal and Queen's Medal for Champion Shot of the Air Force, awarded for skill in rifle shooting. It has the same reverse as the earlier Naval Good Shooting Medal (No. 198).

| | |
|---|---|
| Elizabeth II | £650 |

### 201 Queen's Medal for Champion Shots of the Air Force

The medal was instituted on 12th June 1953 and is competed for annually at the R.A.F. Small Arms Meeting held at Bisley, Surrey.

The medal is in silver and each award carries a bar with the year in relief affixed to the ribbon. Additional year bars are worn for further success in the competition. The recipient's name is engraved on the edge.

The medal was awarded to the Champion Shot of the Royal Canadian Air Force between 1954-67.

| | |
|---|---|
| Elizabeth II | £650 |

### 202 The Queen's Medal for Champion Shots of the New Zealand Naval Forces

The medal was authorised by a Royal Warrant dated 9th July 1958 and took effect from 1st January 1955. The medal was awarded for skill in small arms shooting in an annual competition in the New Zealand Naval Forces.

The medal is very similar to the obsolete Naval Good Shooting Medal 1903-14. The recipient's name is engraved or impressed on the edge and it is awarded with a bar bearing the year of award. Additional bars are awarded for further success

| | |
|---|---|
| Elizabeth II | Rare |

### 203 Union of South Africa Commemoration Medal 1910

A silver medal issued to commemorate the foundation of the Union of South Africa from the states of Cape of Good Hope, Natal, Orange River Colony and Transvaal. The medal was awarded to civilians and military and naval officers and men who took part in the ceremonies, and was issued unnamed.

| | |
|---|---|
| | £200 |

### 204 Shanghai Jubilee Medal 1893

The British settlement in Shanghai was established in 1843 and it formed the nucleus of the International Settlement set up in 1854 and was controlled by an autonomous Municipal Council. A silver medal was issued to commemorate the 50th anniversary of its founding. Obverse: the coat-of-arms of the Municipality,

being the national flags of the twelve nations comprising the Settlement in the shape of a 'Y' with Chinese characters (reading 'Municipal Council') and Latin legend between the arms 'OMNIA JUNCTA IN UNO' (All joined in one), with the foundation date, 'November 17-1843' above. Reverse: a shield with the wording, 'SHANGHAI JUBILEE (recipient's name engraved in block capitals) November 17 1893'. Dragons are to either side with a steamship and setting sun above. Medal edge engraved 'Presented by the Shanghai Municipality'. Issued with a small ring suspension, sometimes found replaced by a straight bar. Ribbon 32mm. wide, equal halves of red (left) and white. Approximately 625 medals were struck in silver. Some 100 are said to have been struck in bronze.

| | |
|---|---|
| Silver | £250 |

## 205 *Shanghai Municipal Council Emergency Medal* 1937

A bronze eight-pointed star with a ring suspension. On the obverse centre, the coat-of-arms of the Municipality; on the reverse, within a wreath, 'FOR SERVICES RENDERED AUGUST 12 TO NOVEMBER 12 1937'. Ribbon: equal bands of red, white, red edged with thin stripes of black, with a thin stripe of yellow at the ribbon edge. Although the medals were issued unnamed each was accompanied by a certificate stating the name and unit of the recipient.

The medal was awarded to members of the Police (regulars and specials), Volunteer Corps, Fire Brigade (regulars and volunteers) and Civilians for services during the emergency of Aug.-Nov. 1937 when fighting between the Chinese and Japanese in and around Shanghai seriously threatened the International Settlement.

| |
|---|
| £45 |

## 206 *Shanghai Volunteer Corps Long Service Medal* 1921

The Shanghai Volunteer Corps was raised in 1853 to assist in the protection of the Shanghai foreign settlements; it saw its first action on 4th April 1854 in the Battle of Muddy Flat. The Volunteer Corps was international in composition but the British provided the largest contingent. The Corps was disbanded in September 1942.

A medal for long service was introduced in 1921 and was awarded for 12 years good service in the Volunteer Corps. The circular medal, in silver, has on the obverse an eight pointed star bearing the arms of the Shanghai Municipality, with the wording 'SHANGHAI VOLUNTEER CORPS'. Below, a band with the words 'FOR LONG SERVICE'. The reverse is plain, engraved with the recipient's name and period of service. With a two ring suspension and a ribbon of equal bands of red, white and blue, the red bisected by a thin stripe of green, the white by black, the blue by yellow.

| |
|---|
| £325 |

### 207 *Shanghai Municipal Police Distinguished Conduct Medal*

This medal instituted in about 1924 was issued in two classes: Class I in silver and Class II in bronze. The medal obverse has the arms of the Municipality and the words 'SHANGHAI MUNICIPAL POLICE', the reverse has the words 'FOR DISTINGUISHED CONDUCT'. Around the edge the medal was engraved in capitals and lower case lettering with the recipient's rank and name. For a second award a sliding bar was provided for the ribbon, this being a plain bar with a small council crest obverse and the reverse engraved with details of the second award. This was apparently only awarded once, being a bronze bar for a bronze medal. Ribbon for the 1st Class was red with a 6mm wide central blue stripe, the 2nd Class was red with a 6mm wide blue stripe near each edge.

| | |
|---|---|
| Silver | £800 |
| Bronze | £650 |

### 208 *Shanghai Municipal Police Long Service Medal (Regulars)*

The Police Force was established in the early days of Shanghai, staffed initially by ex-soldiers and ex-policemen from elsewhere and latterly by Europeans, ex-Sikh troopers, Chinese, Russians and Japanese. Medals for long service were issued from the mid-1920s, possibly earlier, for 12 years good service in the Municipal Police. Medals were awarded up to 1942.

The medal was issued in silver, the obverse portrays the arms of the Municipality with the words 'SHANGHAI MUNICIPAL POLICE'. The reverse has the words, 'FOR LONG SERVICE'. Engraved around the edge with the recipient's rank and name in capitals and lower case lettering. Dated bars for further five year periods of service were awarded. With a swivelling scroll suspender. Ribbon was brown with a central yellow band edged in white.

| | |
|---|---|
| No bar | £300 |
| 1 bar | £375 |

### 209 *Shanghai Municipal Police Long Service Medal (Specials)*

The Shanghai Special Constabulary was created in 1918. In 1929 a silver long service medal was instituted as an award for 12 years efficient and active voluntary service in the Special Constabulary. The qualifying period could also be composed of a minimum of 6 years active service plus sufficient service in the reserve, which counted half, towards a total of 12 years. Service in other voluntary organisations did not count towards the qualifying period, neither did

service in the full-time constabulary. The medal was awarded up to 1942.

The medal obverse portrays the coat-of-arms of the Municipality, the reverse has the words 'SHANGHAI MUNICIPAL POLICE (SPECIALS) FOR LONG SERVICE' or 'FOR DISTINGUISHED AND VALUABLE SERVICES' as appropriate. The entry in the 'Municipal Gazette' would indicate the wording appropriate to the recipient. The edge is engraved with the recipient's rank, number and name in capitals and lower case. Bars were awarded for further 5 year periods of service. With a swivelling scroll suspender. The ribbon is a dark brown with three 6mm white stripes each with a 3mm yellow stripe passing through the centre.

Approximately 52 medals and 8 bars were awarded for Long Service. In 1930 a medal to Mr. A. L. Anderson was awarded for 'Distinguished and Valuable Services'.

| No bar | £450 |
|---|---|

## 210 *Shanghai Volunteer Fire Brigade Long Service Medal*

Established in 1904, this medal was awarded as follows: for 5 years service, a silver medal; for 8 years service, a silver medal with a bar added to the ribbon; for 12 years service, a gold medal. Examples of the medal in bronze are likely to be specimens.

On the medal obverse are the arms and motto of the Municipality surrounded by the inscription 'SHANGHAI VOLUNTEER FIRE BRIGADE. ESTABLISHED 1866'. On the reverse centre are a pair of crossed axes surmounted by a fireman's helmet under which is a scroll on which are engraved the recipient's dates of service. Surrounding this is the inscription 'FOR LONG SERVICE' and 'WE FIGHT THE FLAMES'. The recipient's name is inscribed on the edge in engraved capitals. The medal has a swivel suspender and a ribbon 25mm. wide being red with a white stripe at the edge.

| Silver | £450 |
|---|---|

## 211 *Loyal Service Decoration* 1920

A silver medal instituted by the Union of South Africa in 1920 to officers of the Boer Republics for distinguished service in the 2nd Boer War 1899-1902. On one side, the arms of Transvaal—lion, sentry and wagon, on the other, the arms of Orange Free State—tree, cattle, lion and wagon. It was worn with the appropriate side showing depending on the recipient's state. Similarly the ribbon was worn according to the state, those from Transvaal worn with the red to the centre of the chest, Orange Free State worn with the white to the centre.

A total of 591 awards were made.

| | £250 |
|---|---|

## 212 *Anglo-Boer War Medal* 1920

A silver medal instituted by the Government of the Union of South Africa in 1920. Awarded to officers and men of the Boer Republics for loyal service in the war against the British. The Transvaal or Orange Free State side of the medal was worn to the front according to the recipient's home state. Similarly the ribbon was worn with the green towards the centre of the chest for Transvaal and with yellow towards the centre for Orange Free State.

|  | £65 |
|---|---|

## 213 *Wound Ribbon* 1920

No medal was worn from this ribbon. It is included here to complete the series of awards to servicemen of the Boer Republics.

The ribbon was instituted in 1920 and was awarded with a certificate to servicemen of the Republics wounded during the 2nd Boer War.

## 214 *Commonwealth Independence Medals*

The British Commonwealth comprises of countries and dependencies that were part of the British Empire. The transition from Empire to Commonwealth began in 1931 when the Statute of Westminster gave the legal dates of Independence to Canada as 1837, Australia 1901 and New Zealand 1907. This change to Commonwealth status was often commemorated with the issue of a medal.

| | |
|---|---|
| India Independence Medal 1947, Sanctioned 1948 | £15 |
| Pakistan Independence Medal 1947, Sanctioned 1950 | £10 |
| Nigeria Independence Medal 1960, Sanctioned 1964 | £45 |
| Sierra Leone Independence Medal 1961, Sanctioned 1961 | £60 |
| Jamaican Independence Medal 1962, Sanctioned 1962 | £55 |
| Uganda Independence Medal 1962, Sanctioned 1963 | £55 |
| Malawi Independence Medal 1964, Sanctioned 1964 | £55 |
| Guyana Independence Medal 1966 | £40 |
| Fiji Independence Medal 1970 | £60 |
| Papua New Guinea Independence Medal 1975 | £40 |
| Solomon Islands Independence Medal 1978 | £40 |
| Gilbert/Ellis Islands Independence Medals 1978 | £50 |
| Zimbabwe Independence Medal 1980 Silver | £250 |
| Bronze | £15 |
| Vanuatu Independence Medal 1980, Sanctioned 1981 | £40 |
| St Christopher Nevis Independence Medal 1983 | £40 |

# Jubilee & Coronation Medals

---

### 215 *Empress of India Medal* 1877

This large medal, 58mm in dia., was struck in both gold and silver and was awarded to commemorate the proclamation of Queen Victoria as Empress of India on 1st January 1877. The medal was awarded to Indian princes and various high ranking European and Indian civilians and selected officers and men from the various British and Indian regiments serving in India at the time. The medal was worn around the neck, however officers and men were not permitted to wear it when in uniform.

| | |
|---|---|
| Gold | £3000 |
| Silver | £270 |

---

### 216 *Jubilee Medal* 1887

The medal was issued to commemorate the 50th year of Queen Victoria's reign. It was struck in three metals: gold, silver and bronze. The gold medal was given to members of the Royal Family and Royal guests. The medal in silver was given to members of the Royal Household, distinguished guests, ministers and officials, also to officers including officers in command of ships at the Spithead Naval Review. The bronze medal was awarded to selected 'other ranks' taking

part in the Jubilee processions through London on 21st June 1887 or who were onboard ship at Spithead when the fleet was reviewed. All the medals were issued unnamed.

On the occasion of the 1897 Jubilee, recipients of the 1887 medal who were entitled received the crowned dated bar '1897' which was to be sewn on to the ribbon of the medal.

|  | *1887 medal* | *with 1897 bar* |
|---|---|---|
| Gold | £850 | £950 |
| Silver | £70 | £100 |
| Bronze | £60 | £95 |

## 217 *Jubilee Medal* 1887—Police Issue

The medal was issued to all ranks of the Metropolitan Police and City of London Police in recognition of their services on Jubilee Day, 21st June 1887. The medal was issued in bronze and was named around the edge giving the recipient's rank, name and in the case of the Metropolitan Police the division. Two reverses were issued: 'Metropolitan Police' and 'City of London Police'. It is possible that a very few medals with the reverse 'Police Ambulance' may also have been issued.

On the occasion of the 1897 Jubilee, recipients of the 1887 medal who were entitled, received the bar '1897' which was fixed onto the suspension.

|  | *Bronze* | *Bronze with '1897' bar* |
|---|---|---|
| Metropolitan Police | (14,000) £15 | (8700) £20 |
| City of London Police | (900) £45 | (485) £60 |
| Police Ambulance | — | — |

## 218 *Jubilee Medal* 1897

On the occasion of Queen Victoria's Diamond Jubilee, medals similar to those of 1887 were issued in gold, silver and bronze. Worn from the same ribbon they differed in having the reverse inscription reading '60th', instead of '50th' and '20th June 1897' instead of '21st June 1887'.

Those entitled who held the earlier medal received instead the crowned dated bar '1897' which was to be sewn onto the ribbon.

| | |
|---|---|
| Gold (73) | £850 |
| Silver (3040) | £60 |
| Bronze (890) | £45 |

### 219 *Jubilee Medal* 1897—Mayors Issue

A special diamond-shaped medal was struck in both gold and silver and issued to Mayors and Provosts to commemorate the Jubilee. Issued in gold to Lord Mayors and Lord Provosts and in silver to Mayors and Provosts. The medal was worn from a blue and white ribbon very similar to that of the general issue Jubilee Medal but having the colours reversed.

| | |
|---|---|
| Gold (14) | £1200 |
| Silver (512) | £240 |

### 220 *Jubilee Medal* 1897—Police issue

A medal, very similar to that for the 1887 Jubilee was issued to various officers on duty and involved in the Jubilee celebrations and processions of 20th June 1897. The medal was worn from the same dark blue ribbon as for earlier medal and differed only in the date '1897' replacing '1887' on the reverse. Those officers in possession of the 1887 medal and entitled to the 1897 received instead the bar '1897' which was fixed on to the medal suspension bar.

| | Bronze |
|---|---|
| Metropolitan Police (7500) | £12 |
| City of London Police (535) | £60 |
| Police Ambulance (210) | £140 |
| St John Ambulance Brigade (910) | £60 |
| London County Council | |
|    Metropolitan Fire Brigade (950) | £60 |

### 221 *Hong Kong Diamond Jubilee Medal* 1897

In common with some other colonies e.g. Ceylon, a medal was issued to celebrate Queen Victoria's Diamond Jubilee. As most of the records of the Government in Hong Kong were destroyed during the Japanese Occupation little is known of the circumstances surrounding the award.

The medal is known to have been issued in silver and it is possible that bronze medals were also awarded.

The circular medal has a ring suspender attached to a crown. On the obverse is the veiled bust of Queen Victoria with the inscription, 'VICTORIA REGINA ET IMPERATRIX', with the date '1897' under the bust. In the centre of the reverse is a seascape depicting a British three-masted sailing ship and a Chinese junk with hills in the background and land in the foreground on which two figures stand shaking hands, a third figure stands apart. Above this scene are the words 'HONG KONG' and around in two concentric circles are inscriptions, the inner one reading 'SIR WILLIAM ROBINSON G.C.M.G. GOVERNOR', the outer reading 'TO COMMEMORATE SIXTY YEARS OF HER

MAJESTY'S REIGN 1837-1897'. The medal is named on the edge in engraved capitals. The ribbon is believed to be equal bands of dark blue, maroon, dark blue.

| | |
|---|---|
| Silver | £350 |

## 222 *Ceylon Diamond Jubilee Medal* 1897

Issued by the colony of Ceylon to certain persons in celebration of the Diamond Jubilee. In general the medal has similarities to the Hong Kong issue.

The medal was issued in gold. On the obverse is the veiled bust of Queen Victoria with the inscription, 'VICTORIA · DEI · GRA · BRITT · REGINA · FID · DEF · IND · IMP' with the dates '1837-1897' below the bust. The reverse centre depicts an elephant and a monument with 'CEYLON' above. The scene is enclosed by two concentric lines of inscription, the inner one reading 'TO COMMEMORATE SIXTY YEARS OF HER MAJESTY'S REIGN', the outer 'THE RT. HON. SIR J. WEST RIDGEWAY, K.C.B., K.C.M.G. GOVERNOR'. The ribbon is believed to be a plain red.

| | |
|---|---|
| Gold | £750 |

## 223 *Visit to Ireland Medal* 1900

The medal was issued to commemorate the visit to Ireland of Queen Victoria in 1900 and was awarded to officers of the Royal Irish Constabulary and Dublin Metropolitan Police who were involved in the various events of the visit. It was struck in bronze and had the recipient's rank, name and force engraved on the edge. It was worn from the same dark blue ribbon as for the Police Jubilee Medals and was suspended from an ornate bronze brooch bar bearing shamrock. 2285 medals were struck.

| | |
|---|---|
| | £45 |

## 224 *Coronation Medal* 1902

This medal, struck in both silver and bronze was issued to commemorate the Coronation of Edward VII on 9th August 1902. Members of the Royal Family, distinguished guests, officials and officers of the Army and Navy involved with the celebrations received the silver medal. Selected 'other ranks' of the services received the medal in bronze. All the medals were issued unnamed.

The original date for the coronation was 26th June 1902 and this date appears on the medal reverse. However the coronation was postponed because of the

Kings illness until 9th August 1902. Certain nurses attending the King during this period received the medal. Certain colonial officers and men not present on 9th August who would have been present at the coronation had it gone ahead in June also received medals.

| | |
|---|---|
| Silver (3493) | £45 |
| Bronze (6054) | £35 |

## 225 *Coronation Medal* 1902—Mayor's issue

The medal struck in silver was issued to mayors, provosts and senior civic officials who took part in the coronation celebrations. The medal was issued unnamed.

| | |
|---|---|
| | £240 |

## 226 *Coronation Medal* 1902—Police issue

This medal was issued to all ranks of the Police and associated forces who were on duty and involved in the official coronation celebrations. The medal was struck in both silver and bronze; silver being awarded to certain senior officers, bronze to all other ranks. Medals were issued named around the edge. Five reverse types were issued.

| | Silver | Bronze |
|---|---|---|
| Metropolitan Police | (51) £300 | (16,700) £12 |
| City of London Police | (5) £400 | (1,060) £30 |
| L.C.C.M.F.B. (London County Council Metropolitan Fire Brigade) | (9) £350 | (1000) £30 |
| St John Ambulance Brigade | (?) rare | (912) £40 |
| Police Ambulance Service | (1) rare | (204) £130 |

## 227 *Hong Kong Coronation Medal* 1902

The medal was issued to celebrate the Coronation of King Edward VII; it is believed that medals were awarded to all troops, British and Indian, and police serving in Hong Kong at the time.

Medals were issued in bronze, in a fitted case and without ribbon. The obverse has the crowned busts of King Edward VII and Queen Alexandra with the inscription 'EDWARD VII R.I. ALEXANDRA R'. The reverse is identical to that of the Jubilee Medal with the exception of the inscriptions; the inner one

reads 'SIR HENRY A. BLAKE G.C.M.G. GOVERNOR', the outer one has, 'TO COMMEMORATE THE CORONATION OF THEIR MAJESTIES THE KING & QUEEN'. The year '1902' is situated below the seascape. Medals may be named on the edge in engraved capitals.

| | |
|---|---|
| Bronze | £65 |

### 228 *Ceylon Coronation Medal* 1902

The medal was issued in gold. On the obverse is crowned and robed bust of the King with the legend 'EDWARDUS VII REX ET IMPERATOR'. The reverse is the same as that of the Jubilee Medal with the exception of the two line inscription which reads, 'IN COMMEMORATION OF THE CORONATION OF H.M. KING EDWARD VII 1902'. The ribbon is believed to be a plain blue.

| | |
|---|---|
| Gold | £750 |

### 229 *Delhi Darbar Medal* 1903

The medal was issued to commemorate the Delhi Darbar of King Edward VII on 1st January 1903. The medal was struck in both gold and silver and issued unnamed. Awarded in gold to Indian State rulers and in silver to other dignitaries, officials, officers and men. 140 gold and 2570 silver medals were struck.

| | |
|---|---|
| Gold | £1400 |
| Silver | £60 |

### 230 *Visit to Scotland Medal* 1903

The medal was struck to commemorate the official visit of King Edward VII to Scotland in May 1903. The medal was issued to members of the Scottish Police and associated forces who were on duty. The medal was struck in bronze and was very similar to the Police Coronation Medal, being distinguished by the reverse inscription and plain red ribbon. It was worn suspended from an ornate bronze brooch bar bearing thistles. Medals were issued named with details of the recipient's rank, name and force. Approximately 2950 medals were struck.

| | |
|---|---|
| | £45 |

## 231 *Visit to Ireland Medal* 1903

This medal was struck to commemorate the visit of King Edward VII to Ireland in July 1903. It was issued to members of the police and associated forces who were on duty. The medal was struck in bronze and had the same reverse as the Queen Victoria issue except for the date '1903' replacing '1900' in the exergue. It was worn on a pale blue ribbon from an ornate bronze brooch bar bearing shamrock. The medal was generally named around the edge with the rank, name and force of the recipient. Approximately 7750 medals were struck.

| | |
|---|---|
| | £40 |

## 232 *Coronation Medal* 1911

The medal was issued to commemorate the Coronation of King George V on 22nd June 1911. Issued in silver only and unnamed, approximately 16,000 medals were awarded. For this and succeeding commemorative medals the recipient did not have to be actually present at the occasion to qualify. Recipients of the medal entitled to the Delhi Durbar Medal, 1911, received instead the bar 'Delhi'.

| | |
|---|---|
| Coronation Medal 1911 | £25 |
| With bar 'Delhi' (134) | £300 |

## 233 *Coronation Medal* 1911—Police issue

The medal was issued to various Police Forces and organisations to commemorate the Coronation of George V on 22nd June 1911. The medal was awarded to all ranks of the Metropolitan Police and City of London forces serving on the day and to a percentage of the strength of other Police Forces. Unlike earlier jubilee and coronation medals the 1911 issue was struck in silver only. The medals were usually issued named.

| | |
|---|---|
| Metropolitan Police | £12 |
| City of London Police | £50 |
| County and Borough Police | £50 |
| Police Ambulance Service | £300 |
| London Fire Brigade | £50 |
| Royal Irish Constabulary (585) | £90 |
| Scottish Police (280) | £100 |
| St John's Ambulance Brigade | £60 |
| St Andrews Ambulance Corps | £150 |
| Royal Parks (119) | £300 |

## 234 *Visit to Ireland Medal* 1911

The medal was issued to commemorate the visit of King George V to Ireland in July 1911. The medal was issued to members of the police forces on duty and prominent civic officials involved. The medal was struck in silver and was very similar to the 1911 Police Coronation Medals, being distinguished by the reverse inscription and ribbon. Issued unnamed, approximately 2480 medals were struck.

£50

## 235 *Delhi Durbar Medal* 1911

The medal struck in both gold and silver was issued to commemorate the Delhi Durbar of King George V in December 1911. Unlike the earlier medal a recipient did not have to be present to receive a medal. 200 gold medals were struck mainly for issue to Indian State rulers. 30,000 silver medals were struck 10,000 of which were issued to military personnel throughout India. The medals were issued unnamed. Recipients of the Coronation Medal 1911 entitled to the Durbar Medal received instead the bar 'Delhi' which was worn on the ribbon of Coronation Medal. 134 bars were issued.

| | |
|---|---|
| Gold | £1000 |
| Silver | £25 |

## 236 *Jubilee Medal* 1935

The medal was issued to commemorate the 25th year of the reign of King George V. Issued in silver and unnamed, approximately 85,000 medals were awarded.

£20

## 237 *Coronation Medal* 1937

The medal was issued to commemorate the Coronation of King George VI on 12th May 1937. Approximately 90,000 of these unnamed silver medals were issued.

£20

## 238 *Coronation Medal* 1953

A silver medal, issued to commemorate the Coronation of Queen Elizabeth II on 2nd June 1953. Approximately 129,000 were issued. The medals were issued unnamed, however 37 were named around the edge, 'Mount Everest Expedition' and presented by the Queen to members of the expedition at Buckingham Palace on 16th July 1953.

| | |
|---|---|
| | £25 |

## 239 *Jubilee Medal* 1977

A silver medal, issued to commemorate the 25th year of the reign of Queen Elizabeth II. A Canadian version was also issued having a distinctive reverse. The obverse common to both types has the Queen wearing the Imperial State Crown. 30,000 of each type were issued, all unnamed.

| | |
|---|---|
| Standard issue | £150 |
| Canadian issue | £100 |

# *Meritorious Service Medals*

### 240 *Royal Naval Meritorious Service Medal*

The medal was instituted by an Order in Council dated 14th January 1919. It was awarded without annuity or pension to non-commissioned officers and men of the naval forces for arduous or specially meritorious service or for an act of gallantry whilst not in the presence of the enemy. Forces awarded the medal included R.N., R.N.A.S., R.M., various naval reserves and colonial naval forces. The medal was discontinued by an Order in Council of 1st November 1928, being replaced by the British Empire Medal for Gallantry or Meritorious Service. The medal issued had on the obverse the bust of George V in the uniform of Admiral of the Fleet and had the standard M.S.M. reverse. The medal was named around the edge in large capitals with serifs. The ribbon was crimson with a white stripe at the edges and centre. A total of 1020 medals of this type were gazetted between 1919 and 1923.

The R.N. M.S.M. was re-instituted on 1st December 1977. The medal (without annuity) is available to members of the R.N., R.M., Q.A.R.N.N.S. and W.R.N.S. Recipients must be serving senior non-commissioned officers (P.O., Sgt. or above), the main qualifications are 27 years service (minimum starting age 17½) and possession of the L.S. and G.C. Medal and 3 good conduct badges. The medal is not an automatic award once the requisite number of years have been served and no more than 59 medals per year may be awarded. In appearance the medal is exactly as the Army M.S.M. and may only be differenciated by the naming detail which gives number, rank, name and ship.

| | |
|---|---|
| George V (1919-28) | £220 |
| Elizabeth (1977-    ) | £280 |

### 241 *Royal Marines Meritorious Service Medal*

The M.S.M. for the Royal Marines was sanctioned by an Order in Council of 15th January 1849. A sum of £250 was made available for annuities not exceeding £20 as a reward for distinguished or meritorious service. Serving sergeants having served a minimum of 24 years, the last 14 of which as a sergeant, with an irreproachable and meritorious character were deemed eligible for the annuity and accompanying medal. In 1872 discharged sergeants became

eligible and the service qualification was reduced to 21 years. In 1855 a further sum of £50 was provided specifically for annuities for gallant conduct in action before the enemy on land in the Crimea. The M.S.M. award for gallantry was replaced in 1874 by a reconstituted C.G.M. A total of 6 gallantry M.S.M's were awarded.

The medal awarded was essentially the army version of the M.S.M. and differed only in the naming detail and by being worn from a plain blue ribbon.

Under the terms of the 1916/17/19 Royal Warrants (see Army and Royal Navy M.S.Ms) the Royal Marines became entitled to the M.S.M. 'immediate' awards for valuable services etc. Royal Marine personnel received 72 'Army M.S.Ms' (George V Military bust) and 173 'Naval M.S.Ms' (George V Admiral's bust) during the period 1917-1928. 'Immediate' awards were worn from the military ribbon of crimson with three white stripes. This use of the M.S.M. as an immediate award ended in 1928. The M.S.M. for 'long service' continued to be awarded until 1951.

In 1977 the R.M. M.S.M. was re-instituted, the medal and ribbon being common to all services.

Approximate numbers issued: Victoria 110, Edward VII 40, George V Mil. bust non-immed. 35, George V Mil. bust immed. 72, George V Adm. bust non-immed. 50, George V Adm. bust immed. 173, George V Coinage head 16, George VI Ind. Imp. 55, George VI Fid. Def. 270.

| | |
|---|---|
| Victoria, with '1848' below bust | £425 |
| Victoria | £150 |
| Edward VII | £200 |
| George V 'non-immediate' award | £95 |
| George V 'immediate' award | £75 |
| George VI | £95 |
| Elizabeth II 2nd type | £230 |

## 242 *Army Meritorious Service Medal*

The medal was instituted by Royal Warrant of 19th December 1845. By the warrant a sum of money not exceeding £2,000 was provided each year to be distributed in the form of annuities not exceeding £20, paid for life to N.C.Os of the rank of sergeant and above as a reward for distinguished or meritorious service. Both serving and retired N.C.Os were eligible. In addition to the annuity the recipient was awarded the Meritorious Service Medal. Thus the number of medals issued was limited by the money available and in general annuities and medals only became available on the death of a previous recipient or when the annual sum was increased. Essentially the medal with annuity was an award for long service through occasionally early awards were made in respect of gallantry. Until November 1902 recipients were not permitted to wear both the L.S. & G.C. Medal and M.S.M., thereafter the M.S.M. was worn after the L.S. & G.C. until 1979 when approval was given for the M.S.M. to be worn before the L.S. & G.C. Medal (Military). Prior to 1951 the M.S.M. could only be awarded when an annuity became available, subsequently the medal could be awarded without an annuity being immediately available. Since 1956 a recipient must have served a minimum of 27 years before being eligible.

In addition to the M.S.M. above awarded primarily for long service a second type was awarded, introduced during the First World War. By a Royal Warrant dated 4th October 1916 the medal was made available to all N.C.Os and men for valuable and meritorious service. By a Warrant of 3rd January 1917 this was extended to include gallantry. Such service had to be other than in action with the enemy. The M.S.M. granted under the terms of the Warrants of 1916/17 was available to N.C.Os and men of all services: Army, R.N., R.M., R.A.F. whether U.K. or Colonial. The medal issued was the standard Army type. No annuities were associated with these 'immediate' awards. By a Royal Warrant of 7th September 1928 this use of the M.S.M. was terminated, being replaced by the Empire Gallantry Medal and British Empire Medal. The M.S.M. with annuity for 'long service' was unaffected by the 1928 Warrant. During the period 1916-28 over 27,000 M.S.Ms were awarded under the terms of the 1916/17 Warrants. The vast majority were gazetted for 'valuable service', 435 for 'gallantry' and 144 for 'devotion to duty'. R.M. personnel received 72, R.N. 47 and R.F.C. and Australian F.C. 141.

The medal was worn from a plain crimson ribbon until June 1916 when white stripes were added to the edges, changing again in August 1917 to the current type of crimson with three white stripes. Bars were introduced in 1916 for recipients of the M.S.M. for additional acts of gallantry or saving life; seven were gazetted between 1916-1928. The medal was always issued named. The medal reverse has remained constant throughout its long history. Various types may be distinguished based on obverse, suspension and naming detail:

Victoria, dated '1847' on the edge, swivelling suspension.
Victoria, dated '1848' below the bust.
Victoria, without date below bust.
Edward VII, Military bust.
George V, Military bust. Non-swivelling suspension from 1926 onwards. Awards for 'long service' without recipient's regimental number. Awards for 'valuable service' etc. (1916-1928) with regimental number.
George V, Coinage head
George VI, Coinage head, 'GEORGIUS VI D:G:BR:OMN:REX F:D:IND:IMP.'
George VI, Crowned head, 'GEORGIUS VI DG:BR:OMN:REX ET INDIAE IMP'. Issued during 1942.
George VI, Coinage head, 'GEORGIUS VI D:G:BRITT:OMN:REX FID:DEF:'
Elizabeth II, 'ELIZABETH II DEI GRA:BRITT:OMN:REGINA F:D:'
Elizabeth II, 'ELIZABETH·II·DEI·GRATIA·REGINA·F:D:' Early issues with a fixed suspension, later medals fitted with a swivel suspension.

| | |
|---|---|
| Victoria, dated '1847' on edge | £350 |
| Victoria, dated '1848' below bust | £425 |
| Victoria | £160 |
| Edward VII | £100 |
| George V Mil. bust non-immediate | £45 |
| George V Mil. bust immediate | £35 |
| George V Coinage head | £80 |
| George VI Ind. Imp. | £45 |
| George VI Crowned head | £200 |
| George VI Fid. Def. | £45 |
| Elizabeth II | £200 |

## 243 *Royal Air Force Meritorious Service Medal*

Instituted by Royal Warrant in June 1918, the medal was awarded to warrant officers, non-commissioned officers and men in recognition of valuable services rendered in the field as distinct from actual flying service. The medal had on the obverse the 'coinage head' of George V and had the standard M.S.M. reverse. The naming around the edge was of two distinct types: the first type (1918-20) was associated with awards for the Great War and the war in Russia and had large serifed capitals similar to those on the Naval L.S. & G.C. & D.S.M. Later medals were named in thin sans serif capitals similar to the early G.S.M. Unlike the Army M.S.M. with the similar obverse, the R.A.F. version had a swivelling suspender. The medal was worn from a ribbon of half crimson half blue with a white stripe at the edges and centre. Unlike the Army and Navy M.S.M. the RA.F. medal was worn before the L.S & G.C. Medal. A total of 854 medals of this type were gazetted between 1918 and 1924. The medal was discontinued in 1928 being replaced by the B.E.M.

The R.A.F. M.S.M. was re-introduced on 1st December 1977. The medal, without annuity, is available to airmen and airwomen of the rank of Sgt. or above. The main qualifications being 27 years service (minimum starting age 17½), possession of the L.S & G.C. Medal, irreproachable conduct and a high standard of service. The medal is not an automatic award on completing the required period of service and no more than 70 per year may be awarded. In appearance the medal is exactly the same as the Army M.S.M. and it is worn from the same ribbon, it may only be differenciated by the naming detail which gives rank, name, number followed by 'R.A.F.' As with the 1918 type the R.A.F. medal is worn before L.S. & G.C. medal.

| | |
|---|---|
| George V (1919-28) | £180 |
| Elizabeth II (1977-    ) | £240 |

## 244 *Colonial Meritorious Service Medals*

By a Royal Warrant of 31st May 1895, medals for Distinguished Conduct, Meritorious Service and Long Service were made available to warrant officers, N.C.Os and men of the Colonial forces. The qualifications being as far as possible similar to those governing the award of comparable medals to U.K. forces.

The design of the Colonial M.S.M. was similar to the Imperial issue but had the name of the country on the reverse and was worn from a distinctive ribbon.

Canada

Ribbon crimson, possibly with a central white stripe until 1916, then crimson with white edges and from 1917 onwards crimson with white edges and a central white stripe. With 'Canada' on the reverse until the late 1930s-early 1940s when replaced by the standard Imperial type which was issued until 1958. No Victoria head types issued but specimens exist.

Cape of Good Hope
Ribbon crimson with a central orange stripe. 1 or possibly 2 Edward VII medals issued.

Natal
Ribbon crimson with a central yellow stripe. 15 Edward VII medals issued. Unusual in that it was awarded to non-permanent forces of the Natal Militia.

Commonwealth of Australia
Ribbon crimson with two dark green central stripes. Issued between 1903 and 1975.

New South Wales
Ribbon crimson with a central dark blue stripe. Issued until 1903.

Queensland
Ribbon crimson with a central light blue stripe. Issued until 1903.

South Australia
Ribbon plain crimson. Issued until 1903.

Tasmania
Ribbon crimson with a central pink stripe. Issued until 1903.

New Zealand
Ribbon crimson with a central light green stripe. Issued since 1898.

The medals were issued named. Unnamed specimens exist.

The M.S.M. issued to Colonial forces under the terms of the 1916 and 1917 Royal Warrants were of the Imperial type and worn from the standard ribbon of the time.

|  | Victoria | Edward VII | George V | George VI | Elizabeth II |
|---|---|---|---|---|---|
| Canada | £600 | £500 | £350 | — | — |
| Cape of Good Hope | — | rare | — | — | — |
| Natal | — | £600 | — | — | — |
| Comm. of Australia | — | £500 | £300 | £200 | £200 |
| N.S.W. | rare | rare | — | — | — |
| Queensland | rare | rare | — | — | — |
| S. Australia | rare | rare | — | — | — |
| Tasmania | rare | £1000 | — | — | — |
| New Zealand | £600 | £500 | £350 | £200 | £200 |

## 245 *Indian Army Meritorious Service Medal*

(for Europeans of the Indian Army)

The medal was introduced by the Government of India in the General Order of 20th May 1848. The medal with an annuity not exceeding £20 was awarded to European sergeants, serving or discharged for distinguished or meritorious service.

The obverse of this silver medal bears the head of Victoria, the reverse the arms, crest and motto of the H.E.I.Co. The medal was named around the edge and worn from a plain crimson ribbon.

In 1873 the award of this distinctive medal to Europeans was discontinued.

| Victoria | £260 |
|---|---|

## 246 *Indian Army Meritorious Service Medal*

The medal was instituted in 1888 and was awarded with an annuity to Dafadars, Havildars and Drum, Fife, Trumpet and Bugle-Majors of the Indian Army. The basic requirement was 18 years decidedly meritorious service. The number of medals given was limited by the sum set aside for annuities. Initially one medal was available to each regiment of cavalry and infantry in the three Presidencies, thereafter further medals were awarded when annuities became available through death, promotion or reduction of a recipient. On promotion the medal was retained by the recipient but the annuity relinquished. A recipient in possession of both the M.S.M. and L.S. & G.C. surrendered the latter.

The medal was stuck in silver and was issued named in engraved lettering round the edge. The ribbon was originally a plain crimson, changing in 1917 to one of crimson with three white stripes.

| | |
|---|---|
| Victoria 1888 issue, lotus wreath reverse | £60 |
| Edward VII | £50 |
| George V Kaiser-i-Hind obverse | £45 |
| George V Indiae Imp. obverse | £55 |
| George VI | £35 |

## 247 *African Police Medal for Meritorious Service*

The medal was instituted by Royal Warrant of 14th July 1915 and remained in force until superseded in 1938 by the Colonial Police Medal. It was awarded to non-European, non-commissioned officers and men of the various Colonial police forces of East and West Africa for gallantry, distinguished service or long and meritorious service. For the latter qualification a minimum of 15 years exemplary service was required.

There were three issues, two of George V, distinguished only by the obverse inscription: 1st issue, 1915-31: 'GEORGIUS V REX ET IND:IMP:'; 2nd issue 1931-37: 'GEORGIUS. V. D.G. BRITT. OMN. REX. ET. INDIAE. IMP.' The George VI type was issued during the year 1938.

Medal issued named with details of the recipient's rank, name and force engraved on the edge.

| | |
|---|---|
| George V 1st type | £350 |
| George V 2nd type | £350 |
| George VI | £450 |

### 248 *Union of South Africa Meritorious Service Medal*

The medal was instituted through the Government Gazette of 24th October 1914, being effective from 1st April 1913. It was discontinued in 1952. With the exception of the ribbon it was essentially identical to the standard Imperial military issue. The ribbon was crimson with blue edges with a central band of white blue white. All three types had a swivel suspender. A total of 46 awards were made. In addition to the above medal for 'long service' the M.S.M. was also issued to South Africans under the terms of the 1916/17 Royal Warrants. Over 300 such awards were made, the medals worn from the standard U.K. type ribbon.

The permanent forces of Southern Rhodesia and the police force of Swaziland were also eligible for the M.S.M. worn from the South African type ribbon.

| | |
|---|---|
| George V Military bust | £200 |
| George V Coinage head | £300 |
| George VI Crowned head | £300 |

See opposite page: Issues of Royal Household Faithful Service Medals

# Long Service & Good Conduct Medals

## 249 *Royal Household Faithful Service Medals*

Queen Victoria

The medal was instituted by Queen Victoria in 1872 as a reward to servants of the Royal Household for long and faithful service. Generally awarded for 25 years faithful service; bars for additional 10 year periods of service could be awarded. A silver medal, the obverse has the bust of Queen Victoria facing left, the reverse has the particulars of the recipient engraved upon it, usually name, position in the Household, period of service and year of award. The medal has a complex suspension bearing the Royal Cypher 'V.R.I.' which is in turn attached to a brooch bar. It was not intended that the medal should be worn from a ribbon, however when presented they had a narrow strip of Royal Stuart tartan ribbon behind the cypher between the top and bottom bars.

One medal in gold was struck and presented to Queen Victoria's personal servant, John Brown.

Later Issues

A silver medal, obverse with the head and titles of the monarch, reverse with the words 'FOR LONG AND FAITHFUL SERVICE'. The edge is engraved with the recipient's name. The medal is surmounted by a crowned Royal Cypher attached to a straight bar suspension which is engraved with the recipient's years of service or year of award. Bars for further periods of service could be awarded bearing the words 'THIRTY YEARS', 'FORTY YEARS', 'FIFTY YEARS' as appropriate. Ribbon: George V: Dark blue and red diagonal stripes descending from left to right; George VI: diagonal stripes as above descending from right to left; Elizabeth II: Dark blue with three red stripes.

| | |
|---|---|
| Victoria | £450 |
| George V | £225 |
| Edward VIII (2) | rare |
| George VI | £240 |
| Elizabeth II | £275 |

## 250 *Royal Navy Long Service and Good Conduct Medal* 1831

The medal was instituted by William IV by an Order in Council dated 24th August 1831. It was originally awarded to Petty Officers, seamen and marines for a minimum of 21 years service with irreproachable conduct. The period of service required was reduced to 10 years in 1874 and later increased to 15 years. During the reign of George V bars were authorised for additional 15 year periods of service. In 1981 the medal was made available to officers of the R.N., R.M., Q.A.R.N.N.S. & W.R.N.S. provided 15 years had been served, from the age of 17½ and above, with at least 12 years served as a rating or in the ranks. Similarly, a bar could be awarded for a further 15 years provided a minimum of 7 years had been as a rating or in the ranks. The medal or bar was only awarded to those officers still serving on or after 27th March 1981.

The following types may be discerned:

William IV/Victoria Anchor type (1831-47) 644 issued. Obverse: An anchor with crown above enclosed by an oak wreath. Reverse: The legend, starting at 7 o'clock, 'FOR LONG SERVICE AND GOOD CONDUCT', with the recipient's rank, name, ship and period of service engraved in the centre. The medal is pierced to receive a ring suspension and is worn from a plain blue ribbon. The medal is to be found with various die flaws. A variety of this medal has the reverse inverted relative to the obverse which causes the legend to commence at the 1 o'clock position. Medals of this variety were issued during 1833-35.

Victoria, wide suspender type (1848-74) 3572 issued. Obverse: Victoria, 'Young Head'. Reverse: The legend around the circumference, in the centre a man-of-war at anchor enclosed by a cable tied at the base by a reef knot. With a swivelling straight bar suspender 1½in. long, worn from a ribbon of blue with white edges. The edge of the medal is engraved with the recipient's details.

Victoria, wide suspender '1848' type (1849-50) 100 issued. As above but with the obverse of the Naval General Service Medal 1793 having the year date '1848' below the bust.

Victoria, narrow suspender type with engraved naming (1875-77) 4400 issued. As above but with standard undated obverse. With a straight bar suspender 1¼in. long. Engraved naming around the edge.

Victoria, narrow suspender type with impressed naming (1878-1901) 18,200 issued. As above but with recipient's details impressed in capitals around the edge.

Edward VII type (1901-10) Obverse: bust of Edward VII in admiral's uniform.

George V 1st type (1911-30) Obverse: bust of George V in admiral's uniform. The suspender previously swivelling became fixed in the 1920s and thereafter until about 1956.

George V 2nd type (1930-36) Obverse: 'Coinage head' of George V.

George VI 1st type (1937-48) Obverse: Head of George VI with 'IND IMP' legend.

George VI 2nd type (1949-53) As above but with 'FID DEF' legend.

Elizabeth II 1st type (1953-54) Obverse: Head of Elizabeth II with legend, 'BRITT. OMN.'

Elizabeth II 2nd type 1954-present. Obverse: as above but with the legend 'DEI GRATIA'. Medals with a fixed suspender were issued during the period 1954-55, thereafter the piece was fitted with a swivelling suspender.

Medals were issued giving the name of the ship the recipient was serving on at the time of his qualification. Exceptions to this are those awarded to the Coast Guard, R.M., R.M.A. and R.M.L.I. From the reign of George V onwards medals were also awarded to the various colonial navies. Medals to those navies are distinguished by the appropriate letters on the edge, e.g. R.A.N., R.C.N., R.I.N., R.N.Z.N.

| | | | |
|---|---|---|---|
| William IV/Victoria Anchor type | £420 | George V 1st type Admiral's bust | £20 |
| Victoria wide suspender type | £140 | George V 2nd type Coinage head | £25 |
| Victoria '1848' wide suspender type | £500 | George VI 1st type 'Ind. Imp.' | £25 |
| Victoria narrow suspender, engraved naming type | £50 | George VI 2nd type 'Fid Def.' | £30 |
| Victoria narrow suspender, impressed naming type | £30 | Elizabeth II 1st type 'Brit. Omn.' | £35 |
| Edward VII | £25 | Elizabeth II 2nd type 'Dei Gratia' | £30 |

## 251 *Royal Naval Reserve Decoration* 1908

An oval skeletal badge in silver and silver-gilt, issued unnamed but may be found privately engraved on the reverse. Edward VII issues are hallmarked, later issues often have the year of award engraved on the reverse. When instituted in 1908 the ribbon was a plain dark green, this was changed in 1941 to one of dark green with white edges.

The original qualification for the decoration was 15 years service as a commissioned officer in the R.N.R.; service in the rank of midshipman being excluded. Wartime service counted double. Bars were awarded for additional 15 year periods of service. Recipients of the decoration are entitled to use the postnominal letters 'R.D.' and since 1966 the letters 'V.R.D.'

| | |
|---|---|
| Edward VII | £140 |
| George V | £100 |
| George VI 1st type | £100 |
| George VI 2nd type | £110 |
| Elizabeth II | £120 |

## 252 *Royal Naval Reserve Long Service and Good Conduct Medal* 1908

A silver medal with a straight bar suspension, with impressed naming in capitals around the edge. The medal may be distinguished from similar medals by the initials 'R.N.R.' after the recipient's name on the edge. Certain rare dominion issues may also be distinguished by appropriate initials, e.g. 'R.C.N.R.', 'R.A.N.R.' The ribbon was originally a plain green, changing in 1941 to one of green with white edges and white central stripe. Following the merger of the R.N.R. and R.N.V.R. in 1958, the ribbon changed to one of five equal stripes: blue/white/green/white/blue.

The medal was instituted in September 1908 and granted to men of the R.N.R. for 15 years service including necessary periods of naval training. War service was counted double. A bar was issued for additional 15 year periods of service.

| | |
|---|---|
| Edward VII | £25 |
| George V Admiral's bust | £20 |
| George V Coinage head | £25 |
| George VI 1st type | £20 |
| George VI 2nd type | £25 |
| Elizabeth II 1st type | £30 |
| Elizabeth II 2nd type | £25 |

## 253 *Royal Naval Volunteer Reserve Decoration* 1908

The decoration is similar to that of the R.N.R. Decoration. The ribbon was originally a plain dark-green, this changed in 1919 to one of blue with a central green stripe flanked by red stripes.

The decoration was instituted in 1908 and was awarded to officers of the R.N.V.R. for 20 years service. Qualifying service did not have to be continuous, but commissioned service under the age of 17 was not counted. Commissioned service in the R.N.R., Volunteer and Territorial Forces was allowed to count whilst service in the ranks of the R.N.V.R. and other auxiliary services counted half and war service counted double. Recipients of the decoration were permitted to use the postnominal letters 'V.R.D.' In 1958 the R.N.V.R. merged with the R.N.R. and since 1966 the R.N.V.R. Decoration has been replaced by that of the R.N.R.

| | |
|---|---|
| Edward VII | £140 |
| George V | £100 |
| George VI 1st type | £100 |
| George VI 2nd type | £110 |
| Elizabeth II | £120 |

## 254 *Royal Naval Volunteer Reserve Long Service and Good Conduct Medal* 1908

A silver medal fitted with a straight bar suspension, with impressed naming in capitals around the edge. The medal may be distinguished from similar medals by the initials 'R.N.V.R.' after the recipient's name on the edge. Certain rare dominion issues are also found, indicated by appropriate initials, eg 'R.C.N.V.R.', 'R.A.N.V.R.' The ribbon was originally a plain green as for the R.N.R. L.S. & G.C. Medal; this was changed in 1919 to a more distinctive ribbon.

The medal was instituted in 1908 and was granted to men of the R.N.V.R. for 12 years service with the necessary training. In addition, character during this period had to be assessed as 'very good' or better. War service was counted as double. Bars were awarded for further 12 year periods of service. The medal was issued until 1958 when the R.N.V.R. was merged with the R.N.R.

| | |
|---|---|
| Edward VII | £250 |
| George V Admiral's bust | £35 |
| George V Coinage head | £45 |
| George VI 1st type | £35 |
| George VI 2nd type | £45 |
| Elizabeth II | £65 |

## 255 *Royal Fleet Reserve Long Service and Good Conduct Medal*

A silver medal fitted with a ring suspension, with impressed naming in capitals around the edge. The medal may be distinguished from similar medals by its distinctive ribbon, mode of suspension and by the initials 'R.F.R.' after the recipient's name on the edge.

The medal was granted to men of the R.F.R. for 15 years service, during which time their conduct and training had to be assessed as very good. Service in the Royal Navy was also counted provided a R.N. L.S. & G.C. Medal had not been awarded. Recipients of a R.F.R. L.S. & G.C. Medal later qualifying for a R.N. L.S. & G.C. Medal could receive the latter provided the R.F.R. Medal was returned. Bars were awarded for further 15 year periods of service.

| | |
|---|---|
| George V Admiral's bust | £20 |
| George V Coinage head | £20 |
| George VI 1st type | £25 |
| George VI 2nd type | £30 |
| Elizabeth II 1st type | £55 |
| Elizabeth II 2nd type | £35 |

## 256 *Royal Naval Auxiliary Sick Berth Reserve Long Service and Good Conduct Medal*

A silver medal fitted with a straight bar suspension with impressed naming in small capitals around the edge. The medal is very similar to the R.N.R. L.S. & G.C. Medal and may only be distinguished by the initials 'R.N.A.S.B.R.' after the recipient's name on the edge. The ribbon was originally a plain green, changing in 1941 to one of green with white edges and central stripe.

The R.N.A.S.B.R. has its origins in 1900 when the Medical Director of the Navy invited the St. John Ambulance Brigade to form a reserve of Naval Sick Berth personnel who could be mobilised in times of crisis. The Reserve was then established on the 19th November 1902. The first medal issue was made in 1919, the basic qualification being 15 years service in the Reserve. During the period 1919-1939 the medal, awarded by the Admiralty was presented by the Chief Commissioner of the St. John Ambulance Brigade. Between 1939-1945 the medal was sent direct to the recipient's ship or hospital for presentation, thereafter it was sent to the recipient direct. The Reserve was disbanded in 1949. Approximately 1,500 medals were issued.

| | |
|---|---|
| George V Admiral's bust | £90 |
| George V Coinage head | £100 |
| George VI | £90 |

## 257 *Royal Naval Wireless Auxiliary Reserve Long Service and Good Conduct Medal* 1919

A silver medal fitted with a straight bar suspension, with impressed naming in small capitals around the edge. The medal is very similar to the R.N.R. & R.N.V.R. L.S. & G.C. Medal and can only be distinguished by the initials 'R.N.W.A.R.' after the recipient's name on the edge. It has the same ribbon as the R.N.V.R. L.S. & G.C. Medal.

The medal was instituted in 1919 and issued until 1949. It was awarded for 12 years service in the R.N.W.A.R. with service in the R.N.V.R. allowed to count. A bar was issued for additional 12 year periods of service.

| | |
|---|---|
| George V Admiral's bust | £150 |
| George V Coinage head | £175 |
| George VI | £140 |

## 258 *Royal Naval Auxiliary Services Long Service and Good Conduct Medal* 1965

The medal was instituted by Royal Warrant on 15th July 1965. It is granted to both officers and other ranks for 12 years satisfactory service in the Royal Naval

Auxiliary Service, founded in 1962 or its predecessor, the Royal Naval Minewatching Service, founded in 1952.

The medal is struck in cupro-nickel and is issued named around the edge in impressed capitals.

| | |
|---|---|
| Elizabeth II | £100 |

## 259 *Rocket Apparatus Volunteer Long Service Medal*

1911

Instituted in 1911 by the Board of Trade and awarded for 20 years service with the Rocket Life Saving Apparatus Volunteers. The Board of Trade retained responsibility for the Volunteers until 1942 when the Ministry of Transport took control. The Rocket Apparatus Volunteers became the Coast Life Saving Corps in about 1953 to become the Coastguard Auxiliary Service in about 1968.

There are two reverse types: 1 'Presented by the Board of Trade' (1911-1942). 2. 'Rocket Apparatus Volunteer Medal' (1942-1968).

The medal was struck in silver and was always issued with the recipient's name engraved on the reverse.

| | |
|---|---|
| George V Coinage head | £45 |
| George VI 1st issue | £50 |
| George VI 2nd issue | £65 |
| Elizabeth II 1st issue | £65 |
| Elizabeth II 2nd issue | £65 |

## 260 *Coastguard Auxiliary Service Long Service Medal*

The Coastguard Auxiliary Service Long Service Medal is the present day successor to the Rocket Apparatus Volunteer Long Service Medal. Similar to its forebear it is distinguished by the reverse inscription ''The Coastguard Auxiliary Service''. It is struck in silver and is always issued with the recipient's name engraved on the reverse (specimen illustrated).

| | |
|---|---|
| Elizabeth II 2nd issue | £85 |

## 261 *Army Long Service and Good Conduct Medal* 1830

The medal was instituted in 1830 by King William IV. It was originally awarded to soldiers of irreproachable conduct for 21 years service in the infantry or 24 years in the cavalry. In 1870 the period of service required was reduced to 18 years. During the Second World War the medal was made available to officers provided they had served at least 12 of their 18 years service in the ranks.

Since its inception the medal has undergone a variety of changes, as detailed below:

William IV, 1830-31, Hanoverian coat-of-arms inescutcheon on obverse, large reverse letters, steel clip and small ring suspension, plain crimson ribbon approximately 25mm. wide.

William IV, 1831-37, similar to above but with a large ring or rectangular suspension and a plain crimson ribbon 32mm. wide.

Victoria, 1837-55, similar to above but without the inescutcheon.

Victoria, 1855-74, as above with a swivelling scroll suspension.

Victoria, 1874-1901, as above but with smaller reverse lettering.

Edward VII, 1901-10, obverse with bust of Edward VII in Field-Marshal's uniform.

George V, 1911-20, obverse with bust of George V in Field Marshal's uniform. In 1916 the ribbon was changed to crimson with white edges to more readily distinguish it from the otherwise similar ribbon of the Victoria Cross.

George V, 1920-30, as above but with a fixed suspender.

By a Royal Warrant of 23rd September 1930, the title of the medal was changed, becoming the Long Service and Good Conduct Medal (Military). This was accompanied by a change in design, most significantly the addition of a fixed rectangular suspension bar bearing a title according to the issue. British issues had the title, 'Regular Army', Commonwealth issues, a title as appropriate: 'India', 'Canada', 'Australia', etc.

George V, 1930-36, the first issue of the new style medal had on the obverse, the robed bust of George V.

George VI, 1937-48, head of George VI, obverse legend with 'INDIAE IMP.'

George VI 1949-53, as above but with obverse legend with 'FID. DEF.'

Elizabeth II, 1953-54, head of Elizabeth, obverse legend with 'BRIT OMN'.

Elizabeth II 1954-, as above, obverse legend with 'DEI GRATIA'.

A recipient of the earlier Army L.S. & G.C. Medal who after 1930 served a further qualifying period of 18 years was permitted to receive the new style L.S. & G.C.. Medal (Military).

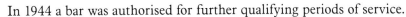

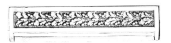

In 1944 a bar was authorised for further qualifying periods of service.

The medal is always found named. Those of William IV and the early issue of Victoria are impressed in large capitals as in the style of the Waterloo Medal, they are also dated with the year of discharge and award. The 1855 issue is found undated and impressed in the style of the Military General Service Medal. Later issued of Victoria are engraved in a variety of styles. Medals from Edward VII onwards are impressed in small capitals of various types. Medals to Europeans in the Indian Army are engraved in running script.

| Army L.S. & G.C. Medal | |
|---|---|
| William IV 1st issue | £425 |
| William IV 2nd issue | £400 |
| Victoria 1st issue | £150 |
| Victoria 2nd issue | £90 |
| Victoria 3rd issue | £35 |
| Edward VII | £25 |
| George V 1st issue | £20 |
| George V 2nd issue | £25 |

| L.S. & G.C. Medal (Military) | | |
|---|---|---|
| | Regular Army | Commonwealth |
| George V 3rd issue | £30 | £85 |
| George VI 1st issue | £25 | £85 |
| George VI 2nd issue | £25 | £85 |
| Elizabeth II 1st issue | £35 | £85 |
| Elizabeth II 2nd issue | £30 | £85 |

## 262 *Volunteer Officers' Decoration* 1892

An oval skeletal badge in silver and silver-gilt having the monarch's cypher in the centre. Issued with an ornate silver brooch bar which formed an integral part of the decoration. Usually with a hallmark on the badge reverse. Issued unnamed but often privately engraved.

This decoration was instituted by a Royal Warrant of 25th July 1892. The basic qualification was 20 years service as a commissioned officer in the Volunteer Force; time spent in the ranks counted half. Recipients were permitted to use the postnominal letters 'V.D.' Recipients of the Volunteer Decoration were not permitted to wear the Volunteer L.S. Medal. By a Royal Warrant of the 24th May 1894 the award of the Decoration was extended to the Volunteer Forces of India and the colonies. The qualifying period in India was 18 years. In 1906 provision was made for the Decoration to be available to officers of the Honourable Artillery Company, to be worn from the special H.A.C. ribbon; but in the event none were awarded.

In 1899 the Decoration was superseded in the colonies by the Colonial Auxiliary Forces Officers' Decoration and in India by the Indian Volunteer Forces Officers' Decoration. In the United Kingdom the award was replaced in 1908 by the Territorial Decoration.

| | |
|---|---|
| Victoria, British issue 'V.R.' cypher | £45 |
| Victoria, Colonial issue 'V.R.I. cypher | £150 |
| Edward VII | £60 |

## 263 *Volunteer Long Service Medal* 1894

A silver medal, issued named though Victorian issues may be found unnamed.

The medal was instituted in May 1894 the main qualification being 20 years service in the Volunteer Force. Officers who had served in the ranks but had not qualified for the V.D. were also eligible. A Royal Warrant of 13th June 1896 extended the award to the Volunteer Forces of the Empire, though with the introduction of the Colonial Auxiliary Forces Long Service Medal these awards were generally restricted to India. In 1906 the medal was made available to the Honourable Artillery Company and was worn from a distinctive ribbon—the racing colours of Edward VII. In the U.K. the Volunteer Long Service Medal was replaced in 1908 by the Territorial Force Efficiency Medal; in India it remained until 1930 when it was replaced by the Efficiency Medal bar 'India', in the rest of the Empire it was generally replaced in 1899 by the Colonial Auxiliary Force Long Service Medal.

| | |
|---|---|
| Victoria U.K. issue 'VICTORIA REGINA' | £25 |
| Victoria India and Colonial issue 'VICTORIA REGINA ET IMPERATRIX' | £45 |
| Edward VII U.K. issue 'EDWARDVS VII REX IMPERATOR' | £25 |
| Edward VII Colonial issue | £60 |
| Edward VII India issue 'EDWARDVS VII KAISAR-I-HIND' | £40 |
| George V India issue | £45 |

## 264 *Territorial Decoration* 1908

An oval skeletal badge in silver and silver-gilt issued unnamed but often privately engraved. Issued with an ornate silver brooch-bar which formed an integral part of the Decoration. There was no difference between a King Edward VII issue V.D. and T.D. other than the hallmark on the reverse.

The Decoration was instituted by a Royal Warrant dated 17th August 1908. It replaced the Volunteer Decoration and was in turn superseded by the Efficiency Decoration in 1930. The basic qualification was 20 years service as a commissioned officer in the Territorial Force, service in the ranks counted only half, service during the Great War counted double. Recipients were permitted to use the postnominal letters 'T.D.'.

| | |
|---|---|
| Edward VII | £70 |
| George V | £40 |

## 265 *Territorial Force Efficiency Medal* 1908

Silver medal with impressed naming. Established by Army Order 128 of June 1908 it replaced the Volunteer Long Service Medal in the U.K., in 1921 it was in turn replaced by the Territorial Efficiency Medal. Awarded to non-commissioned officers and men of the Territorial Force who had completed 12 years service and 12 trainings. Service by members of the Territorial Force during the Great War counted double. A bar was awarded for further 12 year periods of service. By an

Army Order of December 1919 the ribbon was changed from green with a central yellow stripe to one of green with yellow edges.

| | |
|---|---|
| Edward VII | £40 |
| George V | £20 |

### 266 *Territorial Efficiency Medal* 1921

Silver medal with impressed naming. When in 1921 the Territorial Force became the Territorial Army the change of title resulted in a change of reverse inscription. Having the same conditions of award as the earlier version it remained current until replaced by the Efficiency Medal in 1930.

| | |
|---|---|
| George V | £15 |

### 267 *Efficiency Decoration* 1930

An oval skeletal badge in silver and silver-gilt issued unnamed but often privately engraved. Post 1938 U.K. awards are dated on the reverse. As with the earlier Volunteer and Territorial Decorations, officers of the Honourable Artillery Company were permitted to wear the Decoration from a special H.A.C. ribbon.

The Efficiency Decoration was instituted by a Royal Warrant of 23rd September 1930. It replaced the Territorial Decoration in the U.K., the Indian Volunteer Decoration in India and the Colonial Auxiliary Force Decoration in the Colonies. Whilst the Decoration itself became uniform throughout the Empire the brooch bar was inscribed according to the area in which the service was performed. In Britain the Decoration was worn from the bar 'Territorial'; those for service overseas were worn from an appropriate bar: 'India', 'Canada', 'Fiji' etc. Recipients of the Efficiency Decoration bar Territorial are entitled to use the postnominal letters 'T.D.' those of the Empire/Commonwealth the letters 'E.D'.

The basic qualification was originally 20 years service. After 1949 this was changed to 12 years continuous commissioned service in the U.K. Territorial Army and in certain other specified forces, elsewhere in the Empire 20 years commissioned service not necessarily continuous was still required. Service in the ranks counted half, war service counted double. Bars were awarded for further 6 year periods of service, these being dated on the reverse.

In 1969 with the setting up of the Territorial and Army Volunteer Reserve, the Decoration with the bar 'Territorial' was replaced by one of 'T. & A.V.R.' and was worn from a ribbon of half blue and green with a central yellow stripe. In 1982 with another change in title the T. & A.V.R. became the Territorial Army again and the bar to the Decoration reverted to 'Territorial', however, the blue/yellow/green ribbon was retained.

| | *Territorial* | *India* | *Colonial* | *T. & A.V.R.* |
|---|---|---|---|---|
| George V | £50 | £65 | £100 | — |
| George VI 1st Type | £45 | £60 | £100 | — |
| George VI 2nd Type | £60 | — | £100 | — |
| Elizabeth II | £75 | — | £100 | £100 |

## 268 *Efficiency Medal* 1930

Silver medal issued named having a scroll bar suspension upon which is embossed the medals subsidiary title.

The Efficiency Medal was instituted by Royal Warrant on 17th October 1930. It replaced the Territorial Efficiency Medal, Militia L.S. & G.C. and Special Reserve L.S & G.C. in the U.K., the Volunteer Long Service Medal in India and the Colonial Auxiliary Forces Long Service Medal in the Colonies. The suspension bar was named according to the area the service was performed. In Britain the medal had the bar 'Territorial' or 'Militia' as appropriate, whilst overseas auxiliary bodies had the name of the country: 'India', Australia', etc.

The basic qualification was 12 years continuous service, with service in West Africa and war service counting double. For each subsequent 6 year period of service a bar was awarded. The medal with bar 'Militia' was issued to certain categories of the Supplementary Reserve until the formation of the Army Emergency Reserve in the early 1950s.

In 1969 following the formation of the Territorial and Army Volunteer Reserve the medal with the suspension bar 'Territorial' was replaced by one with 'T. & A.V.R.' and was worn from a ribbon of half blue and green with yellow edges. In 1982 with a further change in title the T. & A.V.R. became the Territorial Army again and the suspension bar reverted to 'Territorial', however the yellow/blue/green/yellow ribbon was retained. As with the earlier Volunteer Medal, T.F.E.M. & T.E.M., recipients who are members of the Honourable Artillery Company are permitted to wear the Efficiency Medal from a special H.A.C. ribbon.

| | Territorial | Militia | T. & A.V.R. | India | Colonial |
|---|---|---|---|---|---|
| George V | £20 | £35 | — | £35 | £50 |
| George VI 1st type | £18 | £35 | — | £40 | £60 |
| George VI 2nd type | £18 | £35 | — | — | £60 |
| Elizabeth II 1st type | £30 | — | — | — | £60 |
| Elizabeth II 2nd type | £30 | — | £75 | — | £60 |

## 269 *Army Emergency Reserve Decoration* 1952

An oval skeletal badge in silver and silver-gilt, dated on the reverse, issued unnamed but found privately engraved by the recipient. In form exactly as the Efficiency Decoration but having a top brooch bar bearing the words 'Army Emergency Reserve' and suspended from a ribbon of dark blue with a central yellow stripe.

Instituted on 17th November 1952, the Decoration was awarded for 12 years commissioned service in the Army Emergency Reserve. Officers commissioned in the Army Supplementary Reserve or Army Emergency Reserve of Officers between 8th August 1924 and 15th May 1948 who transferred to the Regular Army Reserve of Officers after 10 years service were also eligible. War service counted double, service in the ranks counted half. Recipients are permitted to use the postnominal letters 'E.R.D.' A bar, dated on the reverse was awarded for each further period of 6 years served.

The Army Emergency Reserve was abolished in 1967 following the formation of the Territorial and Army Volunteer Reserve.

| Elizabeth II | £140 |
|---|---|

### 270 *Efficiency Medal (Army Emergency Reserve)* 1953

Silver medal in the same form as the Efficiency Medal but with the scroll bar reading, 'Army Emergency Reserve' the ribbon being a dark blue with three central yellow stripes.

Instituted by a Royal Warrant of 1st September 1953, it was awarded for 12 years service in the ranks of the Army Emergency Reserve or for service in the Supplementary Reserve between 1924 and 1948 prior to transfering to the Army Emergency Reserve. War service counted as double. A bar was awarded for each further 6 year period served.

The Army Emergency Reserve was abolished in 1967 following the formation of the Territorial and Army Volunteer Reserve.

| | |
|---|---|
| Elizabeth II | £160 |

### 271 *Imperial Yeomanry Long Service and Good Conduct Medal* 1904

A silver medal with impressed naming in sans-serif capitals. Authorised by Army Order 211 in December 1904. Awarded to non-commissioned officers and men of the Imperial Yeomanry of good character and conduct serving on or after 9th November 1904, who completed 10 years service and attended 10 trainings. Service with Auxiliary Forces counted provided that the last five years of service was in the Yeomanry. Service in the Regular Army was not counted. Breaks in service of less than twelve months were permitted. The award became obsolete in 1908 when the Imperial Yeomanry became part of the Territorial Army. A total of 1674 awards were made.

| | |
|---|---|
| Edward VII | £160 |

### 272 *Militia Long Service and Good Conduct Medal* 1904

A silver medal with impressed naming in sans-serif capitals. Authorised by Army Order 211 of December 1904. Awarded to non-commissioned officers and men of the militia of good character and conduct, serving on or after 9th November 1904 who completed 18 years service and attended 15 trainings. Service with Auxiliary Forces was allowed to count provided the last five years of service was in the Militia. Service in the Regular Army was not counted. Breaks in service of less than twelve months were permitted. In 1930 the medal was replaced by the Efficiency Medal with bar 'Militia'. A total of 1587 awards were made of which only 141 were George V issues.

| | |
|---|---|
| Edward VII | £75 |
| George V | £140 |

## 273 *Special Reserve Long Service and Good Conduct Medal* 1908

A silver medal with impressed naming in sans-serif capitals. Authorised by Army Order 126 in June 1908. Awarded to non-commissioned officers and men of the Special Reserve of good character and conduct who completed 15 years service and attended 15 trainings. Service with the Militia, Imperial Yeomanry, Volunteer or Territorial Forces was allowed to count provided the last five years of service was in the Special Reserve. Breaks in service of less than twelve months were permitted. Service in the Regular Army was not counted. Irish Yeomanry could also be awarded the medal if they completed 10 years service with 10 trainings. The medal was issued until 1936. A total of 1078 awards were made.

| | |
|---|---|
| Edward VII | £120 |
| George V | £140 |

## 274 *Indian Army Long Service and Good Conduct Medal* 1848 (for Europeans of the Indian Army)

This medal was introduced by the Government of India in the General Order of 20th May 1848. It was awarded to European non-commissioned officers and soldiers of the Indian Army upon discharge after 21 years meritorious service.

The obverse of this silver medal has a trophy of arms around a shield bearing the arms of the Honourable East Indian Company. The reverse centre is engraved, giving the recipient's rank, name, regiment and date of award. The medal was worn from a plain crimson ribbon.

The award of this distinctive medal continued until 1873 after which Europeans in the Indian Army received the standard Army L.S. & G.C. Medal. In 1859 a batch of 100 medals struck from the wrong die was sent to India and issued. These aberrant medals have on the obverse the diademed 'young head' of Queen Victoria and on the reverse the legend, 'FOR/LONG/SERVICE/AND/GOOD CONDUCT' within two oak branches with a crown above and an anchor below.

| | |
|---|---|
| Victoria 1848 issue, H.E.I.C. arms | £400 |
| Victoria 1859 issue, anchor reverse | £450 |

## 275 *Indian Army Long Service and Good Conduct Medal* 1888

This medal was instituted in 1888 and was awarded to native Indian 'other ranks' for 20 years meritorious service.

The medal was struck in silver and was issued named in engraved lettering around the edge. The ribbon was originally a plain crimson but this changed in 1917 to one of crimson with white edges.

With the Independence of India in 1947 the medal was made obsolete.

| | |
|---|---|
| Victoria 1888 issue, lotus wreath reverse | £40 |
| Edward VII | £35 |
| George V Kaiser-i-Hind obverse | £25 |
| George V Indiae Imp. obverse | £30 |
| George VI | £25 |

## 276 *Indian Volunteer Forces Officers' Decoration* 1899

An oval skeletal badge in silver and silver-gilt generally hallmarked on the reverse, issued unnamed but mostly found engraved on the reverse. Issued with an ornate silver brooch bar which formed an integral part of the Decoration.

The Indian Volunteer Forces Decoration came into being through the Royal Warrant of 18th May 1899, however, its institution did not bring about a new design and the 'Volunteer Decoration' with V.R.I. cypher continued to be issued. The insignia did not change and become distinctive until 1903. The basic qualification was 18 years as a commissioned officer in the Indian Auxiliary Forces, with any service in the ranks counting half. The Decoration was replaced in 1930 by the Efficiency Decoration with brooch bar 'India'.

| | |
|---|---|
| Victoria | £150 |
| Edward VII | £200 |
| George V | £175 |

## 277 *Colonial Auxiliary Forces Officers' Decoration* 1899

An oval skeletal badge in silver and silver-gilt, hallmarked on the reverse, issued unnamed but often privately engraved on the reverse. Issued with an ornate silver brooch-bar which formed an integral part of the Decoration.

The Decoration was instituted by a Royal Warrant of 18th May 1899. The basic qualification was 20 years service as a commissioned officer in the reserve forces of the colonies (except India), whether in the Volunteers or Militia. Half the time spent in the ranks of such forces counted; service in W. Africa counted double, service during the Great War counted double. Recipients were permitted to use the postnominal letters 'V.D.' The Decoration was replaced by the Efficiency Decoration in 1930.

| | |
|---|---|
| Victoria | £200 |
| Edward VII | £175 |
| George V | £150 |

## 278 *Colonial Auxiliary Forces Long Service Medal* 1899

The medal was struck in silver and named in either impressed or engraved lettering around the edge.

Instituted by the Royal Warrant of 18th May 1899 the medal was awarded for 20 years service in the ranks of the Volunteers or Militia of the Dominions and Colonies with the exception of India. Officers who had served in the ranks who had not served sufficiently long to qualify for the Colonial Auxiliary Forces Officers' Decoration were also eligible. Service on the west coast of Africa counted double. Service by members of the Colonial Auxiliary Forces in the Great War also counted double. The Medal was replaced in 1930 by the Efficiency Medal with the appropriate Dominion or Colonial bar.

| | |
|---|---|
| Victoria | £90 |
| Edward VII | £75 |
| George V | £65 |

## 279 *Colonial Long Service and Good Conduct Medals* 1895

By the Royal Warrant of 31st May 1895 medals for Distinguished Conduct in the Field, Meritorious Service and Long Service and Good Conduct were instituted for award to Warrant Officers, non-commissioned officers and men of the Indian and Colonial Forces. The qualifications being as far as possible similar to those governing the award of comparable medals to United Kingdom forces.

The design of the Colonial L.S. & G.C. Medal was similar to that of the contemporary U.K. issue except that it had the name of the country on the reverse. The ribbon was the standard army L.S. & G. C. crimson but with a central stripe, the colour being dependant on the country:

Canada: white
Cape of Good Hope: orange
Commonwealth of Australia: dark green
Natal: yellow
New South Wales: dark blue
New Zealand: light green
Queensland: light blue
South Australia: no stripe
Tasmania: pink

The Australian state medals were replaced in 1902 by the 'Commonwealth of Australia' issue.

The medals were replaced in 1909 with the introduction of the Permanent Forces of the Empire Beyond the Seas L.S. & G.C. Medal.

from £350

## 280 *Permanent Forces of the Empire Beyond the Seas Long Service and Good Conduct Medal* 1909

The medal was instituted in 1909 and replaced the various colonial L.S. & G.C. Medals of 1895. In 1930 it was in turn replaced by the L.S. & G.C. Medal (Military) with the appropriate Dominion or Colony named suspender bar. The medal was awarded to non-commissioned officers and men of the Permanent Overseas Forces of the Empire for 18 years service with good conduct.

The medal was struck in silver and issued named, the naming indicating which particular colonial force.

| | |
|---|---|
| Edward VII | £250 |
| George V | £95 |

## 281 *Royal West African Frontier Force and King's African Rifles Long Service and Good Conduct Medals*

The medal to the West African Frontier Force was sanctioned in September 1903, that to the King's African Rifles in March 1907. They were awarded to native non-commissioned officers and men for 18 years service with good conduct.

The medal in silver was issued named. There were three reverse types: 'West African Frontier Force' (on medals issued prior to June 1928), 'Royal West African Frontier Force' (on medals issued thereafter) and 'King's African Rifles', The ribbon was crimson with a central green stripe slightly wider than those of the Colonial L.S. & G.C. Medals.

| | |
|---|---|
| Edward VII | £275 |
| George V | £250 |
| George VI 1st type | £220 |
| Elizabeth II | £600 |

George VI     £750

## 282 *Trans-Jordan Frontier Force Long Service and Good Conduct Medal* 1938

This rare medal was instituted by a Royal Warrant of 20th May 1938. It was awarded to non-commissioned officers and soldiers of the Trans-Jordan Frontier Force for 16 years service. Service in the Palestine Gendarmerie or Trans-Jordan Arab Legion also counted provided the soldier transferred to the Trans-Jordan Frontier Force without a break.

The medal was issued in silver and is believed to have been engraved around the edge. It was worn from a crimson ribbon having a central green stripe.

A total of 112 medals are known to have been awarded between 1939 and 1948.

## 283 *South African Permanent Force Long Service and Good Conduct Medal* 1939

This medal was instituted by a Royal Warrant of 29th December 1939. It was awarded to warrant officers, non-commissioned officers and other ranks of the South African Permanent Force for 18 years service. The conditions of award were basically the same as the U.K. medal. In form it is essentially the same except for the bilingual reverse and suspension bar. The medal was replaced in 1952 by the Union Medal.

| | |
|---|---|
| George VI 1st type | £150 |
| George VI 2nd type | £200 |

## 284 *South African Efficiency Medal* 1939

This medal was instituted by a Royal Warrant of 29th December 1939. It was awarded to warrant officers, non-commissioned officers and soldiers of the Coast Garrison and Active Citizen Forces of the Union of South Africa for 12 years service. But for the bilingual reverse and suspension bar the medal was essentially the same as the Efficiency Medal issued to the U.K. and colonial forces. The medal was replaced in 1952 by the John Chard Medal.

| | |
|---|---|
| George VI 1st type | £120 |
| George VI 2nd type | £120 |

## 285 *Canadian Forces Decoration* 1949

This decoration was instituted on 15th December 1949 as an award to officers and men of the Canadian Regular and Reserve Forces for 12 years service. Time spent in the Regular, Reserve or Auxiliary Forces of the British Commonwealth also counted provided that (a) the last five years had been spent in the Canadian Forces and (b) the service did not count towards another medal. A bar was awarded for each additional 10 year period served. The decoration replaced all the long service decorations and medals previously issued to Navy, Army or Air Force, regular, reserve or auxiliary. It was issued to those qualifying who joined a service after 1st September 1939, the first award being made in September 1951.

Two substantially different issues have been made. The George VI issue is in silver-gilt and has a suspension bar—'Canada' the reverse of which is engraved with the recipient's rank and name. The Elizabeth II issue is in gilded tombac, has no suspension bar and the recipient's rank and name are impressed upon the lower edge.

| | |
|---|---|
| George VI | £55 |
| Elizabeth II | £40 |

### 286 *Victoria Volunteer Long and Efficient Service Medal* 1881

The medal was first issued on 26th January 1881 although Royal permission for the award of this medal was not given until 21st April 1882. It was awarded to officers and men of the Victorian Volunteers for 15 years effective service. Awards to officers ceased in 1894 with the introduction of the Volunteer Officers' Decoration and existing officer recipients were no longer permitted to wear the medal. With the advent of the Volunteer Long Service Medal in 1896, the other ranks of the Victoria forces continued to receive the Victoria Volunteer Long and Efficient Service Medal for 15 years service. After a total of 20 years they were then eligible to receive the Volunteer Long Service Medal in which case the Victoria Volunteer L. & E.S.M. could not be worn. After the Federation of Australia in 1901 the medal became obsolete being replaced by the Commonwealth of Australia L.S. & G.C. or the Colonial Auxiliary Forces L.S. Medal as appropriate.

Two types of this silver medal were issued, both with impressed naming in capitals around the edge. Type 1, 1881-1893, obverse motto, 'AUT PACE AUT BELLO'. Medals to land forces are impressed with the recipient's name and the year. Type 2, 1894-1901, obverse motto, 'PRO DEO ET PATRIA'. Medals to land forces are additionally impressed with the recipient's rank and regiment. Medals to the Victorian Naval Forces (6 Type 1 medals known) have a variety of naming detail.

£500

### 287 *New Zealand Long and Efficient Service Medal* 1887

This silver medal was instituted on 1st January 1887 originally as an award to members of the New Zealand Volunteer and Permanent Militia Forces for 16 years continuous or 20 years non-continuous service. Active service in the Great War counted double. The medal became obsolete in 1931 following the introduction of the Long Service and Good Conduct Medal (Military) having the bar 'New Zealand'. The medal has the same obverse as the New Zealand Police Long Service and Good Conduct Medal, 1886 (No. 313). The ribbon was originally plain crimson but this was changed in 1917 to one of crimson with two white stripes in the centre. The medal was issued named

£150

### 288 *New Zealand Volunteer Service Medal* 1902

This medal was instituted in 1902 and became obsolete in 1912. It was awarded for 12 years service in the New Zealand Volunteer Forces. The medal was struck in silver, named on the edge and worn from a ribbon of plain drab khaki.

| | |
|---|---|
| Edward VII | £100 |

### 289 *New Zealand Territorial Service Medal* 1912

This medal, which is similar to the New Zealand Volunteer Service Medal was instituted in 1912. It was awarded to officers and men of the Territorial Force for 12 years service. The medal became obsolete in 1931 with the introduction of the Efficiency Medal with suspension bar 'New Zealand'. The medal is silver, named on the edge and was originally worn from a ribbon of plain khaki which was replaced in 1917 by one of dark khaki with crimson edges.

| | |
|---|---|
| George V | £100 |

### 290 *Medal for Long Service and Good Conduct (Ulster Defence Regiment)* 1982

The medal is struck in silver and is issued named around the edge. Instituted in 1982 it is awarded to soldiers of the Permanent Cadre of the Ulster Defence Regiment for 15 years irreproachable service since 1st April 1970. A bar is awarded for each additional 15 year period of service. Officers may also receive the medal provided that 12 of the 15 years had been served in the ranks. A bar may be awarded to an officer provided that 7 of the further 15 years had been served in the ranks. It may thus be seen that an officer receiving the medal is ineligible for the bar.

| | |
|---|---|
| Elizabeth II | £100 |

### 291 *Ulster Defence Regiment Medal* 1982

The medal is struck in silver and is issued named around the edge. It was instituted in 1982 and is awarded to part-time officers and men of the Ulster Defence Regiment for 12 years continuous service since 1st April 1970. A bar for additional 5 year periods of service is also awarded. If the recipient is an officer the postnominal letters 'U.D.' may be used.

| | |
|---|---|
| Elizabeth II | £80 |

## 292 *Cadet Forces Medal* 1950

A medal in cupro-nickel, issued named in impressed capitals for Army and Navy recipients and engraved to the R.A.F.

Instituted in February 1950, awarded to commissioned officers and adult non-commissioned officers for 12 years service in the Cadet Forces of the United Kingdom and Commonwealth. A bar is awarded for each additional 8 year period of service.

| | |
|---|---|
| George VI | £65 |
| Elizabeth II | £50 |

## 293 *Royal Observer Corps Medal* 1950

This medal is struck in cupro-nickel and is issued named around the edge. It was instituted by Royal Warrant on 31st January 1950 and is awarded to officers and observers who have completed 12 years satisfactory service. A bar is awarded for each additional 12 year period of service.

| | |
|---|---|
| George VI | £50 |
| Elizabeth II | £35 |

## 294 *Civil Defence Long Service Medal* 1961

Instituted by Royal Warrant in March 1961, produced in cupro-nickel and issued unnamed. Awarded for 15 years service in a variety of civil defence organisations. A bar was awarded for further 12 year periods of service. Two types of medal differing only in the reverse detail were issued. The General issue had on its reverse the initials of three of the major organisations originally eligible—Civil Defence, Auxiliary Fire Service and National Hospital Service Reserve. The Ulster issue had the initials of the Civil Defence, Auxiliary Fire and Rescue Service and Hospital Service Reserve. Other organisations eligible were the Warning and Monitoring Organisation and the Industrial Civil Defence Organisation. Time spent in certain wartime bodies (pre-1st June 1945) was also counted, they include the Warden Service, Decontamination Service, Ambulance Service, First Aid Service, Civil Nursing Reserve and Air Raid Warning Organisation to name a few. In 1963 the medal was made available to Civil Defence personnel in Gibraltar, Hong Kong and Malta. In 1968 the Civil Defence Corps and Auxiliary Fire Service were disbanded, however the medal was still awarded to those eligible in the remaining organisations.

| | |
|---|---|
| Elizabeth II | £20 |
| Elizabeth II, Ulster issue | £75 |

## 295 *Women's Voluntary Service Long Service Medal* 1961

The medal is produced in cupro-nickel and is issued unnamed. Authorised by Queen Elizabeth II in 1961. Awarded for 15 years service in the Womens Royal Voluntary Service (became 'Royal' in 1966) with bars for each additional 12 year period of service.

| | |
|---|---|
| | £15 |

## 296 *Voluntary Medical Service Medal*

A silver and cupro-nickel medal issued with the recipient's name on the edge. Awarded to members of the British Red Cross Society and the St. Andrew's Ambulance Association for 15 years active and efficient service. A bar is awarded for each additional 5 year period of service, bearing either a St George or St Andrew's Cross.

| | |
|---|---|
| Silver | £15 |
| Cupro-nickel | £12 |

## 297 *Service Medal of the Order of St. John* 1898

The medal was instituted in 1898 and is awarded for service to the Order and its establishments, the usual qualifying period being 15 years (12 years in respect of service in Australia, Canada, New Zealand and South Africa, and 10 years in other countries). A silver bar was instituted in 1911 for additional five year periods of service. Between 1911 and 1924 the bar issued had the inscription '5 YEARS SERVICE', in 1924 the bar design was changed to one having a Maltese Cross at the centre and a spray of St John's Wort to each side. Gilt bars were later introduced, each representing an additional 20 years service. The medal though remaining remarkably constant throughout its history has undergone a few changes. From 1898 to 1947 it was struck in silver, between 1947 and 1960 in a silvered base metal, between 1960 and 1966 in silvered cupro-nickel and from 1966 onwards in cupro-nickel rhodium plated. The suspension was originally by means of a ring but this changed in about 1913 to a straight bar suspender. In 1960 a new die was prepared, very similar to the earlier one but with the obverse bust slightly smaller and the lettering less ornate. Medals are named around the edge giving the medal reference number, recipient's rank, name and unit.

| | |
|---|---|
| Silver medal ring suspension | £45 |
| Silver medal straight bar suspension | £20 |
| Later issues (base metal) | £12 |

## 298 *Royal Air Force Long Service and Good Conduct Medal* 1919

A silver medal, named around the edge with engraved or impressed lettering usually in block capitals. Instituted by Royal Warrant of 1st July 1919 it was awarded to non-commissioned officers and men of the R.A.F. who had served 18 years with irreproachable conduct. In 1977 the period of service was reduced to 15 years. In 1944 provision was made for a bar for further 18 years (post 1977, 15 years) periods of service. Prior to 1945 it was possible for airmen with conduct below the required standard to be eligible if they had shown highly exemplary conduct against the enemy, displayed gallantry or rendered some special service in time of emergency. From 1944, service in the army and navy was allowed to count; prior to this only a maximum of 4 years service was counted provided there was no break of any more than 5 years. In 1947 officers became eligible to receive the medal provided they had served at least 12 years in the ranks. Officers awarded the medal could not then qualify for the bar.

| | |
|---|---|
| George V | £65 |
| George VI 1st type | £30 |
| George VI 2nd type | £40 |
| Elizabeth II 1st type | £40 |
| Elizabeth II 2nd type | £30 |

## 299 *Royal Air Force Levies (Iraq) Long Service and Good Conduct Medal* 1948

In form, the medal was the same as the standard R.A.F. L.S. & G.C. Medal but was in addition fitted with the bar, 'ROYAL AIR FORCE LEVIES IRAQ'. It was instituted in 1948 as an award to the locally commissioned officers and men of the R.A.F. Levies (Iraq) for 18 years service, the last 12 of which had to of an exemplary nature. A bar for further service was also instituted but in the event never issued.

The levies had their origin in the First World War, to be formally constituted as the 'Iraq Levies' in 1919. Following the war, the R.A.F. became responsible for maintaining peace and a British presence in Mesopotamia. This presence consisted of R.A.F. aircraft and armoured cars together with locally recruited Iraq Levies which came under R.A.F. control in 1922. In March 1943 this locally recruited force was renamed the Royal Air Force Levies (Iraq). The force survived until the British withdrawal from Iraq in 1955 when the Levies were disbanded.

Approximately 300 medals were issued.

| | |
|---|---|
| George VI | £525 |

### 300 *Air Efficiency Award* 1942

Instituted in September 1942 to reward 10 years long and efficient service in the Auxiliary and Volunteer Air Forces of the U.K. and Commonwealth. A bar is awarded for further 10 year periods of service. The medal was struck in silver and was issued with engraved naming around the edge.

| | |
|---|---|
| George VI 1st type | £65 |
| George VI 2nd type | £75 |
| Elizabeth II 1st type | £75 |
| Elizabeth II 2nd type | £65 |

### 301 *Police Long Service and Good Conduct Medal* 1951

The award was instituted by Royal Warrant dated 14th June 1951. The basic qualification is 22 years service in an approved police force of the United Kingdom, the medal being available to any full-time officer.

By a Royal Warrant of 1st May 1956 the award was extended to police forces of Australia, Papua New Guinea and Nauru. The Australian award was replaced in 1976 by the 'National Medal'.

The Police L.S. & .G.C. Medal is struck in cupro-nickel and issued named in small impressed capitals.

| | |
|---|---|
| George VI | £20 |
| Elizabeth II 1st type: 'Dei Gratia Regina' | £22 |
| Elizabeth II 2nd type: 'D:G: Regina' | £20 |

### 302 *Special Constabulary Long Service Medal* 1919

The medal is struck in bronze and is named around the edge in small impressed capitals. Three reverse types exist; that of the standard British issue has the reverse, 'FOR FAITHFUL SERVICE IN THE SPECIAL CONSTABULARY'. The medal was instituted on 30th August 1919 and was made available to all ranks of the Special Constabulary. The qualification required is 9 years unpaid service with 50 or more duties per year. During the two World Wars each year served with 50 or more duties counted triple. A bar, 'THE GREAT WAR 1914-18' was awarded with the medal to those who qualified during the war. A bar 'LONG SERVICE (year)' is awarded for additional 10 year periods of service, the year date varying according to the date of award.

A medal with the reverse, 'FOR FAITHFUL SERVICE IN THE ULSTER SPECIAL CONSTABULARY' was introduced in 1970 for 15 years service in the Ulster Special Constabulary. A third reverse type, 'FOR FAITHFUL SERVICE IN THE ROYAL ULSTER CONSTABULARY RESERVE' was introduced in 1982 for 15 years service in the R.U.C. Reserve. Service in the

Ulster Special Constabulary which had not been counted for the award of the Medal or bar, may be aggregated with service as a member of the R.U.C. Reserve.

| | |
|---|---|
| George V (Robed bust) | £8 |
| George V (Coinage head) | £8 |
| George VI 1st type | £8 |
| George VI 2nd type | £12 |
| Elizabeth II 1st type | £12 |
| Elizabeth II 2nd type | £8 |
| Elizabeth II 2nd type 'Ulster' reverse | £100 |
| Elizabeth II 2nd type 'R.U.C. Reserve' reverse | £100 |

## 303 *Royal Ulster Constabulary Service Medal* 1982

The medal is in cupo-nickel and is named around the edge. It was instituted in 1982 and awarded to members of the Royal Ulster Constabulary and Reserve for 18 months continuous service since 1st January 1971. Service in the R.U.C. & R.U.C. Reserve may be aggregated. An award of a British Order, decoration or medal (Queen's Gallantry Medal or above) or a Queen's Commendation in respect of service also qualifies the recipient for the Royal Ulster Constabulary Service Medal. Service curtailed by death, wounds or disability as a result of that service is also a qualification for the medal.

| | |
|---|---|
| Elizabeth II | £130 |

## 304 *Colonial Police Long Service Medal* 1934

A silver medal, named around the edge with details of rank, name and force. Instituted in 1934 and awarded to junior officers and below for 18 years full-time and exemplary service in a Colonial Police force. Bars were awarded for additional periods of service.

| | |
|---|---|
| George V | £75 |
| George VI 1st type | £45 |
| George VI 2nd type | £45 |
| Elizabeth II 1st type | £50 |
| Elizabeth II 2nd type | £50 |

## 305 *Colonial Special Constabulary Long Service Medal* 1957

A silver medal, named around the edge with details of rank, name and force. Instituted in 1957 and awarded for 9 years unpaid or 15 years paid service in a Colonial Special Constabulary. A bar was awarded for further 10 year periods of service.

| | |
|---|---|
| Elizabeth II 2nd type | £200 |

## 306 *Royal Canadian Mounted Police Long Service Medal* 1933

The medal is issued in silver and is engraved around the edge with the recipient's rank and name.

The medal was established by an Order-in-Council of 14th January 1933. It was awarded to all regular or retired members who had served 20 years in the force and were of good conduct. For further service bars were awarded: bronze for 25, silver for 30 and gold for 35 years service. Only one bar was permitted to be worn.

| | |
|---|---|
| George V (Coinage) | £500 |
| George V (Robes) | £500 |
| George VI (1st type) | £400 |
| George VI (2nd type) | £400 |
| Elizabeth II | £250 |

## 307 *Ceylon Police Long Service and Good Conduct Medal* 1925-1934

Instituted in 1925 and awarded to members of the Ceylon Police Force for 15 years active service. Time spent as an orderly, store-keeper etc. was not counted. The medal was silver, had a ring suspender and was worn from a ribbon of white, red, white with blue stripes bisecting the white. The medal was replaced in 1934 by the Colonial Police Long Service Medal.

| | |
|---|---|
| George V | £350 |

## 308 *Ceylon Police Long Service and Good Conduct Medal* 1950-1972

The medal was instituted in 1950 and was awarded for 18 years service with good conduct in the Ceylon Police Force. Bars were awarded for 25 & 30 years. The medal was struck in cupro-nickel, had a straight bar suspender and was named around the edge with the recipient's rank, name and date of award. Ribbon was dark blue edged in khaki, white and pale blue. The medal became obsolete when Ceylon (Sri Lanka) became a republic in 1972.

| | |
|---|---|
| George VI | £300 |
| Elizabeth II | £300 |

### 309 *Cyprus Military Police Long Service and Good Conduct Medal* 1929

This short-lived silver medal was instituted in October 1929 and superseded in 1934 by the Colonial Police Long Service Medal. Medals were issued named around the edge and worn from a ribbon of yellow, dark green, yellow in equal bands.

It was awarded to 'other ranks' of the Cyprus Military Police who (i) possessed three good conduct badges (ii) had served 6 years with good conduct following the award of the third badge (iii) had no more than four entries in the defaulters book (iv) had served a minimum of 15 years. Only active service counted. Officers who had risen through the ranks and whose service in the ranks complied with the conditions of award were also eligible.

A total of 7 officers and 54 men are known to have been awarded the medal.

| | |
|---|---|
| George V | £550 |

### 310 *Hong Kong Police Medal for Merit*

The medal was introduced in the mid 1800s and awarded for long, faithful or extraordinary service. The obverse had the bust of the monarch and legend, the reverse had the inscription in three lines within a laurel wreath and beaded circle 'HONG KONG/POLICE FORCE/FOR MERIT'. It was awarded in the following classes:
1st Class, gold medal with a watered red ribbon.
2nd Class, silver medal with a plain yellow ribbon.
3rd Class, bronze medal, ribbon yellow with a central black stripe.
4th Class, bronze medal, ribbon yellow with two central black stripes.
The class was in addition engraved on the reverse above the wreath. Medals were fitted with a ring suspender and were issued named around the edge. Two types are known for George V. Type 1 obverse: coinage head 'GEORGIVS V D:G: BRITT: OMN: REX F:D: IND: IMP:' reverse: as above Type. 2 obverse: crowned and robed bust 'GEORGIVS V. DG. BRITT. OMN. REX. ET. INDIAE. IMP.' reverse: inscription in four lines, 'HONG KONG/FOR/ MERIT/ POLICE FORCE'.

The above medals were replaced in April 1937 by the similar but short lived Hong Kong Police Silver Medal (1 awarded). In November 1937 this medal was replaced by the Colonial Police L.S. Medal.

A 5th Class of the Medal for Merit was that awarded to the Hong Kong Police Reserve. The medal was bronze and worn from a green ribbon having two central black stripes.

| | 1st Class | 2nd Class | 3rd Class | 4th Class | Reserve |
|---|---|---|---|---|---|
| Victoria | Rare | £500 | £400 | £250 | — |
| Edward VII | Rare | £450 | £350 | £225 | — |
| George V | (1) Rare | £400 | £300 | £200 | Rare |

### 311 *Hong Kong Royal Naval Dockyard Police Long Service Medal* 1920

The medal was instituted in 1920 as an award to members of the Hong Kong Royal Naval Dockyard Police for 15 years service.

A bronze-gilt medal, engraved on the edge with the recipient's rank and name. The obverse bears the monarch's head, the reverse has the words, 'ROYAL NAVAL/DOCKYARD/POLICE/HONG KONG' within a laurel wreath and beaded border. The medal has a swivel ring suspender and a ribbon 32mm wide, yellow with two 5mm wide royal blue stripes in the centre separated by a 4mm wide yellow stripe.

| | |
|---|---|
| George V | £250 |
| George VI 1st type | £250 |
| George VI 2nd type | £250 |

### 312 *Malta Police Long Service and Good Conduct Medal* 1921

A silver medal with engraved naming around the edge giving the recipient's number, rank and name. Instituted in 1921 and awarded to 'other ranks' of the Malta Police who had served 18 years with good conduct. Officers of Sub-Inspector and above who had risen from the ranks and had completed 18 years service in the ranks were also eligible. The medal was replaced by the Colonial Police Long Service Medal in 1934. A total of 99 medals are known to have been awarded.

| | |
|---|---|
| George V coinage head | £350 |
| George V robed bust | £450 |

### 313 *New Zealand Police Long Service and Good Conduct Medal* 1886

This medal was instituted in 1886 and was issued with relatively minor changes until 1976 when a new Police L.S. & G.C. Medal was introduced. The medal was awarded to members of the New Zealand Police Force for 14 years service, the last three of which had to be served without an entry in the defaulters sheet. Bars were introduced in 1959 and awarded for further 8 year periods of service, reduced in 1963 to 7 years, the total length of service being indicated on the bar e.g. '22 YEARS SERVICE', '30 YEARS SERVICE'. Since 1901 the medal was also awarded to Justice Department Prison Officers for long service. Several early 20th Century examples of the very similar New Zealand Long and Efficient Service Medal are also known to have been awarded to Prison Officers. The

medal was struck in silver and was always named on the edge, the usual details being number, rank, initials, surname followed by 'N.Z.P.' or 'N.Z. Police', some also with the year of award added. Medals issued prior to the mid-1940's are found excellently engraved, thereafter the quality deteriorated. From 1971 onwards the medals were impressed. The ribbon was originally a plain crimson but this changed towards the end of the Great War to one similar to the Permanent Forces of the Empire Beyond the Seas L.S. & G.C. Medal.

The 1886 medal was replaced by one instituted by a Royal Warrant of 8th September 1976. The obverse portrays the bust of Queen Elizabeth II, the reverse is remarkable in that it closely resembles the obverse of the earlier medal.

|  |  |
|---|---:|
|  | £120 |

314 *South Africa Police Good Service Medal* 1923

Silver medal, named around the edge. Instituted in 1923 and awarded to 'other ranks' for 18 years service with an irreproachable character or for service of a gallant or particularly distinguished nature. In the latter case the medal was worn with the bar 'MERIT-VERDIENSTE'. Three versions of the medal were issued: 1st type 1923-1932 obv. 'POLITIEDIENST' rev. 'VOOR TROUWE DIENST'; 2nd type 1932-1951 obv. 'POLIESIE DIENS' rev. 'VIR GETROUE DIENS'; 3rd type 1951-1963 obv. 'POLISIEDIENS' rev. 'VIR TROUE DIENS'. The medal was replaced in 1963 by the South African Medal for Faithful Service issued by the Republic of South Africa.

| | |
|---|---:|
| 1st type | £25 |
| 2nd type | £20 |
| 3rd type | £20 |

315 *South African Railways and Harbour Police Long Service and Good Conduct Medal* 1934-60

A silver medal, issued named around the edge and worn from a ribbon similar to that of the South African Police Good Service Medal 1923 but with the colours reversed, having a green central stripe, white stripes to either side and blue edges. The obverse legend was originally 'S.A.R. & H. POLICE, 'S.A.S.- EN HAWEPOLISIE but changed in about 1953 to read, 'S.A.S. POLISIE S.A.R.POLICE'. The medal was instituted in 1934 and awarded to members of the Railway and Harbour Police below commissioned rank for 18 years exemplary service. Also awarded for particularly gallant or distinguished service denoted by the bar 'MERIT—VERDIENSTE' (later 'VERDIENSTE— MERIT'). The medal was replaced in 1960 by the similar Railways Police Good Service Medal.

| | |
|---|---:|
| | £100 |

## 316 *Fire Brigade Long Service Medal* 1954

Instituted by Royal Warrant dated 1st June 1954. Awarded to all ranks of local authority fire brigades whether full or part-time, for 20 years service with good conduct.

Struck in cupro-nickel, issued named on the edge.

| | |
|---|---|
| Elizabeth II | £35 |

## 317 *Colonial Fire Brigade Long Service Medal* 1934

A silver medal, named around the edge giving details of rank, name and brigade. Instituted in 1934 and awarded to junior officers and below for 18 years full time and exemplary service in a Colonial Fire Brigade. Bars were awarded for additional periods of service.

| | |
|---|---|
| George V | £300 |
| George VI 1st type | £250 |
| George VI 2nd type | £250 |
| Elizabeth II 1st type | £250 |
| Elizabeth II 2nd type | £250 |

## 318 *Ceylon Fire Brigade Long Service and Good Conduct Medal* 1950-1972

Very similar to the Ceylon Police L.S. & G.C. Medal 1950 but with the reverse inscription 'CEYLON FIRE SERVICES'. The ribbon differs by having an additional thin central white stripe passing through the dark blue.

| | |
|---|---|
| George VI | £350 |
| Elizabeth II | £350 |

## 319 *Colonial Prison Service Long Service Medal* 1955

A silver medal, named around the edge giving details of the recipient, worn from a ribbon similar to that of the Colonial Fire Brigade L.S. Medal but with a single central white stripe instead of three. It was instituted in October 1955 and awarded to the ranks of Assistant Superintendant and below for 18 years exemplary service in a Colonial Prison Service. Bars were awarded for further periods of service.

| | |
|---|---|
| Elizabeth II | £250 |

### 320 *South Africa Prisons Good Service Medal* 1922-1966

Silver medal, issued named around the edge and worn from the same ribbon as the South Africa Police Good Service Medal. Instituted in September 1922 and awarded to Prison Officers for 18 years service with an irreproachable character or for service of a particularly gallant or distinguished nature. In the latter case the medal was awarded with the bar, 'MERIT-VERDIENSTE'. Two types were issued: 1st type 1922-1959 obv. 'PRISON SERVICE—GEVANGENIS DIENST' rev 'FOR FAITHFUL SERVICE—VOOR TROUWE DIENST' 2nd type 1959-1965 obv. 'DEPARTEMENT VAN GEVANGENISSE—PRISONS DEPARTMENT' rev. 'VIR TROUE DIENS—FOR FAITHFUL SERVICE'. The medal was replaced in 1966 by the Prisons Department Faithful Service Medal issued by the Republic of South Africa.

| | |
|---|---|
| 1st type | £35 |
| 2nd type | £35 |

# *Medals for Life Saving*

Prior to the institution of the Govenment's first official life-saving medals: the Sea Gallantry Medal in 1854 and the Albert Medal in 1877, the only awards were those presented by the various life-saving societies from as far back as the latter part of the eighteenth century. These private awards are keenly sought after by collectors, with many of the citations being available.

### 321 *Royal National Lifeboat Institution Medals*

The Institution was founded on the 4th March 1824. Medals have been awarded by the Institution since 1825 in gold, silver and since 1917, in bronze to 'persons whose humane and intrepid exertions in saving life from shipwreck on our coasts are deemed, sufficiently conspicuous to merit honourable distinction'. Five obverse and two reverse types have been issued. The first medals issued in 1825 bore the head of George IV, medals with this obverse were issued throughout the reign of William IV and into that of Victoria. In 1862 medals were issued with the head of Victoria and thereafter with the effigies of Edward VII and George V. With the accession of George VI it was not possible for the Institution to use the King's head on its medals, therefore from that time medals were struck with the head of the Institutions founder, Sir William Hillary. The medal reverse for all

issues except those of Edward VII depict a man being rescued by three men in a boat, with the legend, 'LET NOT THE SEA SWALLOW ME UP'. Edward VII issues portray the seated figure of Hope adjusting the lifejacket of a lifeboatman. The medal is worn from a plain garter-blue ribbon, originally by means of a two-ring fitting, the medal being pierced, later ones had a ring soldered onto the medal, then during the 1850s the 'double dolphin' suspension was introduced. Medals are issued engraved around the edge with the recipients name and the date the award was voted. The bar 'Second Service', 'Third Service' etc. is awarded for further acts of gallantry, the bar having the voted date on the reverse.

|  | Gold | Silver | Bronze |
|---|---|---|---|
| George IV | £1200 | £200 | — |
| Victoria | £1200 | £225 | — |
| Edward VII | £1600 | £560 | — |
| George V | £1300 | £350 | £300 |
| Sir William Hillary | £1300 | £200 | £175 |

## 322 *Liverpool Shipwreck and Humane Society Medals*

The Society was formed in 1839 originally to administer funds raised to assist those who suffered and reward those who distinguished themselves in saving life as a result of a hurricane that swept the Irish Channel in January 1839.

Medals awarded by the Society may be divided into three main categories.
1. For Saving Life at Sea. 2. For Saving Life from Fire 3. For Saving Life on Land.

## *1. Liverpool Shipwreck and Humane Society's Marine Medals*

The Society's first medal dating from about 1844 was a medallion 56mm in diameter named around the edge but not intended for wear. This was replaced in about 1871 by an oval silver medal with the distinctive 'Liver Bird' suspension, worn from a plain dark blue ribbon. The medal was engraved on the reverse and the edge with details of the recipient's name, ship and date. In 1874 the oval medal was in turn replaced by a circular medal, similar to the 1st type medallion but only 38mm diameter and intended for wear.

*Marine Medal 2nd type*

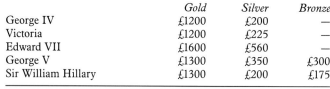

*Marine Medal 3rd type*

These medals are issued in gold, silver or bronze, worn from a plain dark blue ribbon attached to a scroll suspender. Medals are engraved around the edge. For further acts of gallantry in saving life, plain bars are issued having the date of award engraved upon them.

Two other medals for saving life at sea issued by the Society from separate funds were the Camp and Villaverde Medal and Bramley-Moore Medal. The medals are very similar to the 3rd type Marine Medal and differ only in the reverse legend, 'CAMP AND VILLAVERDE MEDAL FOR SAVING LIFE AT SEA 1847' and BRAMLEY-MOORE MEDAL FOR SAVING LIFE AT SEA 1872' in place of the standard title of the Society.

A medal was also issued to the next-of-kin of those who died in attempting to save life. These 'In Memoriam' medals were similar to the 1st type Marine Medallion in silver, being framed and glazed, with details engraved around the edge of the framing.

*Fire Medal*          *General Medal*

*Marine Medal 3rd type*

## 2. Liverpool Shipwreck and Humane Society's Fire Medal

Instituted in 1882 and awarded in gold, silver and bronze for bravery in saving life from fire. The medal reverse is the same as that of the 3rd type Marine Medal, the obverse depicts a fireman descending the stairs of a burning house carrying three children to their kneeling mother who has her arms outstretched to receive them. The medal is worn from a scarlet ribbon attached to a scroll suspender. For further acts of bravery, plain bars engraved with the date of award are given.

## 3. Liverpool Shipwreck and Humane Society's General Medal

Instituted in 1894 and awarded in gold, silver and bronze for saving life on land. The reverse is the same as the 3rd type Marine Medal, the obverse has a cross

pattée with a wreathed crown in the centre and the circumscription 'FOR BRAVERY IN SAVING LIFE 1894'. The ribbon is five equal stripes, three red and two white. For subsequent acts, plain bars engraved with the date of award are given.

## 4. Liverpool Shipwreck and Humane Society's Swimming Medal

An ornate silver medal with double dolphin suspender. Engraved on the reverse with the recipient's name and date, worn from a ribbon of five equal stripes, three blue and two white. Presented by the Society to encourage competition with the view of teaching the art of swimming with the object of saving life.

| | Gold | Silver | Bronze |
|---|---|---|---|
| 1.  Marine Medals | | | |
|     Marine Medal 1st type, medallion | £2000 | £280 | — |
|     Marine Medal 2nd type, oval | — | £375 | — |
|     Marine Medal 3rd type, circular | £1200 | £55★ | £40★ |
|     Camp and Villaverde Medal | | — (37) £400 | (8) £350 |
|     Bramley-Moore Medal | (1) Rare | (22) £450 | (17) £350 |
|     'In Memorian' Medallion | | — (19) £400 | |
| 2.  Fire Medal | (2) Rare | £200 | £120 |
| 3.  General Medal | (1) Rare | £75 | £45 |
| 4.  Swimming Medal | — | £60 | — |

*Medals awarded for High Seas rescues command a premium of 50-80%.

323 ## Shipwrecked Fishermen and Mariners Royal Benevolent Society Medals

The Society was founded in 1839 with the object of providing aid to shipwrecked mariners and to the dependants of those mariners lost at sea. Since 1851 medals in gold and silver have been awarded by the Society for 'heroic or praiseworthy exertions to save life from shipwreck etc.'. Medals are engraved on the edge with the recipient's name and date of award. The ribbon is navy blue 25mm. wide. Earlier medals had a straight bar suspension which was altered to a double dolphin suspension in the 1850s.

| | |
|---|---|
| Gold | £1200 |
| Silver | £150 |

## 324 *C.Q.D. Medal*

On 21st January 1909 in heavy fog the Italian Steamship 'Florida' came into collision with the White Star Liner 'Republic'. In response to a C.Q.D. signal ('Come Quick Danger'—a forerunner of S.O.S.) by wireless the Liner 'Baltic' went to the rescue. Passengers and crew of the 'Republic' were transferred to the 'Florida', then together with passengers of the 'Florida' transferred to the 'Baltic'. The 'Republic' later sank. A medal struck in silver and worn from a blue ribbon was awarded to officers and crews of all three ships by the saloon passengers of the 'Baltic' and 'Republic' for their exertions in rescuing over 1700 lives.

£95

## 325 *Life Saving Medal of the Order of St John*

Instituted on 15th December 1874 and awarded for gallantry in saving life. Issued in silver and bronze, and since 1907 in gold. The 1st type medal issued 1874-1888 had on the obverse the cross of the Order without embellishment, with the legend, 'AWARDED BY THE ORDER OF ST JOHN OF JERUSALEM IN ENGLAND'. The ribbon was an unwatered black bearing the cross of the Order embroidered in white. The 2nd type medal issued since 1888 has on the obverse the cross of the Order with embellishments and the legend, 'FOR SERVICE IN THE CAUSE OF HUMANITY'. The ribbon, until 1950 was a plain watered black, since 1950 the ribbon has been a watered black with white inner and red outer stripes at the edge. All medals were issued named around the edge. Bars for further acts were instituted in 1892.

|  | Gold | Silver | Bronze |
|---|---|---|---|
| 1st type | — | £450 | £225 |
| 2nd type | £1500 | £300 | £150 |

## 326 *Medals of the Society of the Protection of Life from Fire*

The Society was founded in 1836 and awarded medals, watches, certificates and money to those saving life from fire. Several types of medal may be discerned: Type 1, issued in 1836 was in silver, 52mm. dia. and fitted with a swivelling ring suspender and worn from a scarlet ribbon. The obverse portrays an eye with the word 'VIGILO' below and the circumscription, 'SOCIETY FOR THE PROTECTION OF LIFE FROM FIRE 1836'. The reverse engraved with the recipient's name, details of the action and date within an oak wreath. Type 2 introduced in about 1844 was similar but had 'ROYAL' added to the obverse title and the year changed to 1844. Type 3 introduced in the early 1850s was 45mm. diameter and struck in silver and bronze. The obverse portrays a man carrying a woman over his shoulder from a fire; on the reverse the recipient's details engraved enclosed by a crowned wreath and the title of Society with the date '1843'. Royal Patronage ended with the death of Queen Victoria, and a new medal was then produced. The 4th type 41mm. in diameter was struck in silver and bronze and fitted with a straight bar suspender. The obverse portrays a man rescuing a woman and two children from a fire; the reverse has the words 'DUTY AND HONOR' within an oak wreath with the new title of the Society and the year '1843' on the outside. The recipient's details were engraved on the edge.

|  | Silver | Bronze |
|---|---|---|
| Type 1 & 2 | £450 | — |
| Type 3 | £220 | £120 |
| Type 4 | £220 | £120 |

## 327 *Royal Humane Society Medals*

The Society was founded in 1774 originally to promote the art of resuscitation. Medals are awarded by the Society in gold, silver and bronze to those who, at risk to themselves save or attempt to save others. The first medals issued were gold and silver medallions, 51mm. diameter, with the reverse legend outside a wreath reading, 'HOC PRETIVM CIVE SERVATO TVLIT' (He has obtained this reward for saving the life of a citizen), with the name of the recipient and details of the award engraved within the wreath. Later, medallions were also struck in bronze. Where the rescue attempt was unsuccessful the reverse legend outside the wreath was omitted. Although not designed for wear many of these medallions were fitted with a suspension.

In 1869 permission was given for the Society's medals to be worn on the right breast. Concurrently the diameter of the medal was reduced to 38mm., the medal fitted with a scroll suspension and worn from a navy blue ribbon. Accompanying the change in size was a minor modification in design. The reverse of the small 'unsuccessful' medal had within the wreath the legend, 'VIT. PERIC. EXPOS. D.D. SOC. REG. HVM' (The Royal Humane Society presented this gift, his life having been exposed to danger). The reverse of the small 'successful' medal had within the wreath the legend, 'VIT. OB. SERV. D.D. SOC. REG. HVM' (The Royal Humane Society presented this gift for saving life), whilst retaining the legend outside the wreath. Details of the recipient and award were engraved on the edge. In 1921 the ribbon of the silver medal was changed to navy blue with a thin central yellow stripe and a thin white stripe at each edge; that of the bronze medal remained unchanged. Scroll type bars with an oval plaque bearing the initials R.H.S. were awarded for further acts of bravery.

The Stanhope Gold Medal was instituted in 1873 in memory of Capt. C.S.S. Stanhope R.N. and is awarded annually by the Society, to the person performing the bravest act of life-saving during the year. The 1st type Stanhope Medal was similar to the Society's silver medal and differed only by the addition of a suspension bar reading 'STANHOPE MEDAL' with the year of award above. In the 1930s this bar was removed and apart from being gold the award was identical to the other medals. In 1921 the ribbon of the Stanhope Gold Medal was changed from navy blue to one of blue with yellow and black edges.

| | | Gold | Silver | Bronze |
|---|---|---|---|---|
| Stanhope Gold Medal | | | | £2000 |
| Large Medal | successful | rare | £180 | £65 |
| | unsuccessful | — | £280 | £95 |
| Small Medal | successful | — | £100 | £40 |
| | unsuccessful | — | £110 | £40 |

## 328 *Lloyd's Medal for Saving Life at Sea*

The medal was instituted in 1836 as an award to those who, by their exertions contributed to the saving of life at sea. When first instituted the medal was 73mm. in diameter and not intended for wear. In 1896 the diameter was reduced to 36mm., the medal was fitted with a ring suspension and was worn from a ribbon of blue with stripes of white, red, white in the centre. The recipient's name, ship and date of deed were engraved on the edge. The design of both large and small medals is similar, with the obverse depicting the rescue of Ulysses by Leucothöe and the legend, 'LEUCOTHÖE NAUFRAGO SUCCURRIT'.

| | | |
|---|---|---|
| 1st type large | silver | £400 |
| | bronze | £300 |
| 2nd type small | gold | rare |
| | silver | £250 |
| | bronze | £150 |

## 329 *Lloyd's Medal for Meritorious Service*

Instituted by the Committee of Lloyds in 1893 and awarded to officers and men for extraordinary services in the preservation of vessels and cargoes from peril.

The 1st type medal issued in 1893 was a nine pointed bronze star, obverse with the arms of Lloyds, worn from a ribbon of red with blue bands towards the edge.

The 2nd type introduced in 1900 was an oval silver medal worn from a blue ribbon with broad white bands towards the edge. The medal reverse was engraved with the recipient's name, ship and date.

In 1913 a 3rd type was introduced, this being a circular medal struck in both silver and bronze, with a shield bearing the Arms of Lloyds on the obverse.

The 4th and current type dates from 1936 and has on the obverse the full Arms of Lloyds with supporters, crest and motto. Both the 3rd and 4th types are named on the edge.

| | *Silver* | *Bronze* |
|---|---|---|
| Star 1st type | — | £125 |
| Oval 1st type | £400 | — |
| Circular 3rd type | £300 | £270 |
| Circular 4th type | £300 | £270 |

## 330 *Lloyd's Medal for Services to Lloyds*

Instituted by the Lloyds Committee in November 1913 as a reward for services of a general nature rendered to Lloyds. Issued in gold and silver. The obverse depicts Neptune in a chariot drawn by four horses, the reverse has a wreath of oak leaves enclosing a scroll enscribed 'FOR SERVICES TO LLOYDS'. The medal is named around the edge. The ribbon is the same as for the Lloyds M.S.M.

| | |
|---|---|
| Gold (14) | £1600 |
| Silver (10) | £600 |

## 331 *Lloyd's Medal for Bravery at Sea*

The medal was instituted by the Committee of Lloyds in December 1940 for award to officers and men of the Merchant Navy and Fishing Fleets for exceptional bravery at sea in time of war. The medal is struck in silver and named on the edge with the recipient's name, the date of deed and ship. The ribbon is white with broad blue side stripes.

| | |
|---|---|
| | £650 |

## 332 *Hundred of Salford Humane Society Medal*

This, one of the local Humane Societies, was originally founded in 1789 and revived in 1824. Until 1922 the Society issued medals for life-saving in the Salford and Manchester area. The 1st type medal was circular and issued in silver and bronze. The design changed in about 1884 to the distinctive cross shaped medal issued in both gold and silver. Both types were named on the reverse and were worn from a plain dark blue ribbon.

| | | |
|---|---|---|
| 1st type circular | silver | £120 |
| | bronze | £100 |
| 2nd type cross | gold | rare |
| | silver | £90 |

### 333 *Hartley Colliery Medal*

The medal was awarded to those involved in the rescue operations at Hartley Colliery, Northumberland, following a disastrous accident on 10th January 1862. Despite the strenuous efforts of the rescuers, a total of 204 miners perished in the disaster. One gold and thirty-seven silver medals were presented.

| | |
|---|---|
| Silver | £300 |

### 334 *Drummond Castle Medal* 1896

This special commemorative silver medal was bestowed by Queen Victoria upon certain inhabitants of Brest, Ushant and Molène for their generosity, humanity and kindness in connection with the loss of the S.S. 'Drummond Castle'. The ship struck a reef off Ushant on 16th June 1896 and of the 143 passengers and 104 officers and crew only 3 escaped. A total of 252 medals were issued to those who assisted in the rescue of the living and the recovery and burial of the dead. The silver medal was issued unnamed and worn from a crimson ribbon

| | |
|---|---|
| | £135 |

## 335 *R.M.S. Carpathia, S.S. Titanic Medal*

On the night of 14th April 1912, in one of the greatest disasters at sea, the White Star liner 'Titanic' on her maiden voyage, struck an iceberg in the N. Atlantic and sank within three hours with the loss of 1490 lives. The survivors, 711 in all, were rescued by the 'Carpathia'. It was in gratitude to the officers and crew of the 'Carpathia' that the survivors had a medal struck. The medal was issued in gold, silver and bronze according to the rank of the recipient and was worn from a dark blue ribbon.

| | |
|---|---|
| Gold | £1600 |
| Silver | £400 |
| Bronze | £250 |

## 336 *Tayleur Fund Medal*

Medals for saving life from shipwreck were struck in silver with details of the award engraved on the reverse and worn from a dark blue ribbon. The Fund responsible for the medal originated from surplus funds raised for the benefit of survivors of the emigrant ship 'Tayleur' which was wrecked in Bantry Bay in January 1854. In Dec. 1913 the Fund was transferred to the R.N.L.I. and no further medals were issued.

| | |
|---|---|
| | £300 |

# *Bibliography*

| | |
|---|---|
| Abbot P. E. and Tamplin J. M. A. | *British Gallantry Awards,* 1981 |
| Alexander E. G. M., Barron G. K. B. and Bateman A. J. | *South African Orders, Decorations and Medals,* 1986 |
| Biddulph, Major H. | *Early Indian Campaigns and the Decorations Awarded for them,* 1913 |
| Blatherwick, Surg. Cmdr. F. J. | *Canadian Orders, Decorations and Medals,* 1983 |
| Carter T. | *War Medals of the British Army,* 1893 |
| Cole H. N. | *Coronation and Royal Commemorative Medals 1887-1977,* 1977 |
| Douglas-Morris, Captain K. J. | *The Naval General Service Medal Roll, 1793-1840,* 1982 |
| Douglas-Morris, Captain K. J. | *Naval Medals 1793-1856,* 1987 |
| Everson G. R. | *The South Africa 1853 Medal Roll,* 1978 |
| Fevyer W. H. and Wilson J. W. | *The China War Medal 1900 to the Royal Navy and the Royal Marines,* 1985 |
| Fevyer W. H. and Wilson J. W. | *The Queen's South Africa Medal to the Royal Navy and the Royal Marines,* 1983 |
| Foster Colonel Kingsley O. N. | *The Military General Service Medal Roll 1793-1814,* 1947 |
| Gordon, Major L. L. | *British Orders and Awards,* 1959 |
| Gordon, Major L. L. (Joslin E. C. editor) | *British Battles and Medals,* 1979 |
| Gould R. W. and Douglas-Morris, Captain K. J. | *The Army of India Medal Roll 1799-1826,* 1974 |
| Hailes, Colonel D. A. | *Naval General Service Medal Roll 1793-1840* |
| Hastings Irwin D. | *War Medals and Decorations,* 1910 |
| Hibbard M. G. | *Boer War Tribute Medals,* 1982 |
| Jocelyn A. | *Awards of Honour,* 1956 |
| Joslin E. C. | *Spinks Catalogue of British and associated Orders, Decorations and Medals,* 1983 |
| Joslin E. C., Litherland A. R. and Simpkin B. T. | *British Battles and Medals,* 1988 |
| Mackinnon J. P. and Shadbolt S. H. | *The South Africa Campaign of 1879,* 1882 |
| Magor R. B. | *African General Service Medals* |
| Mayo J. H. | *Medals and Decorations of the British Army and Navy,* 1897 |
| McInnes I. | *The Meritorious Service Medal to Naval Forces,* 1983 |
| McInnes I. | *The Meritorious Service Medal to Aerial Forces,* 1984 |
| | *The Medals Yearbook A-Z of Medals* |

| | |
|---|---|
| Milford Haven, Admiral The Marquis of | *British Naval Medals,* 1919 |
| Monick S. | *South African Military Awards 1912-1987,* 1988 |
| Monick S. | *Awards of the South African Uniformed Public Services 1922-1987,* 1988 |
| | |
| Parritt, Colonel B. A. H. | *Red with Two Blue Stripes,* 1974 |
| Payne A. A. | *A Handbook of British and Foreign Orders, War Medals and Decorations awarded to the Army and Navy,* 1911 |
| | |
| Sainsbury, Major J. D. | *For Gallantry in the Performance of Military Duty,* 1980 |
| Santamas M. L. | *British Awards in Cyprus,* 1986 |
| Scarlett R. J. | *The Naval Good Shooting Medal 1903-1914,* 1990 |
| | |
| Tamplin J. M. A. | *The Army Emergency Reserve Decoration and The Efficiency Medal (Army Emergency Reserve),* 1989 |
| Tamplin J. M. A. | *The Colonial Auxiliary Forces Long Service Medal,* 1984 |
| Tamplin J. M. A. | *The Colonial Auxiliary Forces Officers' Decoration, The Indian Volunteer Forces Officers' Decoration,* 1981 |
| Tamplin J. M. A. | *The Efficiency Decoration Instituted 1930,* 1987 |
| Tamplin J. M. A. | *The Imperial Yeomanry Long Service and Good Conduct Medal,* 1978 |
| Tamplin J. M. A. | *The Militia Long Service and Good Conduct Medal,* 1979 |
| Tamplin J. M. A. | *The Special Reserve Long Service and Good Conduct Medal,* 1979 |
| Tamplin J. M. A. | *The Territorial Decoration 1908-1930,* 1983 |
| Tamplin J. M. A. | *The Territorial Force Efficiency Medal 1908-1921 and The Territorial Efficiency Medal 1922-1930,* 1985 |
| Tamplin J. M. A. | *The Volunteer Long Service Medal,* 1980 |
| Tamplin J. M. A. | *The Volunteer Officers' Decoration,* 1980 |
| Tancred G. | *Historial Record of Medals and Honorary Distinctions* 1891 |
| Taprell-Dorling H. | *Ribbons and Medals,* various editions |
| Tozer C. W. | *The Insignia and Medals of the Grand Priory of the Most Venerable Order of the Hospital of St. John of Jerusalem,* 1975 |
| | |
| Whitaker, Captain A. E. | *British War Medals and Decorations,* 1890 |
| Williams R. D. | *The Victoria Volunteer Long and Efficient Service Medal and The Volunteer Officers' Decoration,* 1976 |
| | |
| Wilson, Sir A. and McEwen, Capt. J. H. F. | *Gallantry,* 1939 |

The Journal of the Orders and Medals Research Society
The Life Saving Awards Research Journal
The London Stamp Exchange Medal List
The Medal Collector
The Numismatic Circular
The Orders and Medals Research Society
   The Miscellany of Honours
The Seaby Bulletin

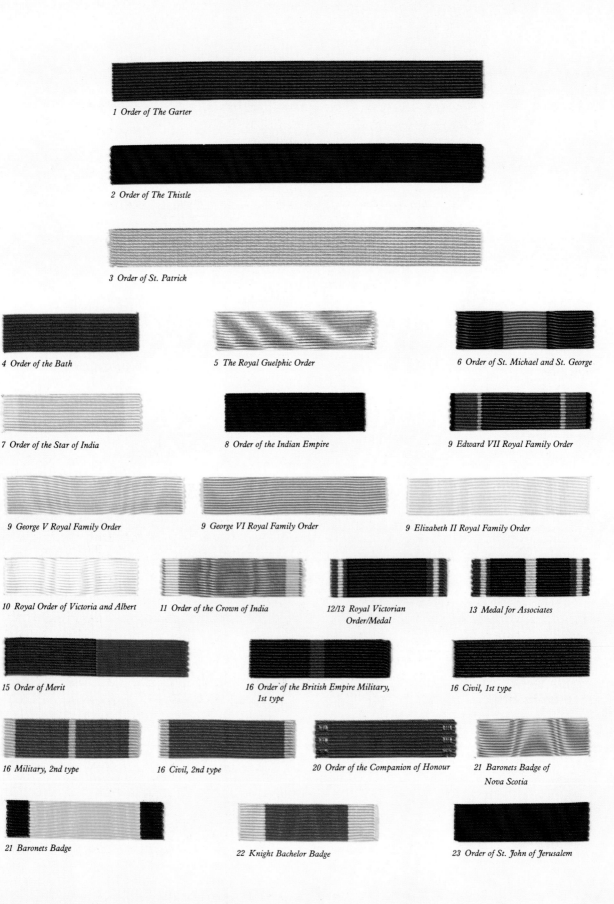

*1 Order of The Garter*

*2 Order of The Thistle*

*3 Order of St. Patrick*

*4 Order of the Bath*

*5 The Royal Guelphic Order*

*6 Order of St. Michael and St. George*

*7 Order of the Star of India*

*8 Order of the Indian Empire*

*9 Edward VII Royal Family Order*

*9 George V Royal Family Order*

*9 George VI Royal Family Order*

*9 Elizabeth II Royal Family Order*

*10 Royal Order of Victoria and Albert*

*11 Order of the Crown of India*

*12/13 Royal Victorian
Order/Medal*

*13 Medal for Associates*

*15 Order of Merit*

*16 Order of the British Empire Military,
1st type*

*16 Civil, 1st type*

*16 Military, 2nd type*

*16 Civil, 2nd type*

*20 Order of the Companion of Honour*

*21 Baronets Badge of
Nova Scotia*

*21 Baronets Badge*

*22 Knight Bachelor Badge*

*23 Order of St. John of Jerusalem*

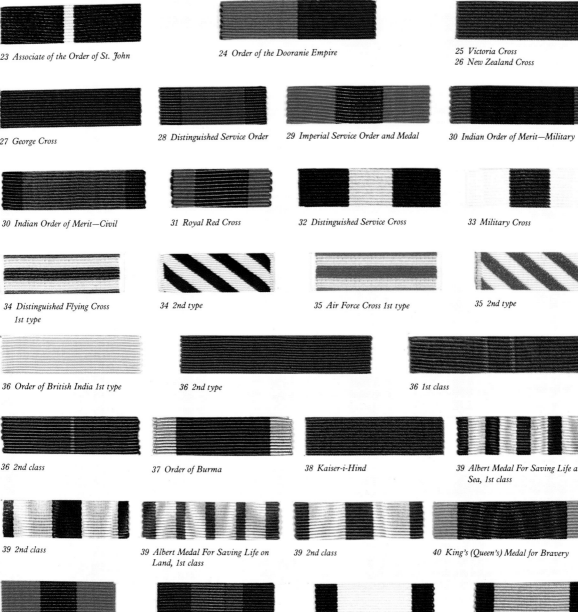

*23 Associate of the Order of St. John*

*24 Order of the Dooranie Empire*

*25 Victoria Cross*
*26 New Zealand Cross*

*27 George Cross*

*28 Distinguished Service Order*

*29 Imperial Service Order and Medal*

*30 Indian Order of Merit—Military*

*30 Indian Order of Merit—Civil*

*31 Royal Red Cross*

*32 Distinguished Service Cross*

*33 Military Cross*

*34 Distinguished Flying Cross 1st type*

*34 2nd type*

*35 Air Force Cross 1st type*

*35 2nd type*

*36 Order of British India 1st type*

*36 2nd type*

*36 1st class*

*36 2nd class*

*37 Order of Burma*

*38 Kaiser-i-Hind*

*39 Albert Medal For Saving Life at Sea, 1st class*

*39 2nd class*

*39 Albert Medal For Saving Life on Land, 1st class*

*39 2nd class*

*40 King's (Queen's) Medal for Bravery*

*41, 42 Distinguished Conduct Medal*

*43 WAFF & KAR DCM*

*44 Conspicuous Gallantry Medal, Naval*

*44 Conspicuous Gallantry Medal Royal Air Force*

*45 George Medal*

*46, 47 King's/Queen's Police Medal Gallantry*

*46, 47 K.P.M./Q.P.M. Distinguished Service*

*46 Queen's Fire Service Medal Gallantry*

*46 Q.F.S.M. Distinguished Service*

*48 Edward Medal*

*49 Indian Distinguished Service Medal*

*50 Burma Gallantry Medal*

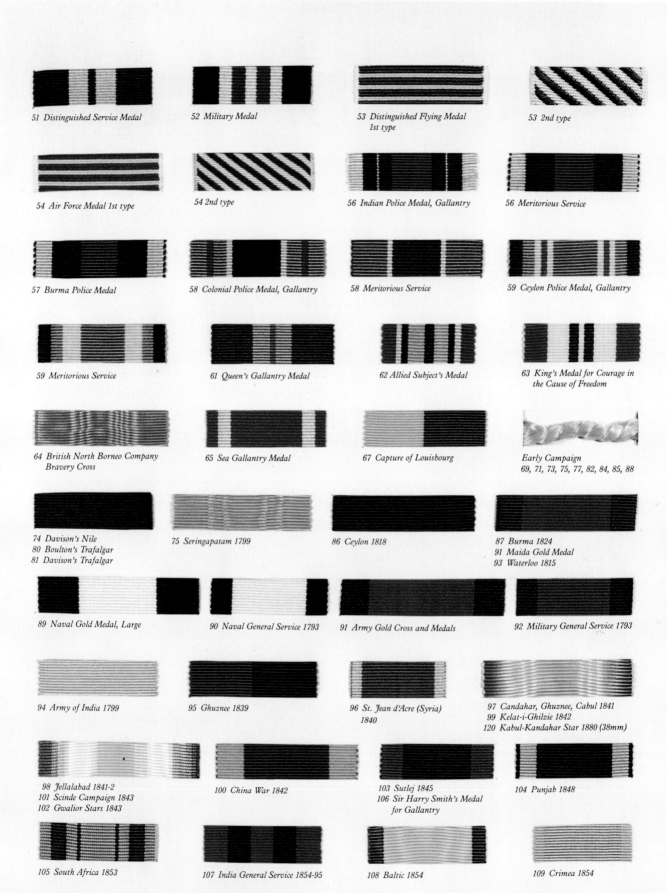

51 Distinguished Service Medal

52 Military Medal

53 Distinguished Flying Medal
1st type

53 2nd type

54 Air Force Medal 1st type

54 2nd type

56 Indian Police Medal, Gallantry

56 Meritorious Service

57 Burma Police Medal

58 Colonial Police Medal, Gallantry

58 Meritorious Service

59 Ceylon Police Medal, Gallantry

59 Meritorious Service

61 Queen's Gallantry Medal

62 Allied Subject's Medal

63 King's Medal for Courage in
the Cause of Freedom

64 British North Borneo Company
Bravery Cross

65 Sea Gallantry Medal

67 Capture of Louisbourg

Early Campaign
69, 71, 73, 75, 77, 82, 84, 85, 88

74 Davison's Nile
80 Boulton's Trafalgar
81 Davison's Trafalgar

75 Seringapatam 1799

86 Ceylon 1818

87 Burma 1824
91 Maida Gold Medal
93 Waterloo 1815

89 Naval Gold Medal, Large

90 Naval General Service 1793

91 Army Gold Cross and Medals

92 Military General Service 1793

94 Army of India 1799

95 Ghuznee 1839

96 St. Jean d'Acre (Syria)
1840

97 Candahar, Ghuznee, Cabul 1841
99 Kelat-i-Ghilzie 1842
120 Kabul-Kandahar Star 1880 (38mm)

98 Jellalabad 1841-2
101 Scinde Campaign 1843
102 Gwalior Stars 1843

100 China War 1842

103 Sutlej 1845
106 Sir Harry Smith's Medal
for Gallantry

104 Punjab 1848

105 South Africa 1853

107 India General Service 1854-95

108 Baltic 1854

109 Crimea 1854

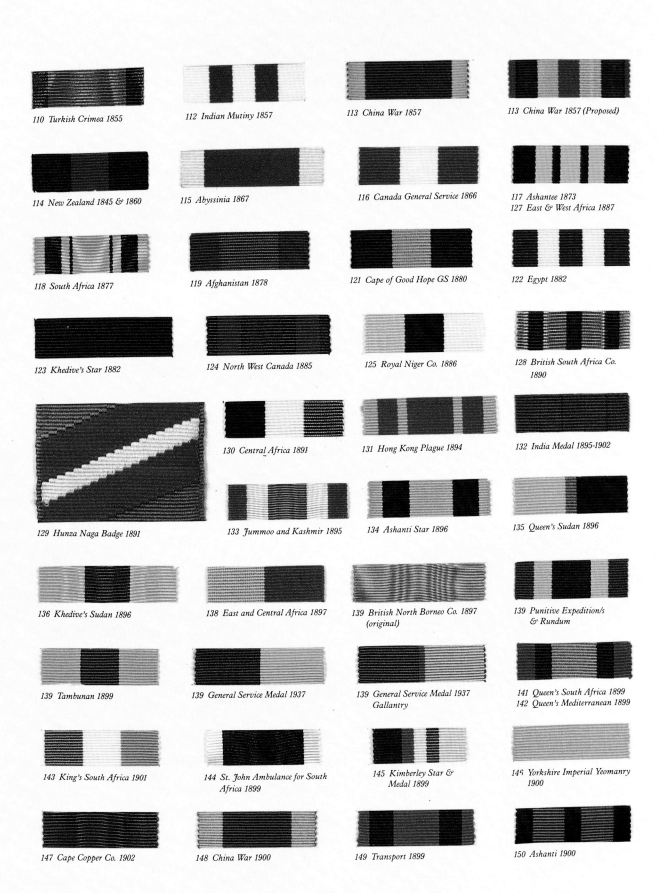

110 Turkish Crimea 1855

112 Indian Mutiny 1857

113 China War 1857

113 China War 1857 (Proposed)

114 New Zealand 1845 & 1860

115 Abyssinia 1867

116 Canada General Service 1866

117 Ashantee 1873
127 East & West Africa 1887

118 South Africa 1877

119 Afghanistan 1878

121 Cape of Good Hope GS 1880

122 Egypt 1882

123 Khedive's Star 1882

124 North West Canada 1885

125 Royal Niger Co. 1886

128 British South Africa Co. 1890

129 Hunza Naga Badge 1891

130 Central Africa 1891

131 Hong Kong Plague 1894

132 India Medal 1895-1902

133 Jummoo and Kashmir 1895

134 Ashanti Star 1896

135 Queen's Sudan 1896

136 Khedive's Sudan 1896

138 East and Central Africa 1897

139 British North Borneo Co. 1897 (original)

139 Punitive Expedition/s & Rundum

139 Tambunan 1899

139 General Service Medal 1937

139 General Service Medal 1937 Gallantry

141 Queen's South Africa 1899
142 Queen's Mediterranean 1899

143 King's South Africa 1901

144 St. John Ambulance for South Africa 1899

145 Kimberley Star & Medal 1899

146 Yorkshire Imperial Yeomanry 1900

147 Cape Copper Co. 1902

148 China War 1900

149 Transport 1899

150 Ashanti 1900

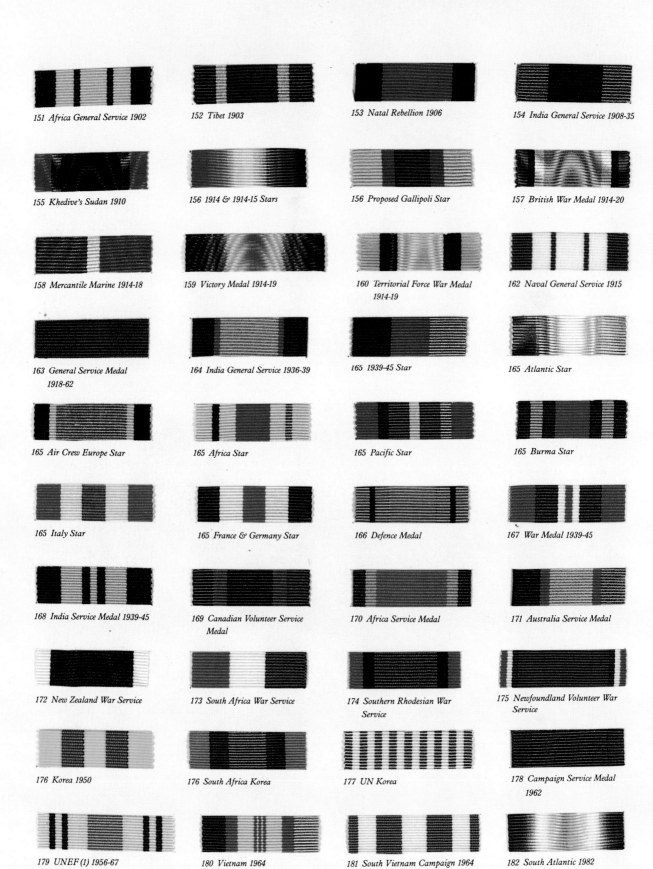

151 Africa General Service 1902

152 Tibet 1903

153 Natal Rebellion 1906

154 India General Service 1908-35

155 Khedive's Sudan 1910

156 1914 & 1914-15 Stars

156 Proposed Gallipoli Star

157 British War Medal 1914-20

158 Mercantile Marine 1914-18

159 Victory Medal 1914-19

160 Territorial Force War Medal 1914-19

162 Naval General Service 1915

163 General Service Medal 1918-62

164 India General Service 1936-39

165 1939-45 Star

165 Atlantic Star

165 Air Crew Europe Star

165 Africa Star

165 Pacific Star

165 Burma Star

165 Italy Star

165 France & Germany Star

166 Defence Medal

167 War Medal 1939-45

168 India Service Medal 1939-45

169 Canadian Volunteer Service Medal

170 Africa Service Medal

171 Australia Service Medal

172 New Zealand War Service

173 South Africa War Service

174 Southern Rhodesian War Service

175 Newfoundland Volunteer War Service

176 Korea 1950

176 South Africa Korea

177 UN Korea

178 Campaign Service Medal 1962

179 UNEF (1) 1956-67

180 Vietnam 1964

181 South Vietnam Campaign 1964

182 South Atlantic 1982

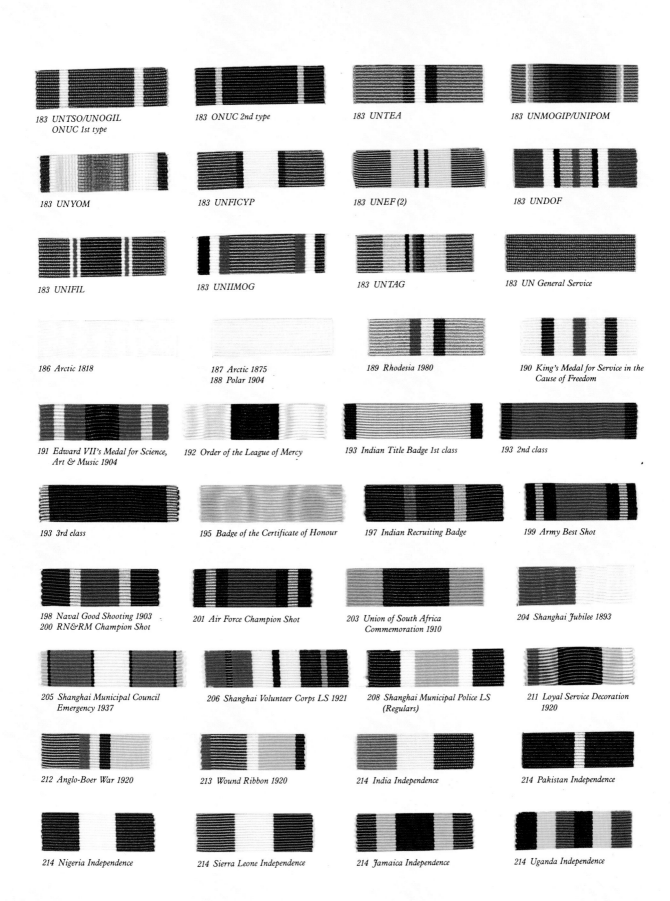

183 UNTSO/UNOGIL
ONUC 1st type

183 ONUC 2nd type

183 UNTEA

183 UNMOGIP/UNIPOM

183 UNYOM

183 UNFICYP

183 UNEF (2)

183 UNDOF

183 UNIFIL

183 UNIIMOG

183 UNTAG

183 UN General Service

186 Arctic 1818

187 Arctic 1875
188 Polar 1904

189 Rhodesia 1980

190 King's Medal for Service in the
Cause of Freedom

191 Edward VII's Medal for Science,
Art & Music 1904

192 Order of the League of Mercy

193 Indian Title Badge 1st class

193 2nd class

193 3rd class

195 Badge of the Certificate of Honour

197 Indian Recruiting Badge

199 Army Best Shot

198 Naval Good Shooting 1903
200 RN&RM Champion Shot

201 Air Force Champion Shot

203 Union of South Africa
Commemoration 1910

204 Shanghai Jubilee 1893

205 Shanghai Municipal Council
Emergency 1937

206 Shanghai Volunteer Corps LS 1921

208 Shanghai Municipal Police LS
(Regulars)

211 Loyal Service Decoration
1920

212 Anglo-Boer War 1920

213 Wound Ribbon 1920

214 India Independence

214 Pakistan Independence

214 Nigeria Independence

214 Sierra Leone Independence

214 Jamaica Independence

214 Uganda Independence

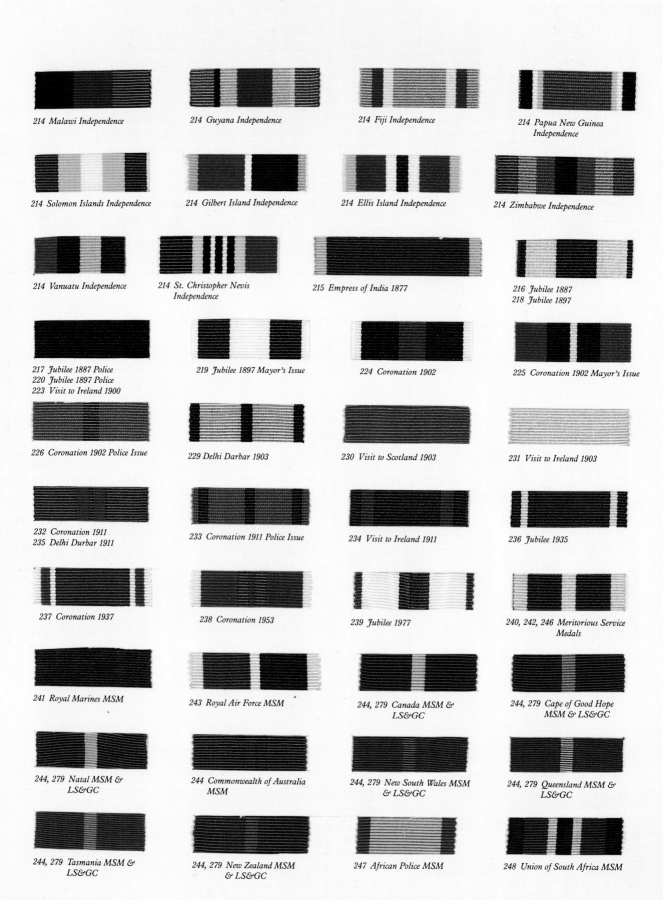

214 Malawi Independence

214 Guyana Independence

214 Fiji Independence

214 Papua New Guinea
Independence

214 Solomon Islands Independence

214 Gilbert Island Independence

214 Ellis Island Independence

214 Zimbabwe Independence

214 Vanuatu Independence

214 St. Christopher Nevis
Independence

215 Empress of India 1877

216 Jubilee 1887
218 Jubilee 1897

217 Jubilee 1887 Police
220 Jubilee 1897 Police
223 Visit to Ireland 1900

219 Jubilee 1897 Mayor's Issue

224 Coronation 1902

225 Coronation 1902 Mayor's Issue

226 Coronation 1902 Police Issue

229 Delhi Darbar 1903

230 Visit to Scotland 1903

231 Visit to Ireland 1903

232 Coronation 1911
235 Delhi Durbar 1911

233 Coronation 1911 Police Issue

234 Visit to Ireland 1911

236 Jubilee 1935

237 Coronation 1937

238 Coronation 1953

239 Jubilee 1977

240, 242, 246 Meritorious Service
Medals

241 Royal Marines MSM

243 Royal Air Force MSM

244, 279 Canada MSM &
LS&GC

244, 279 Cape of Good Hope
MSM & LS&GC

244, 279 Natal MSM &
LS&GC

244 Commonwealth of Australia
MSM

244, 279 New South Wales MSM
& LS&GC

244, 279 Queensland MSM &
LS&GC

244, 279 Tasmania MSM &
LS&GC

244, 279 New Zealand MSM
& LS&GC

247 African Police MSM

248 Union of South Africa MSM

249 *Queen Victoria
Royal Household
Faithful Service*

249 *George V Royal
Household
Faithful Service*

250 *Royal Navy LS&GC 2nd type, 1848*

249 *George VI
Royal Household
Faithful Service*

250 *3rd type, 1875*

249 *Queen Elizabeth
Royal Household
Faithful Service*

251 *Royal Naval Reserve Decoration
2nd type, 1941*

252 *RNR LS&GC 2nd type 1941*
256 *RN Aux. Sick Berth Res.
LS&GC, 2nd type 1941*

252 *3rd type, 1958*

253 *Royal Naval Volunteer Res.
Decoration 2nd type, 1919*

254 *RNVR LS&GC 2nd type, 1919*
257 *RN Wireless Auxiliary
Reserve LS&GC*

255 *Royal Fleet Reserve LS&GC*

258 *Royal Naval Auxiliary Services
LS&GC*

259 *Rocket Apparatus
Volunteer LS*
260 *Coastguard Aux. LS*

261 *Army LS&GC 1831-1916*
274, 275 *Indian Army LS&GC
1st type*

261 *Army LS&GC 1916-*
275 *Indian Army LS&GC
2nd type*

262 *Volunteer Decoration*
251 *(1st type), 253 (1st type)*
276, 277

263 *Volunteer LS*
252 *(1st type), 254 (1st type)*
278

264 *Territorial Decoration*
267 *Efficiency Decoration 1930-*

267 *Efficiency Decoration (T&AVR)
1969-*

262, 264, 267 *Efficiency Decoration,
HAC*

265 *Territorial Force Efficiency
Medal, 1st type, 1908-19*

266 *Territorial Efficiency Med.*
268 *Efficiency Medal 1930-*
265 *TFEM, 2nd type*

268 *Efficiency Medal (T&AVR)
1969-*

263, 265, 266, 268 *Efficiency Medal
HAC*

269 *Army Emergency Reserve
Decoration*

270 *Efficiency Medal (Army
Emergency Reserve)*

271 *Imperial Yeomanry LS&GC
1904*

272 *Militia LS&GC 1904*

273 *Special Reserve LS&GC 1908*

279 *Commonwealth of Australia
LS&GC*

280 *Permanent Forces of the
Empire Beyond the Seas
LS&GC, 1909-30*

281 *RWAFF & KAR LS&GC*

285 *Canadian Forces Decoration 1949*

286 *Victoria Volunteer Long and
Efficient Service 1881*

287 *New Zealand Long and
Efficient Service, 2nd type
1917-31*

288 *New Zealand Volunteer
Service 1902-12*

289 *New Zealand Territorial Service,
2nd type 1917-31*

290 *Ulster Defence Regiment
LS&GC 1982*

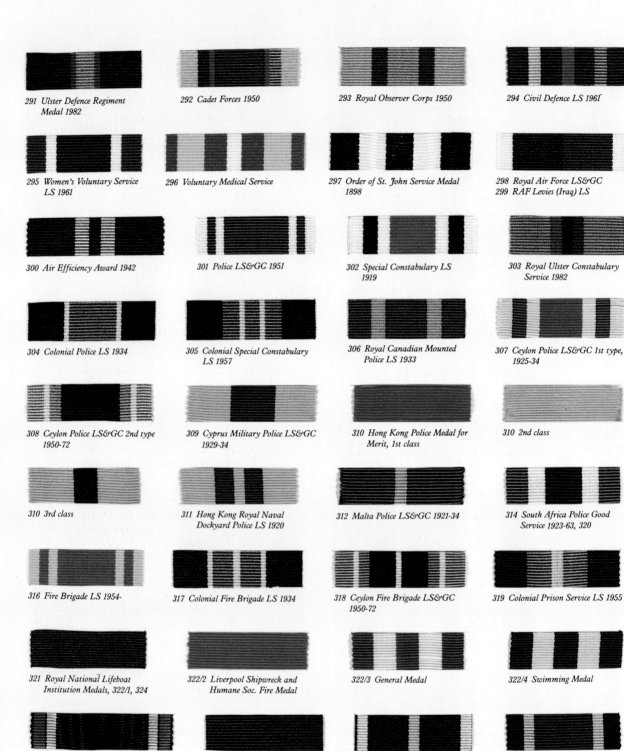

291  Ulster Defence Regiment
     Medal 1982

292  Cadet Forces 1950

293  Royal Observer Corps 1950

294  Civil Defence LS 1961

295  Women's Voluntary Service
     LS 1961

296  Voluntary Medical Service

297  Order of St. John Service Medal
     1898

298  Royal Air Force LS&GC
299  RAF Levies (Iraq) LS

300  Air Efficiency Award 1942

301  Police LS&GC 1951

302  Special Constabulary LS
     1919

303  Royal Ulster Constabulary
     Service 1982

304  Colonial Police LS 1934

305  Colonial Special Constabulary
     LS 1957

306  Royal Canadian Mounted
     Police LS 1933

307  Ceylon Police LS&GC 1st type,
     1925-34

308  Ceylon Police LS&GC 2nd type
     1950-72

309  Cyprus Military Police LS&GC
     1929-34

310  Hong Kong Police Medal for
     Merit, 1st class

310  2nd class

310  3rd class

311  Hong Kong Royal Naval
     Dockyard Police LS 1920

312  Malta Police LS&GC 1921-34

314  South Africa Police Good
     Service 1923-63, 320

316  Fire Brigade LS 1954-

317  Colonial Fire Brigade LS 1934

318  Ceylon Fire Brigade LS&GC
     1950-72

319  Colonial Prison Service LS 1955

321  Royal National Lifeboat
     Institution Medals, 322/1, 324

322/2  Liverpool Shipwreck and
       Humane Soc. Fire Medal

322/3  General Medal

322/4  Swimming Medal

325  Life Saving Medal of the Order of
     St. John, 2nd type 1950-

327  Royal Humane Society Medal
     Bronze, 332

327  Silver

327  Stanhope Gold

328  Lloyd's Medal for
     Saving Life at Sea

329  Lloyd's MSM 2nd
     type 1900
330  Medal for Service to
     Lloyd's

331  Lloyd's Medal for Bravery
     at Sea

334  Drummond Castle Medal
     1896

# *Index of Medals*

# Index of Bars

**Dated Bars**

# NOTES

# NOTES